In Permanent Crisis

Ethnicity in Contemporary European Media and Cinema

Ipek A. Celik

UNIVERSITY OF MICHIGAN PRESS • ANN ARBOR

Published in the United States of America by the
University of Michigan Press
Manufactured in the United States of America
♾ Printed on acid-free paper

2018 2017 2016 2015 4 3 2 1

A CIP catalog record for this book is available from the British Library.
ISBN 978-0-472-07272-9 (hardcover : alk. paper)
ISBN 978-0-472-05272-1 (paperback : alk. paper)
ISBN 978-0-472-12121-2 (ebook)

For Alexis Rappas

Contents

Acknowledgments

In preparation of this manuscript, I was privileged to be a Postdoctoral Fellow in International Humanities at the Cogut Center for the Humanities and Comparative Literature Department at Brown University. I am indebted to these institutions that have provided congenial and stimulating environments for me to develop the ideas that have formed this book.

The semester of leave I took from Bilkent University was instrumental in finalizing my manuscript. I am grateful to the director of Program of Cultures, Civilizations and Ideas, Mustafa Nakeeb, for making this happen. I deeply appreciate the support of LabexMed (Le laboratoire d'excellence sur les études méditerranéennes) at Aix-Marseille Université for inviting me as a visiting researcher and the TELEMME research group for hosting me through this time.

Vangelis Calotychos, Kenneth Haynes, and Kristin Ross have provided continuous inspirations for the book and for me with their scholarship, integrity and ingenious ways of thinking. Their intellectual guidance and generous mentorship have been of inestimable value for my growth as a scholar.

I was fortunate to be surrounded with a wonderful group of colleagues during my stay at Brown. My friends Bianca Dahl and Ipek Türeli read and generously commented on my earlier thoughts on the project. Rina Bliss motivated me to begin writing the book and supported me with her wit and humor even when there did not seem much light at the end of the tunnel. Michelle Cho encouraged me and helped me immensely in shaping the idea behind this book. I deeply appreciate her generosity in sharing her extensive knowledge of genre cinema and film theory.

I thank my former students Sarah O'Hare and Christian Aguiar, who have patiently copyedited the earlier versions of the manuscript. Thanks also go to the two anonymous readers for the University of Michigan Press, who offered productive suggestions for revision. I am grateful to my editor, Aaron McCollough, and his editorial team for their belief in and commitment to this project. Part of the material I discuss in chapter 2 appeared in "'I Wanted You To Be Present': Guilt and the History of Violence in Michael Haneke's *Caché*," in *Cinema Journal*, Vol. 50, No. 1 (Fall 2010), pp. 59–80. I thank *Cinema Journal* for granting me the permission for reprint.

No words are enough to thank Özlem Köksal, my dear friend and colleague, who read the entire manuscript more than once and provided brilliant suggestions. Her insights endlessly improve my vision in film analysis and criticism. My heartfelt thanks to my parents and my sister for their unwavering support through the numerous years and great distances that separated us. My deepest gratitude goes to Alexis Rappas, who accompanied me from the initial stages to the very end of the writing process supporting me every day with his profound insights, endless patience, enthusiasm for the project, and constant encouragement.

Introduction

Mapping the Representation of Ethnicity in Europe

As always in times of emergency people bow to the imperatives of "presentism" and tend to forget the deep causes.

—ACHILLE MBEMBE, "THE REPUBLIC AND ITS BEAST: ON THE RIOTS IN THE FRENCH *BANLIEUES*"[1]

Persons categorized as degenerate typically enter the national register through stereotype, scandal, or unusually horrible death: otherwise their lives are not timely.

—LAUREN BERLANT, *THE ANATOMY OF NATIONAL FANTASY*[2]

Grainy archival footage captures a tense confrontation in a French *banlieue* in the nighttime. The camera shoots from behind a solitary man standing on a well-lit road. He faces the police who cover the distant horizon in multitudes, protected by their shields. The unarmed man shouts at them: "You murderers! It's easy to gun us down! We only got rocks!" The image freezes and the film's title, *La Haine* (Hate), appears calculatedly in the middle of the space between the man and the police. The next frame shows an icon of the globe as the voice-over narrates an anecdote that both opens and closes the film: "It's a story of a guy who falls off a skyscraper. On his way down past each floor he keeps saying to reassure himself: so far so good, so far so good. It's not the fall that matters . . . it's the landing." A Molotov cocktail slowly descends and explodes over the globe and flames cover the entire frame. As the credits roll, the soundtrack of Bob Marley's "Burning and Looting" accompanies a collage of footage from demonstrations in the 1980s and 1990s against the numerous instances of racist police violence that led to deaths of minority youth in Paris. The archival footage smoothly proceeds into the film narrative: a fictional riot in a Parisian *banlieue*.

In 1995, Matthieu Kassovitz's *La Haine* exploded into political and film circles just like the Molotov cocktail that explodes over the image of the earth in the opening sequence of the film. Kassovitz gained the best director award at Cannes and the best film award at the Cesars. The film's impact rippled into the government as much as the film establishment. President Jacques Chirac congratulated the director on his achievement, while Prime Minister Alain Juppé demanded that the film be screened to government officials.[3] The film's influence and Kassovitz's reputation as a spokesman for racial and social issues in the *banlieues* has extended into the 2000s, marked by wide press coverage of the director's heated correspondence with then minister of internal affairs Nicolas Sarkozy in the aftermath of the 2005 riots.[4]

The opening sequence above is key to understanding the two interrelated elements that give *La Haine* its continued popularity among the films that set out to represent minority youth in French *banlieues*: its message of historical urgency and its affective charge. Mathieu Kassovitz decided to shoot *La Haine* after attending a demonstration against the murder of seventeen-year-old Makomé M'Bowole, killed at point blank range as he was handcuffed to a radiator in a Parisian police station.[5] The archival footage used in the opening sequence attempts to give a historical depth to the cycle of events that still haunt France in their repetition—racist police violence and the demonstrations or riots against it that follow. The soundtrack of Bob Marley adds a spatial breadth to this history as an extension of the anticolonial struggle. As its title implies, the film articulates a circulation of affects between the *banlieue* youth and the French police: the cycle of hate and rage, that of *la haine*, the word rendered productive in its double meaning, "hate" in standard French and "rage" in the colloquial.

This "affective economy"[6] is embedded in the film's temporal structure. The anecdote of the falling man is an allegory for the impending social crisis. The film conveys the feeling of crisis through sequences fragmented by a ticking clock that gives the effect of a time bomb as well as through stylistic sharp cuts, disorienting camera angles, pans, and zooms. Stretching between two instances of police brutality, Kassovitz's narrative reveals state racism and the marginalization of minority youth in the *banlieues*. In order to render the urgency of this critical situation, the film juxtaposes the immediacy of climactic clashes (often with the police) and static periods of waiting or strolling (indicative of the social crisis of youth with no job prospects and no education as they burn their own schools). The use of alternate temporalities in *La Haine* keeps the suspense alive while it alludes to and mobilizes media-induced fears of crisis and explosions in the *banlieues*.

La Haine's "affective economy," the circulation of hate and rage, instills in its audience the fear and thrill of an imminently explosive social crisis. In that sense, the film is representative of a particular treatment of temporality when it comes to ethnic and racial minorities in France, mirrored in the larger European context. The temporality assigned to minorities of migrant origin is that of violent events followed by periods of incurable social crisis pregnant with the threat of impending rupture. While the film reveals the historical and affective complexities of violent events that frequently bring minority youth in the French *banlieues* to the media's attention, it also contributes to the media-articulated temporality of crisis and urgency assigned to Europe's Others. The clock ticks, the bomb is about to explode, the society will imminently crash, as it is on its way down.

This book explores how and why violence and temporality of crisis have become central to the articulation of ethnic and racial difference in today's Europe. Refugees, migrants,[7] and minorities of migrant origin frequently appear in European mainstream news in relation to emergency situations: victims of human trafficking, suspects of terrorism, "bogus" asylum seekers who pose an imminent threat to social welfare systems, hyperfertile minorities within a declining "European" population,[8] or some other potential threat to European safety and welfare states. The news items often take injury as the basis of political identity of ethnic and racial Others, giving them roles either as perpetrators of or sufferers from violence.[9] These social, economic, humanitarian, and racial states of crises often call for urgent security measures or humanitarian intervention: in the name of Muslim women threatened by their paternalistic traditional families or HIV-positive refugees who need urgent health care.[10] The lives and experiences of ethnic and racial Others of Europe are marginalized into extreme temporalities defined by rupture, crisis, and emergency. This urgency at the heart of Europe calls for immediate action against violence and violation and leaves no time for reflection.[11]

The chapters that follow thus attempt to pause and contemplate the catastrophism that frames ethnic and racial Otherness in Europe, a language of crisis that is even more pronounced in the 2000s, after

September 11 and then the July 7 bombings in London. Detailed analyses of European film productions pay close attention to key events—particular riots, terrorist and criminal acts, and honor killings—that have brought Europe's minorities to the forefront of public visibility and often reduced their identity to that of perpetrators or victims of violence. Closely examined films provide the basis to explore the thick historicity of these violent events beyond the claims of eruption in sensationalized media representations. All shot in the mid-2000s, the films explored in this book—*Children of Men* (Alfonso Cuarón, 2006), *Hidden* (Michael Haneke, 2005), *Hostage* (Constantinos Giannaris, 2004) and *Head-On* (Fatih Akın, 2004)—reveal and challenge the limited and often generic frames of visibility imposed on Europe's Others in the media's histrionic approach to such events. Each film reconsiders a sensational minority-related event by taking into account the fragments of temporalities other than its immediate present, and its repercussions and affective depth that extend to more than one country.

The films analyzed here do not propose "more truthful" representations of the particular historical events or of the migrants and minorities in question. In that sense, the book attempts to go beyond the dilemma of documentarism that frequently shapes audience expectations in films that capture ethnic and racial Others. Rather, these films open a space for the exploration of violent media events and crisis situations in their full complexity that involves historical and geographical implications as much as affects entangled in their representation. They make visible and thinkable the underrepresented dynamics of a minority-related violent event. Moreover, each chapter unravels how the event's mediatic representation renders certain affects through an appeal to generic conventions, be it the fear of minority youth embedded in thrilling narratives of eruptive *banlieue* violence, compassion for Muslim women's victimhood in honor crime melodramas or dystopias of humanitarian crisis involving refugees. It is these affective residues of events that the films unfold through revealing and mobilizing the generic frameworks of ethnicity and race in the European media. The cinematic appropriation of genre conventions used in the media renders an affective access point to the "crisis" situations involving refugees, migrants, and minorities. The use of genre conventions articulates the landscape of social anxieties in Europe's relation to its Others, the fears that display themselves in a thriller or dystopic science fiction, and the pity that is pursued in melodrama or tragedy.

Migrants, refugees, and ethnic and racial minorities of migrant origin are categories whose definitions and legal implications are worlds apart. What puts these categories side by side in this book is not people's histories of migration or their origins per se. Refugees, migrants, and ethnic and racial minorities are brought together in their common experience as targets of racism and racialization framed in cultural and especially visual and temporal terms.[12] As the quote from Lauren Berlant in the epigraph suggests, these "degenerate" communities commonly enter the national registers through "untimely" acts such as "honor" crimes that seem to emerge from a distant temporality, instead of being placed within the more general framework of domestic violence.

Before proceeding any further, it is necessary to underscore that while inquiring into contemporary European articulations of ethnic and racial Otherness, "Europe" is by no means conceptualized as a bounded or a homogeneous space in this study. The directors, film narratives, characters, and production processes are transnational in many ways that break any given borders of (and within) Europe. The case studies include an Austrian filmmaker whose film is deeply entrenched in French history (Haneke's *Hidden*), a Mexican director's portrayal of contemporary Britain produced with a company in Hollywood (Cuarón's *Children of Men*), a Greek director's depiction of a controversial Albanian hero in a film produced partially by a Turkish company (Giannaris's *Hostage*), and a minority director whose success is claimed by both Germany and Turkey (Fatih Akın's *Head-On*). Each chapter, however, provides situated analyses of films, close readings that pay attention to historical and geographic specificities as well as context-specific debates on migration and minority communities in each country. These debates range from the colonial heritage of migration and its contemporary repercussions in France, to the frequent appeal to women's rights as a litmus test of minority integration in Germany,[13] the stigmatizing media campaigns against asylum seekers and refugees in Britain, and the intense migration from the Balkans as a demographic and identitarian challenge in Greece.[14] While differing in their articulations, these transnational filmmakers reveal the pervasive anxieties that see European identity under an urgent risk, anxieties that Talal Asad succinctly describes: "if Europe cannot be articulated in terms of complex space and complex time that allow for multiple ways of life (and not merely multiple *identities*) to flourish, it may be fated to be no more than the common market of an imperial civilization, always anxious about exiles within its gates and barbarians beyond."[15]

Borders and Mobility in the Post-1990s European Cinema

In the aftermath of the Cold War, with the union of two Germanies, the breakup of the Soviet Union and Yugoslavia, and the collapse of all communist regimes in Eastern Europe and the Balkans, European borders became unstable. Concurrently, the EU pursued its path of expansion and further integration beginning with the Maastricht Treaty, heralding the advent of a politically unified Europe. Redefining the borders of new Europe gained salience, that is, both extra-European border control and flexible movement within the European space became central components in an otherwise elusive European identity.[16] On the one hand, flexible travel is promoted for heritage and cultural tourism profitable for most European states, and on the other hand, migration and mobility are tightly controlled through border policies.[17] "Border reinforcing" has become as much a substance of European citizenship as "border crossing."[18]

As Europe began to define itself more and more with mobility and movement beyond national borders (with a single market, a single currency, and for the most part, a single visa) the experiences of diaspora, exile, border crossing, and tourism have become more pronounced in European cinema.[19] Studies on post-1990s European cinema have inquired into how films critique and go beyond spatial frames of national and European identity, partly as a reaction to the rise of "Fortress Europe," a space of tight border control against outside interventions. Some studies probe into European films that portray borders and discriminations that inhibit mobility, focusing on films that explore troubled journeys, human trafficking, refugee camps, and cities' margins to identify a crisis of European identity in its preoccupation with Others.[20] Other studies celebrate the work of migrant and diasporic directors as well as themes of migration and mobility for their contribution to the transnationalization of European cinema (or for getting European films out of their national framework by bringing in hybrid identifications and multiculturalism).[21] Concerned with the post-1990s European space and identity, and the possibilities that cinema may offer to make them more inclusive, Thomas Elsaesser, for instance, explores films that break "Fortress Europe" by introducing itinerary elements. The scholar suggests that new European cinema (even films that are not directly about race or ethnicity such as Lars von Trier's *Dogville* [2003] or commercial films such as Jean-Pierre Jeunet's *Amélie* [2001])] pursues more inclusive identity politics in which "boundary-drawing gives way to general recognition of co-habitation, mutual interference and mutual responsibility as necessary forms of a new solidarity and sense of co-existence."[22]

The exploration of borders and celebration of mobility in European films have made a strong contribution to studies in European cinema and identity. Yet their predominant focus on space and movement at times neglects historicity and eventfulness, a gap in European film studies that this book intends to fill. In other words, this study approaches "Fortress Europe"—which has so far been challenged predominantly through cinematic mobility—with an inquiry into temporality in film.[23] The idea behind the emphasis on historicity and eventfulness is to examine a dimension of this "fortress" of Europe that is not spatial and cannot be located on a map. The symbolic fortress I refer to may be defined as the "racialized understanding of proper Europeanness" that excludes European citizens of migrant origin and their children as much as migrants and refugees from the category of "proper" European. [24] As Etienne Balibar writes:

> Borders are vacillating [in Europe]. This does not mean that they are disappearing. . . . on the contrary, borders are being multiplied and reduced in their localization and their function; they are being doubled, becoming borders zones, regions or countries one can reside and live.[25]

Balibar argues that Europe is constructed as an ever-shifting borderland in which the external borders are duplicated in the form of internal borders that stigmatize certain populations "whose presence in European societies are nonetheless increasingly massive and legitimate."[26] As Europe's borders increase and become deterritorialized, what remains inside shrinks while the obsessive protection of this realm inflates the concerns and measures of security and control, carried away from the geographical borderlines into the heart of public space.

At this moment, these internal and symbolic borders are predominantly drawn with references to a temporality of permanent crisis—an assumed temporal non-coevalness and violent eventfulness of minorities. In contrast to earlier works on the spatial cartography of Otherness in European cinema, this study brings to the fore a temporal dimension and pays a particular attention to historicity constructed in relation to ethnic and racial Others in Europe. An analysis of this historicity of crisis and catastrophe has deeper significance in this decade as sensationalized media events increasingly provide the frames of visibility through which ethnic and racial Others are seen. As these media events are representative of what I mean by the stigmatized temporality of Others (conceived through crisis between moments of stasis and explosion), it is necessary to address how ethnic and racial Others are typically depicted in European mass media.

On Ethnic and Racial Others in Mainstream European Media

In the first week of April 2009, BBC news alarmed its readers with reports of "anti-terror searches" in the UK, in which "twelve men—11 of them Pakistani, and most of them students—are still being questioned over the alleged plot."[27] This news has reinitiated the debate about the potential threat of young Muslim migrants who come to Britain on student visas, reminiscent of the way September 11 hijackers had entered the United States.[28] The same week the Athenian daily *I Kathimerini* published a statement by the Greek prime minister of the time, Kostas Karamanlis, in which he attributed a large share of the responsibility for the December 2008 riots in Athens to illegal migrants. Karamanlis presented statistical data showing migrant identification with crime and implied that migrants (as well as the activists of the extreme Left) have a tendency to consider themselves immune from laws; as he stressed, "the laws apply to everyone."[29] At the time of the riots, the mainstream Greek media reflected all migrant participation negatively; they were depicted as looters, outlaws, and criminals, scapegoats for worst kinds of violence. Such limited depiction dismissed their active participation in nonviolent protests and in the attempt to remake Greek politics, often at the risk of losing their legal status as residents.[30]

The numbers of such European news media articles that cast migrants as threatening and thereby fuel public anxieties about security continue to soar. A media content research study conducted in 2003 involving fifteen countries in Europe and examining nearly three thousand news items shows that refugees, migrants, and ethnic minorities are overrepresented in stories of crime and deviation (including illegal migration) and religious fundamentalism, while minority voices, even involving issues concerning ethnic relations, are scarcely heard.[31] Moreover, the Minority Rights Group's report in 2010 reveals that it is often minorities worldwide who suffer the aftereffects of September 11 and the so-called war on terror through escalating state-sanctioned discriminatory practices that take the shape of religious profiling and stops and searches under counterterrorism laws.[32] Such discriminatory practices have increased as a result of events such as the 2004 murder of director

Theo van Gogh in Amsterdam, the 2005 and 2007 riots in the suburbs of Paris, and the 2004 and 2005 terror bombings in Spain and London.

Migrant and minority communities, especially European Muslims, in addition to being associated with criminality and terrorism, are depicted as inassimilable aliens unwilling or unable to embrace democratic values. Again in 2009, a *Der Spiegel* article titled "Foreign Forever" discussed a survey conducted by the Berlin Institute for Population and Development. The article blended demographic anxiety related to migration with concerns over so-called failed integration claming that one-third of children born in Germany have immigrant parents who are "poorly integrated into German society."[33] Representing a social emergency prone to eruption, the article declared: "an alarmingly high percentage of [Germany's immigrants] live in a parallel world with poor prospects of a decent education and career advancement." The article concluded with a reference to Islam and its treatment of women as the main problem that makes integration difficult if not impossible. Hence, minorities appeared as a threat to the alleged stability of Western democracy not only because of their actions but also by their absence of action, the inability to adapt and "integrate" that makes them easy victims of grand forces that accompany the processes of globalization.

The negative representations in the mainstream British, Greek, and German presses in 2009 were all the more striking amid the economic devastation to the well-being of migrants as they were among the communities hit hardest by the global financial crisis.[34] Moreover, there has been a visible increase of support for European far-right parties that pursue outright discriminatory politics against minorities.[35] This increase of far-right representation in the European Parliament brought anti-immigration and Islamophobic politics into the mainstream political arena. Overall, 2009 was marked by intense discriminatory attacks such as those on a Muslim prayer center in Greece, mosques set on fire in France, and anti-Islam laws and boycotts such as the "Stop the Islamization" rally in Cologne,[36] the antimosque campaign in Denmark, and the Swiss ban on minarets following an intense campaign by the conservative Swiss People's Party.

The Swiss antimosque campaign, for example, was promoted with a poster associating Islam with niqab-wearing women with hostile looks and missile-like minarets invading the national territory represented by the flag, alarming the public with the alleged dangers of religious jihad. Hence, the depiction of Muslim migrants and minorities as threats has been frequently exploited by the far Right to pursue a public discourse that is fundamentally averse to the freedom of thought and belief; in an ironic twist, simultaneously claiming to protect these very "European" freedoms from the imagined Muslim attack. Similarly associating Muslim religious symbols with violence, the cartoons published in the Danish daily *Jyllands-Posten* also claimed to promote freedom of speech and cultural tolerance. In fact, the cartoon controversy in 2005 was framed as the clash of the liberal values of a democratic society with the antimodern and authoritarian values of Muslims.[37]

This openly anti-Muslim and alarming discourse is different from public debates and policies concerning migrants and minorities in the 1980s and the 1990s. Earlier discourses and policies were geared toward the promotion of multiculturalism and were, to some extent, optimistic about the possibility of these communities' integration into European societies through cultural work. In France, Germany, Great Britain, and the Netherlands social-democratic governments initiated multiculturalist policies to promote diversity. In Germany, for instance, cities where there were high concentrations of migrants and minorities, such as Berlin and Frankfurt, opened offices of "multicultural affairs" with commissioners for "foreigners." These offices were established on the assumption that "each ethno-national group of immigrants had its own 'culture' and that . . . cultural traditions and differences were a major factor to be reckoned with when it came to social integration."[38] Hence, while multiculturalist policymaking had the underlying understanding of "Other" cultures as homogeneous, it assumed that maintaining one's own culture was key to peaceful cohabitation. As Slavoj Žižek observes, the European multicultural ideal carried cultural essentialisms and elements of commodification that turned it into an "inverted, self-referential form of racism, a 'racism with a distance'—it 'respects' the Other's identity, conceiving the Other as a self-enclosed 'authentic' community towards which he, the multiculturalist, maintains a distance rendered possible by his privileged universal position."[39] The marketing and packaging of difference did not critique but rather promoted certain power relations between Europe's "natives" and minorities, in a context in which cultural integration stood as an impossible goal on a horizon that was ever flexible and extending.

In the new century, with the augmentation of antimigration and racist discourses, unabashed policies of integration replaced multicultural policies. Among these more forceful integrationist policies have been language and citizenship tests imposed on the naturalizing migrants in the UK, Netherlands, and Denmark, the ban on the hijab in French schools in 2004, the subsequent ban on niqabs in 2010, and Sarkozy's creation of the controversial Ministry of Immigration, Integration and National Identity and Co-development (2007–10). In this general context, German chancellor Angela Merkel's alarmist speech in 2010, which declared the defeat of multiculturalism, describing it as an "utterly failed" approach in the face of an alleged increase in the number of minorities, symbolizes the sharp turn toward the regime of state-enforced integration.

Toward the end of the first decade of the 2000s, the predominant mode of European politics appears to be one that centers itself on the administration and protection of life as it mobilizes people through the language of "defense from potential victimization or harassment."[40] At a moment when the continent is characterized by economic instability, growing support for a politics of fear has taken extreme right-wing discourses of racism and exclusion into the mainstream, and debates on ethnicity and race have increasingly focused on violent occurrences. The tropes of the threatening and inassimilable minority appear in discourses of illegality, criminality, and terrorism, but also as more insidious and diffuse threats to European ways of life—exemplified by the inflated discourses on Islam and its so-called paternal traditions that victimize women and fail to integrate with European democracy. At the heart of the constellation of these discussions on migrants and minorities of migrant origin is European identity, conceptualized as at risk, an anxiety that creates an affective economy dictated by a temporality of crisis associated with Europe's Others.

In Permanent Crisis: The Temporality of Europe's Others

What does temporality have to do with political visibility of communities that are underprivileged and discriminated against? In *The Nights of Labor* (1981) Jacques Rancière addresses the role that the politics of temporality plays in the subjugation of workers through the early nineteenth century.[41] As he explores the poems composed by the proletariat in the hours after work, through the nights, he argues that poetry becomes a form of speech that crosses the temporal borders allocated to workers. The partition of the day for the worker was clear-cut: labor during the day and sleep during the night for recuperation and to ensure that the body functions effectively during the next workday. To be a good worker meant to follow this regulated schematization of time.[42] The social configuration of workers' temporality was essential to keeping them "in their place," that is, outside visibility and speech, assigning them to the space of the nonpolitical life. Hence for Rancière, temporality is distributed along class lines, and such allocation of time gives form to social inequality. At the core of emancipation, which is opening a space for a new subjectivity and new relations to speech and visibility, lies the dislocation of such nonegalitarian compartmentalization of time.

Around the time Rancière discussed the allocation of temporality along class lines, anthropologist Johannes Fabian published *Time and the Other* (1983), in which he articulated a parallel politics of nonegalitarian temporality in the subjugation of the colonial and postcolonial Other. Fabian explores the "denial of coevalness," the temporal distancing and the rejection of cohabiting in the same temporality that the Western anthropologist constructs over his objects of study, the distancing that reinforces Western knowledge and domination over the so-called backward natives. The geographical, racial, and ethnic Other is assigned a temporality of underdevelopment, stagnation, and tradition: "*geopolitics* has its ideological foundation in *chronopolitics*."[43] While in Rancière's description the segregated temporality is imposed to domesticate the working class, or to create good workers, according to Fabian, in the case of racial and ethnic Others this segregation justifies difference and hierarchy based on a linear conception of temporality and progress.

Such categories of bounded temporality and temporal stagnation were used throughout the 1980s and 1990s to approach ethnic and racial minorities in Europe, a stagnation that goes hand in hand with their assumed cultural fixity. The calls for integration of "Blacks" in Britain and "Beurs" in France promoted the idea of temporal progress as a form of emancipation, a progressive rupture both in temporality and in culture.[44] In public debates in the 1990s, Turkish youth in Germany, for instance, were assigned to a temporality of "timeless traditions and unbridgeable cultures," considered misplaced and disoriented within the accelerating pace of urban life in Germany, standing "at an incommensurable distance from the modernity and present of the West. Their co-evalness denied, they [became] Turks in narratives of criminality, isolation, and (dis)integration."[45] This designation of temporal fixity and "incommensurable cultural difference"[46] between Turks and Germans is even more striking when one considers the simultaneous rise of neo-Nazism at an intensity that resulted in numerous instances of racist violence during the same period.[47] Hence, post-Wall urban contexts and times were those of conflict and rise of fundamentalism, but not only or necessarily on the side of Turkish minorities.

In the 2000s, the allocation of temporality for Europe's Others has moved from that of a static crisis that can be healed with the medicine of multiculturalism to an imminent crisis that requires stringent measures. The static periods of waiting, disorientation, attachment to tradition, and temporal gap become reasons in and of themselves for potential explosion waiting to happen. This conception of the temporality of the Other as that of crisis or impending violent eventfulness is connected to a changing conception of temporality and historicity in the aftermath of September 11. In the twenty-first century a more static temporality of crisis lent itself to the explosive temporality of catastrophe. The quasi-Hegelian discourses of "end of history"/history coming to final stop that emerged in the post–Cold War epoch shifted gears toward a conception of history moving through the ruptures of catastrophes.[48] The representation of ethnic and racial Others, I argue, became central to this emergent temporality.

The focus on temporality and its politics observed in the works of Rancière and Fabian has been taken over by declarations of "endisms" after 1989, an ironic twist in political philosophy especially considering the intense historical change in Europe after the fall of the communist regimes thanks to migration from the east as well as the rise of nationalisms, xenophobia, and racism. Francis Fukuyama declared the end of history, claiming that the past no longer determines the present.[49] On the other end of the political spectrum, Fredric Jameson similarly argued for the death of temporality in the postmodern era and claimed that spatial categories take over the modernist emphasis on the temporal.[50]

This relatively static figuration of reaching the end of history that emerged in the 1990s has been replaced with an explosive endism in this century. In the aftermath of September 11 and July 7, the event has gained salience as a category that ruptures and expands the present. Such a punctuated present marks the end of the past and the inability to move toward the future: "an endless present committed solely to waging war with an unseen and unknown enemy."[51] Hence, in this century there emerged a conception of temporality marked by fear-inducing immediacy and punctuality, a time of imminent threats that justify immediate actions. In the Global North fear and terror assumed a new significance as mobilizing principles in politics and affective tools used to legitimize government violence, inducing eventfulness, especially as it relates to ethnic and racial Others. As declarations of the end of history and a focus on the present gained a strong edge of catastrophism (history proceeding in traumatic disasters) in the aftermath of September 11 and July 7, refugees, migrants, and minorities have started to come to the forefront exceedingly through violent events and imminent crises in Europe.

In this context, the terms crisis and catastrophe have become interchangeable in relation to ethnic and racial Others. Film scholar Mary Ann Doane, while admitting the frequent collision of the two terms, articulates the difference between crisis and catastrophe as one of agency: while the former often connotes a decision and "can be attributed to a subject," the latter simply happens, is "subject-less" and instantaneous.[52] This crucial difference between the two categories is eliminated by the fact that the subject position of European Others almost always stands in between agents of crisis and victims of catastrophes. Indeed a crisis involving Europe's Others, similar to the way mass media treats economic crisis, "is often disguised as catastrophe and hence naturalized, contained, desystematized."[53] It is a conception of history moving through disasters that are at the crux of European eventfulness (major media scandals such as events of criminality, riots, and honor killings) involving refugees, migrants, and minorities.

Event and Its Other

In the post–September 11 context that associates the present and the movement of time with crises and catastrophes, theoretical discussions on the event have gained renewed interest. The delayed translation of Alain Badiou's *Being and Event* (*L'être et l'événement*,1988) into English in 2005 and the publication of his *The Rebirth of History* (2012) have a significant place within these debates.[54] Badiou's event theory prioritizes the revolutionary event as the mover of history, an event that creates a new temporality that follows it, a new language that sheds light onto the relationships it brings forth, and a new form of subjectivity. For Badiou, the event is an unpredictable break, an exceptional and singular realm. It is excessive, arrives to displace categories that define and divide people and places, and offers new avenues for thought. In *The Rebirth of History* Badiou confronts the declarations of the end of history or of utopias as he considers the awakening of history through events such as the Arab Spring. Especially in Egypt, he claims, what took place was a "historical riot," defined as such as a result of its ability to expand to the whole population and allow people who were previously not part of decision-making to engage with the process.

According to the philosopher, in opposition to the "historical riot" stands the category of the "immediate riot." An event that often starts as a reaction to the despotic acts of the state, the "immediate riot," Badiou describes, is often the initial form of the "historical riot." However, the former fails to assume a historical dimension as a consequence of its lack of political direction and organization. It is circumscribed by outbursts of violence as the intention of the participants is not separated from their rage: "it does not make it possible clearly to distinguish between what pertains to a partially universalizable intention and what remains confined to a rage with no purpose other than the satisfaction of being able to crystallize and find hateful objects to destroy or consume."[55] Temporally, "immediate riot" is not enduring and is a singularly intense moment, spatially it remains stagnant and local, incapable of expanding to larger parts of the city, hence eventually destroying its own space of existence. Furthermore, it is limited in its social appeal as it finds itself incapable of including larger segments of population, across gender, class, and race divides.

In the category of "immediate riot" Badiou analyzes the 2005 riots in France, and points out how these riots remained predominantly limited to violent destructions of property and categorically remained as male, underclass, and minority events spatially limited to the ghettos of urban France. In his analysis, Badiou explores the police violence that lead to the riots and the government and media's stigmatizing of minority youth during and after the riots. He points out that in the government and media discourses economic costs were deemed more important than human costs, especially because the individuals involved were minority youth: "the death of the young man—'a black hooligan,' no doubt, or an Arab 'known to the police'—is nothing compared with all these additional costs. Let us not grieve for the death, but for the insurance companies."[56]

The debates around the 2005 riots in France have been predominantly about its minority participants, declaring these communities as violent outcasts, the root and the evidence of a social crisis. Within this larger context of stigmatization, Badiou's analysis has shown the larger scope of violence against minorities, the structural violence embedded in state institutions and the media. Yet, his focus on the French riots as the "immediate riot" par excellence—for instance the absence of a comparative exploration of the London riots of 2011 or the Greek riots of 2008 that had more or less similar characteristics yet less of a minority presence than the 2005 riots in France—generates questions regarding the limits in his approach toward a "minority event." Such a focus places a predominantly minority-involved event at the center of debates on explosive uprisings that are deemed outside the movement of history.

Badiou's analysis associates minority youth with riots that are eventually described as "violent, anarchic and ultimately without enduring truth," lacking organization and an idea behind them, remaining a minority event that "rages on itself, destroys what it is used to."[57] The fact that these "immediate events" did not expand to a larger section of the population might as well be explained by the minority status of their participants instead of a lack of organization. But more significantly, within this theorization, the political visibility of Europe's minorities is once again limited to an imminent crisis that lacks proper historicity. Badiou's influential conceptualization of the event, when it comes to a minority event, akin to the Marxist dilemma with regard to peasants and the colonized, considers these populations as potentially failing historicity. Or rather, "the good Arab" of Egypt moves history through the "historical riot," while the "bad Arab" of the *banlieues* remains outside history.[58]

On the one hand, Alain Badiou has provided a refreshing perspective to the consideration of the event at a moment when the event is conceived as something that should never happen again, a trauma; the conception crystallized after September 11. On the other hand, his influential theory of the event as an unpredictable eruption or disruption, a singular and exceptional realm in Marxist revolutionary vocabulary, has its problems that emerge from the historicity that took shape in the post–September 11 context. At the core, Badiou's event, be it imminent or historical, shares a language of eruption associated with catastrophism and the discourse on security in the face of the tenacious dangers of terrorism in the 2000s.[59] The language of rupture or event as a vertical point in history, as unpredictable as it is, gives the sense of a certain visibility (detected by the intellectual) when it takes place, with a beginning and an end, bounded duration and location. Such peculiar treatment of event circumscribes its disorderly existence. The event gives the impression of clear readability and absorbability in the face of the vague multiplicity of archives "distracted from sources, distracted at times from its context and the long duration of its temporality, transformation even of its essence, the event becomes a reliable source," while the silences, irregularities, disorders, and enigmas it carries are often disregarded for narrative clarity.[60]

Gilles Deleuze rejects the image of clarity that "great resounding events" give in their declaration as such. He considers the event as a geological phenomenon where "the struggle is underground, and if we want to grasp an event, we must not show it, we must not pass along the event, but plunge it. . . . to grasp an event is to connect it to the silent layers of earth which make up its continuity."[61] Hence, in order to uncover its geological depths, silences and disorders that are inherent to it, an event needs to be approached as unfinished since its geographical and historical background and repercussions move beyond the moment of its present temporality. "To plunge" the event entails not to see it as an eruption of some visible truth but rather to search for the hidden "layers [that] make up its continuity," to horizontalize the event as a process in which certain historical, geographical, social, and affective forces converge.[62]

Harry Harootunian counters the conception of the present as a rupture marked by the extraordinary temporality of crisis with the Husserlian conception of "thickened present." Such thickening connects the present to its past and future, situates it within everyday life and in relation to the individual's interaction with the world.[63] The films analyzed in the following chapters unfold minority-related events not as momentous eruptions that puncture an otherwise uneventful present but as openings to explore the convergence of multiple temporalities that always already exist in the "eventful" present. For instance, the recurrent fearmongering in analyses of the 2005 French riots as an explosive social crisis related to minorities cannot be explained within the immediacy of 2005 and without the multiple layers of temporality that date back to the history of anticolonial struggles (explored by Haneke's *Hidden*). Such thick temporality also includes multiple spatialities as, for instance, zones of immigration cannot be separated from those of emigration, even though these zones are at times considered to live in different temporalities (for instance, the European past imagined as Balkan present, a discourse countered in Giannaris's *Hostage*).

Beyond its multiple layers of temporality and spatiality the minority-related event's invisible depth is often aggrandized by its constructedness in the media. Going back to Deleuze's comment about the event as a geological phenomenon that can only be revealed through plunging into the earth, the minority-related event is often overly exposed and scandalous, yet for this reason all the more deeply rooted and buried. The underrepresented elements are often silenced by those that are boisterously overrepresented in the media, and for this reason the film that deals with the event cannot ignore the mass media's approach to it. All of the films explored in this book explicitly refer or implicitly react to the ways in which mass media construct the events that involve European Others. These historical events, through mass media's silencing (Algerian demonstrations in 1961) or overrepresentation (honor crimes in Germany), have significant resonances and aftereffects and shape the affective intensities in relation to ethnicity and race in the European countries explored. As they probe into migrant and minority-related violent events, or rather the stigmatized temporality of ethnic and racial Others in Europe, *Children of Men*, *Hidden*, *Hostage*, and *Head-On* capture the invisible temporal and spatial depths as much as the affective repercussions of these events that are often constructed through the mass media.

Verisimilitude and Affect from Media to Cinema

The relationship between cinematic and media representations of migrant and minority-related events needs to be considered beyond the assumption of truthfulness to the event so to confront the frequent assumption of "documentarism" in the cinematic construction of Europe's Others. The question of the verisimilitude of the image appears again and again in instances when the characters portrayed are ethnic and racial Others. The question of how to represent the Other is frequently considered as an ethnographic problem in the realm of journalistic, sociological, or anthropological analysis rather than an aesthetic concern within the realm of fiction. These communities have become, in Rey Chow's words, the new "primitives" of Europe: the oppressed classes or the underprivileged that provide a creative source of fascination for European and diasporic filmmakers alike, who at times take the opportunity to produce ethnographic or auto-ethnographic representations, while at other times being curtailed into this social function either due to the minority personalities they depict or due their own diasporic heritage.[64] The "epistemological hierarchy" assigns the Western, the European, what is theoretically, aesthetically and temporally "the general" or the norm, while the third world, refugee, migrant, and minority remains the temporally distant ethnographic particular. A constricted politics of visibility divides the world into those who can afford a fictional self and those who need to or are assumed to reveal themselves in verisimilitude.

In consequence, when it comes to the reception of minority representations the mediatic and filmic visibility is often collapsed. In France, for instance, "the reception of *beur* cinema can be understood through a series of political and social conjunctures in the accretion of current events . . . These terms [*immigration*, *integration*, *beurs*, *marches*, and *banlieues*] act as indexical sites that facilitate the social interpenetration of cinema and establish it as a form of visual currency."[65] This transference between journalism and filmmaking does not only apply to the films made by *beur* directors. As mentioned earlier in the introduction, when

La Haine came out in France, the prime minister insisted that the film be screened to government officials, treating the filmmaker and the film as authorities on representing a deeply rooted social problem. Just as the film's opening sequence, where the archival footage from actual riots moves smoothly into the film's fictional riot, the film itself moved into the realm of journalism as it was considered to provide a privileged insight into the "*banlieue* reality." Tom Conley in his analysis of *La Haine* claims that "As it recedes from recent memory the film blends into a syndrome of frenzied opposition to civil chaos that runs from the memory of Rodney King to the O.J. Simpson trial and the idea of suburbs in perpetual disaster."[66] Conley's comparison of the film with two media events asserts the former's power of transference from the realm of fiction to that of documentary of so-called *banlieue* reality "in perpetual disaster"; a transference, as his examples from the U.S. media suggest, that is racially conditioned.

While this book is not concerned with a more accurate portrayal of minority-related events in comparison to those in the media, in response to the rapid and frequent transference between media and film representations of ethnic and racial communities, it is very much concerned with the ways that the mass media represent these events, and the generic conventions they use to promote certain affects. To better understand what is meant by generic conventions used by the mass media we need to consider a number of questions: what constitutes a media event that involves migrants and minorities in Europe? What is left in the shadows or disregarded in this realm of violent eventfulness? What kinds of events bring migrants and minorities to the forefront and create media visibility and media sensations?

An illustrative example is one of the most mediatic instances of minority-related violence in Germany: the murder of Hatun Sürücü. The twenty-three-year-old German citizen of Turkish-Kurdish descent was killed in Berlin by her brother in February 2005, allegedly for becoming too modern or Western. The crime quickly became a media sensation. After Sürücü's murder the media retroactively labeled other minority-related domestic murders as "honor killings," isolating them from domestic violence in nonminority households in Germany. Every year at the anniversary of the murder, articles that analyze the incident continue to appear in the news giving the murder the status of a cautionary tale in debates about Islam, patriarchy, tradition, and the so-called lack of integration of minorities in Germany. In contrast to the Sürücü case, the murder of Marwa Sherbini did not get the attention it deserved in

German media. Sherbini, a Muslim minority woman of Egyptian origin, took a neo-Nazi youth to court for hate speech in Dresden in 2009. At the court the accused stabbed Sherbini. Meanwhile, mistaking Sherbini's husband as the attacker, the court police shot the husband, who was trying to protect his wife. Both the German police's racial profiling of the husband and the racist murder of a minority Muslim woman pursuing her rights in a German court were significantly underrepresented in the German media.[67]

The German media's particular focus on Sürücü's as opposed to Sherbini's murder gives an insight into the particular generic component of minority visibility. While the sensational and ethnic "honor crime" melodrama is overrepresented with the yearly updated news items, the interethnic court drama depicting both quotidian and institutional racisms is reduced to a nonevent. In the former story there is a clear-cut separation of villain versus victim along ethnic and gendered lines, which allows the reading of Otherness through Manichaean dichotomies: the aggressive Turkish-German Muslim man and the submissive Turkish-German Muslim woman meet in a domestic melodrama.[68] The films analyzed in the book reflect on such relationship between the event and generic conventions when it comes to the representation of ethnic and racial Others in Europe. They probe into the media-constructed affective intensities around events by themselves appealing to genre conventions.

Genre Conventions

The main reason why this book approaches minority eventfulness through genre is the excess of generic tropes through which minorities appear in the media. The Sürücü and Sherbini cases show that within a state of eventfulness not all minority-related violence counts; there is a tight connection between genres and generalities about minorities and the media's eventualization of a minority-related event. The kind of events that become central to the visibility and knowability of Europe's Others are thoroughly generic: ethnic and racial minorities are publicly visible in family melodramas in honor crimes, thrilling menaces to safety, and humanitarian "disasters" or "tragedies."

Their subjectivity is represented as a form of generality "repeated until it takes on truth value, a truth that is repeated until its resonance dies."[69] The dynamics of genres, in their repetition and failure of conventions, determine how ethnic and racial Otherness is reproduced as an affect, to be feared and to be pitied in Europe. As the historical signification of the media event is inherently linked to the punctuation of affects created around it, especially when it concerns a repetition of certain affects in events that have ethnic and racial dimension, adoption of media genres into films allows the films' access to the affects conjugated around the event.

Lauren Berlant's definition of genre underscores this affective component in its relationship with the individual who interacts with it. She describes genre as "an aesthetic structure of affective expectation . . . promising that the persons transacting with it will experience the pleasure of encountering what they expected, with details varying the theme."[70] Berlant uses this description to explain how femininity is constructed in the United States, while in a parallel manner, I use genre to understand how ethnicity and race (or Otherness) of refugees, migrants, and minorities are made visible and legible in Europe. While generic conventions in the media present repetitions that frame the visibility for the ethnic and racial Others in Europe, the films explored in this book appropriate these "aesthetic structures" to convey a better sense of the "affective expectations" and intensities constructed around ethnicity and race in Europe. Repeating and failing genre conventions provide these films a certain grammar into which the affect related to the event and that in connection to its representation is codified. Attaching themselves to conventional generic framings of Europe's Others in the media (the Other's story as dystopic, tragic, thrilling, or melodramatic) the films explored in this study both profit from and bend conventionality from within. As the repetition of victim and criminal identities in the mass media form a minority generality, the films inquire into this generality as a sensuality stimulated by event-/crisis-based representation, a generality (established in generic conventions) that reflects anxieties about the multicultural composition of Europe.

The use of genre conventions that I track in these films does not neatly correspond to popular film genre categorizations. In chapter 3, for instance, I explore a crime narrative that blends the elements of ancient Greek tragedy with conventions of a road movie. In the Greek context the audience reactions to a tragedy with an Albanian criminal as its noble hero are so much more intense than they would be in a context where tragedy does not have the connotation of the national genre par excellence. Hence, the affective expectations particular to the context define my analysis of genre rather than structural market categorizations. Thus, Berlant's definition of genre is especially applicable in this study that focuses on the affective relationship between "the aesthetic structure" and "the person transacting with it" rather than on a formalist set of popular genre conventions that are predominantly concerned with the commercial value of the film.[71]

Moreover, the book does not deal with works that are categorized immediately under popular genre films; it rather deals with auteur films that appeal to genre conventions to wield the affective potential of genre tropes. Despite the effort to reconceptualize the supposed polarity between European art and Hollywood genre cinemas,[72] scholarship that breaks the artificial dichotomy between genres as repetition of conventions and auteur cinema as unique and original,[73] and an increase in popular genre films in certain national cinemas of Europe (such as Spanish horror films), there still seems to be a resistance against inquiring into genre conventions in auteur films. This reaction is partly conditioned by the directors' own statements against genre. Michael Haneke explains in an interview, "As a European filmmaker, you cannot make a genre film seriously. You can only make a parody . . . because the genre film, by definition, is a lie. And a film is trying to be art, and therefore must try to deal with reality. It cannot do this by means of lies."[74] Haneke's claim notwithstanding, the relationship between auteurs and genre conventions has always been more complicated than what "parody" may surmise. Fassbinder's melodramas and his praise for Douglas Sirk's films as "the most beautiful in the world,"[75] Wim Wenders's film noirs, Claude Chabrol's and Jean-Pierre Melville's persistent appeal to the crime thriller, and Costa Gavras's political thrillers have all provided insights on the appeal of genre conventions for auteurs. These directors transgress genre conventions as they exploit many genre expectations.

The auteurs whose works are explored in this book, however, do not have a comfortable relationship with popular film genres. Michael Haneke outright rejects the genre film as a "lie," and even Cuarón, whose oeuvre consists of several popular films and Hollywood productions, insists that his film (*Children of Men*) is not a conventional science fiction. These comments by directors are not anecdotal, as they have shaped the analyses of their films.[76] The films, however, call to be evaluated differently and beyond the directors' own claims about their filmmaking. The most ardent critic of genre films, Haneke, could very well be making a thriller, at times repeating and at other times bending genre conventions, just as the director of any good thriller film does.

Among the reasons for this relative neglect of auteurs' use of genre conventions is the depreciation of the affective relationship of genre with its audience. The affective appeal of genres or the affective intensities they produce in their spectators is often dismissed as "mere cliché."[77] For instance, in relation to melodrama, which is often considered the genre of sentimentality par excellence, respectable examples such as Douglas Sirk's films have been valued for their affective excess only in the potential of this excess for stimulating an ideological critique. Seeing the affective excess as a path to an enlightened ideological contradiction divides the spectators into two: the unthinking members of the popular audience who are drawn to the affective versus the intellectual ones who are distanced from it.

The relative lack of focus on the affective potential of genre conventions, thus, has roots in the theories of spectatorship that prioritize cognitive estrangement over emotional attachment. In order to avoid such endorsement of cognitive estrangement in approaching genre conventions Jacques Rancière's critique of theories of spectatorship[78] is instrumental. Rancière reveals the patronizing approach of theories of spectatorship which take spectators as mindless passive consumers of images, and assume the role of visual art is to transform them into informed and active citizens. For the philosopher, in contrast, the spectator "observes, selects, compares"; he or she is an "active interpreter" of images who translates them into his or her own realm of experience and memory, be it personal or collective.[79] Hence, the influence of visual art shall not be considered within the limits of a cognitive alienation and realization of a previously unknown fact, but as a perceptual break, "the shift from a given sensory world to another sensory world which defines other capacities and incapacities, other forms of tolerance and intolerance. What works out are processes of dissociation: the break in a relation between sense and sense—between what is seen and what is thought, what is thought and what is felt."[80]

Rancière, however, does not delve further into the sensory or affective consequences of his approach to spectatorship. While endorsing Rancière's critique of the theories of distanciation and cognitive estrangement, the question that concerns this book is how auteur films use generic conventions to approach and narrate the media event in full awareness of its affective potential, at times questioning yet always exploiting this potential. The conceptualization of affect instigated by popular genre conventions often explains the spectator's reaction as unconscious bodily excess, which once again segregates the body and the mind and assigns the former to genre film.[81] I suggest that there are more complicated reaction schemes at play that involve memory (discussed in chapter 2) as well as ideological conditioning (discussed in chapter 3) in the reception of genre conventions. Hence affect is conceived, in this book, not only as a visceral reaction but as a field that breaks the separation between cognitive and emotional states. It calls for a wider sense of perceiving reality, a more embodied and multisensory relationship to image (see chapter 4).

In that sense the book attempts to connect the study of genres with the growing field of affect theory in visual and diaspora studies. The analyses of exilic and diasporic filmmaking by Hamid Naficy[82] and Laura Marks[83] have explored the ways in which intercultural films form a multisensory connection with their spectators. Both scholars emphasize the altered sensibilities of films by exilic and diasporic filmmakers, sensibilities that deprioritize the ocular and explore the aural and the tactile so to instigate the memory of home and the experience of uprootedness in a wealth of affective registers. They both call for a different epistemology that destabilizes the Cartesian division between the spectator's body and mind, weaves together the sensual and the conceptual, breaks the hierarchy between the sensation and cognition in their analyses of memory and embodied experiences in postcolonial and transnational films. The "accented cinema" for Naficy, or "intercultural cinema" for Marks, includes more tactile details as a marked shift away from the centrality of the gaze. These films call for a broader sense of reception through a bodily identification, intend to collapse the border between the film and its audience and provide a more sensual experience of spectatorship.

The analyses of films that portray Europe's Others in this book build on this movement initiated by Hamid Naficy and Laura Marks toward a more multisensory exploration of filmmaking and spectatorship. In their analysis both scholars focus on exilic and diasporic directors who work between two cultures. The works explored in this book are chosen in an attempt to go beyond the bounds of migrant cinema explored through directors of migrant origin or descent. Though I accept the particularly sharp sensibility that the experience of exile and minority status provides in the representation of discrimination and Otherness in cinema, *In Permanent Crisis* focuses on directors who take up these issues due to political attachment and positioning along with those with a sensibility provided by personal experience.[84]

Chapter Outline

The following chapters explore genres as transnational and historically situated aesthetic forms that frame the affective economy transferred from media events to film and unfold the affects that surround the public visibility of Europe's Others. I sustain the significance of the Other in the articulation of European identity, not necessarily as a hybrid "color" but as an essential component that keeps on challenging and also holding it together. So the chapters track films that represent Europe's minorities in the twenty-first century for a consideration of how an impasse of historicity finds its language in a growing sensibility of the relationship between events and affects. This book explores the presence and centrality of ethnic and racial Others in the channeling of anxieties that are at their core attached to the fragility of European identity (ever increasing since 2007 with the economic crisis that many European countries have been undergoing) as a cohesive entity. This identitarian precariousness within the changing frame of historicity since the end of Cold War, and accelerated with the September 11 and July 7 attacks, takes an alternate appearance, that of an emergency related to migrants and minorities. At the heart of the constellation of discussions on crisis, stable European identity is conceptualized as at risk. Within European temporality constructed as a series of catastrophes, refugees, migrants, and minorities play a crucial yet always generic role as the primary subjects or objects of the catastrophic present. These migrant and minority roles appear in cinema through genre conventions that at times poke a finger at or undermine and at other times fuel this conception of emergency and crisis and the affective intensities attached to its temporality.

The first chapter provides insights into the centrality of September 11, 2001, and July 7, 2005, for a reconceptualization of history as a string of disasters. The chapter inquires into the role of refugees within this philosophy of history through Alfonso Cuarón's *Children of Men.* Appealing to disaster and action conventions, the dystopian science fiction portrays the Britain of the near future as that of human infertility, anarchical chaos, and extreme forms of discrimination against noncitizens. *Children of Men* insightfully interweaves certain anxieties of the twenty-first century—declining birthrates, security threats, and so-called bogus refugees in desperate need of humanitarian aid—that are all related to the increasingly multicultural composition of the population in London and in other European cities. *Children of Men* is exemplary of a moral economy distinguished by the contemporary global ascendance of humanitarianism, an economy in which the portrayal of the victimized and silent bodies of refugees plays a central role in presenting how the world's misery that once remained distant, has come dangerously close to the homes of European spectators.

The second chapter explores the thick historicity of minority-related violent events. It discusses the colonial history of police violence in Paris as well as the generic terms of visibility and invisibility of minorities of Algerian origin in France. "The Thrill of French Colonial History: Michael Haneke's *Hidden*," is centered on the connection between the Paris riots of 2005, during which Haneke's film prophetically made its French premiere, and the 1961 demonstrations organized by the Front de Libération Nationale (FLN) in Paris, an event at the core of the film's narrative. Michael Haneke's film *Hidden* underscores the problem that the rioters were revolting against: the unbroken repetition of colonial values through the policing of the minority population in the name of security measures. *Hidden* captures the fear-mongering that mobilizes the affective dimensions of the historical memory of Algerian anticolonial resistance in the heart of France. Fear of the eruption of repressed colonial history is an element that Haneke skillfully embeds in his film by appealing to the generic conventions of thriller. The thriller anticipates the tense emotional landscape surrounding the riots.

The third chapter examines migrant-related violent events in their geographical extension, as linked to and influencing multiple geographies, including those of immigration and emigration. It delves into a high-profile crime event in Europe's primary illegal migrant entry point, the 1999 bus hijacking in northern Greece by an Albanian migrant. This shift to Greece moves the discussion of migration in Western Europe to that within southeast Europe. Greece is the now much-discussed European country undergoing a current rise of neo-Nazi party Golden Dawn and with a major financial crisis. The chapter gives clues about the pre–Golden Dawn identitarian exclusions and discriminations in the country and the relations and conflicts with its Balkan neighbors at the height of its economic power before the crisis. The chapter, in its analysis of the film, explores the long-standing migration from Albania and the gray areas of migration regimes in Greece. Constantinos Giannaris's documentary drama, *Hostage*, represents a seemingly simple migrant crime. The film makes visible the complex networks of power politics in the Balkans: neoliberal economics and the hierarchies that shape politics between the country of immigration, the "center" (Greece/Europe), and that of emigration, "periphery" (Albania/Balkans). Comparing *Hostage* to

Gianni Amelio's *Lamerica* (1994), this chapter shows how Giannaris avoids Amelio's crude ethnography of Albania in cinemascope by mobilizing the politics of ancient Greek tragedy in *Hostage.* It explores the problems of documentary aesthetics in framing minorities: at a moment when social realism turns migrant lives into tragedies, the affective dimension of a theatrical tragedy gives historical depth to a minority character, specifically evoking the affective relationship the Greek audience has with the genre.

The fourth chapter establishes the link between genre and minority event by asking what makes the minority-related violent event an event in the first place and what sort of visibility it provides for minorities. "Ethnicity and Melodrama in the German Media and Fatih Akın's *Head-On*" looks into honor killings of minority women in Germany as mediatic and melodramatic events. German-Turkish filmmaker Fatih Akın's *Head-On* (2004) thrusts itself into the public debates around domestic melodramas, all of which rhetorically place Muslim and Turkish women in Germany as the ultimate victims of Islam and its presumed patriarchal culture. Akın mobilizes aspects of melodramatic representations, the aggressive Turkish-German man, and the victimized Turkish-German woman, in order to revise both clichés. The director capitalizes on the conventions of melodrama while eliminating its moral legibility through multisensory perception, rendering the visible ambiguous with the help of the aural and the haptic. While the chapter acknowledges the director's and the critics' declaration of the transnational quality of Akın's filmmaking, it focuses on the film's approach to the routines of ethnic visibility in Germany and the strategies that undermine the demanded ethnic authenticity from a minority director.

The book traces a commonality despite generic differences between the films explored in each chapter: the similar difficulty that all these directors face in getting away from the trope of victimhood. The epilogue suggests that, beyond all their political efforts, these films cannot distance themselves from the systematic association of Europe's refugees, migrants, and minorities of migrant origin with suffering and victimization, which perpetuates a liberal sense of European self that validates itself through humanitarian conscience. Refugees, migrants, and minorities in Europe today are central to the notion of liberal subjectivity and its self-legitimization through a state of contradiction between the need for security and the call for humanitarian intervention. The book concludes in affirming the need to reconceptualize the visibility of racial and ethnic Others, especially as detached from the overarching trope of victimhood.

ONE

Refugees and Humanitarianism in a Dystopic Europe

Alfonso Cuarón's Children of Men

The opening scene of Alfonso Cuarón's *Children of Men* (2006) depicts the London of 2027 in a state of chaos. The black screen directs the spectator's attention to the voice of the newscaster: "Day 1000 of the siege of Seattle," "The Muslim community demands an end to the army's occupation of mosques," "Homeland security bill is ratified, after eight years British borders will remain closed." The news describes a world that has become a war zone with sieges, occupations, and closed borders. The news items of the near future recall familiar global events of the immediate past: the 1999 Seattle protests during the World Trade Organization meeting, September 11 and the ensuing surveillance of Muslim minorities in the Global North, the occupation of Iraq and Afghanistan, and homeland security acts in the United States and the United Kingdom. The future depicted in the film is a version of the postmillennial present, recognizable yet more catastrophic.

The lead story on the news explains the reason behind the global chaos: the slow death of humankind due to infertility. In a London coffee shop a sad crowd gazes at the TV screen that announces the death of the youngest person in the world at eighteen years old. As the main character Theo (Clive Owen) leaves the coffee shop, the shaky handheld camera follows him, soon letting him go off-screen and panning to capture the city. The London of 2027 is gray and dull, streets are covered with flat-screen TVs, uncollected garbage, and recognizable post–

September 11 and post–July 7 announcements: "Please report suspicious activity." The moment after Theo steps outside, an explosion takes place inside the coffee shop. Catching sight of the event in the background, the camera moves forth to capture the aftermath of the explosion as a woman comes out of the coffee shop holding her own detached limb. In this world of the near future there is a thin line between watching disasters on TV and being part of a disaster. Just like the sound of the explosion that remains in Theo's ears and extends to the following scene with a sound bridge, the world of catastrophe in which Theo lives in a detached state of drunken oblivion will soon pull the character in and give him a humanitarian cause to pursue: saving a pregnant refugee from being captured by the authoritarian state as well as an antigovernment resistance group.

Despite the rumored lack of support by its production company, Universal Pictures,[1] *Children of Men* made around $70 million worldwide and was the most watched film in Britain the weekend of its release, for "clearly, the film spoke to many people's anxieties."[2] The film evokes urgent anxieties and fears that define our historical moment and are represented by two iconic images of the twenty-first century, the September 11 attacks as the epitome of the "traumatic spectacle of mass destruction," and Dolly the Sheep as the image of the insidious biological threat that involves reproduction.[3] *Children of Men* articulates a number of anxieties felt in millennial London and continental Europe: public security, declining birthrates, and a third anxiety tightly connected to the previous two—the increasing multiethnic composition of the societies involved.

A year before the film's release, on July 7, 2005, London was shaken with the news of coordinated suicide bombings. Four fundamentalist Muslim terrorists detonated bombs in London's transportation system during the morning rush hour. Fifty-six people were killed and nearly seven hundred people were injured. The bombers were British citizens of minority descent raised in the Leeds area with no established connections to al-Qaeda. Regardless, Tony Blair declared that the event signified both an external and an internal threat: "The [roots of] terrorism we are fighting in Britain . . . are in schools and training camps and indoctrination thousands of miles away, as well as in the towns and cities of modern Britain."[4] Blair's speech opened the way to fortify the security measures already established with the UK's Anti-terrorism, Crime and Security Act adopted after September 11. The regime of surveillance is extended from border control to measures that target ethnic minorities in the UK. Shadow home secretary David Davis declared multiculturalism as "outdated," while Blair's government proposed laws for removal of citizenships for dual citizens who "act in a way that is contrary to [British] interests," suggested compulsory citizenship tests, and promoted the screening of clerics and the right to close down mosques.[5]

In the first decade of the century, the other social anxiety that frequently appeared in the British and the continental European headlines was declining birthrates. Soon after the millennium the *Sunday Times* ran the following headline: "The nightmare scenario of the human race waking up one morning and realizing it cannot reproduce itself is not just scaremongering . . . if we carry on like this, it will be a reality."[6] In the subsequent years, major EU-funded conferences such as "Families, Change and European Social Policy" (Dublin, 2004) and "The Demographic Future of Europe—from Challenge to Opportunity" (Brussels, 2006) revealed the upsurge of institutional interest in population policies and the well-being of families.[7] In Sweden, demographic concern was popularized in a government-sponsored Björn Borg underwear advertisement campaign in 2001. The ad features a group of midwives gathered in the empty hospital nursery. Sixteen midwives, each representing an EU member state, look sternly at the camera. Underneath their photo is Borg's advice for the people of Europe: "One quick, and you're home free! We have a bit of a delicate problem here in the Western world: there aren't enough babies born, if nothing drastic happens soon there won't be anyone who can work and put up for our pensions. . . . Get to it! Fuck for Future."[8] While Borg's advice alerted the people of Europe to the future economic consequences of the population decline, the group of all-white nurses suggests the particular urgency of white European procreation.

In 2006 when the former Italian prime minister Silvio Berlusconi's offered baby-bonuses to parents who had a second child, those migrant parents who were accidentally sent baby bonuses were asked to return the money.[9] The same year renowned Italian journalist Oriana Fallaci announced her conspiracy theories about the invasion of Europe by so-called Islamic expansionism in her book *Force of Reason*:

> The Policy of the Womb, that is, the strategy of exporting human beings and reproducing in abundance, has always been the most direct means for taking control of a territory, of dominating a country, of substituting a people or subjugating it. . . . In all European mosques, the Friday prayers are accompanied by the exhortation to all Muslim women to "give birth to at least five children each." Well, five children

> are not that few. In the case of the immigrant with two wives, the five become ten. Or at least ten. In the case of the immigrant with three wives, they become fifteen. Or at least fifteen.[10]

While Fallaci considers Muslim men as the masterminds of a reproductive conspiracy theory, the women are deemed the passive "wombs" that carry out the insidious project that intends to make Europe "a colony of Islam." The supposedly hyperfertile polygamous bodies of Muslim migrant and minority women are imagined to pose a major threat to European integrity. As Berlusconi's policy and Fallaci's conspiracy theories manifestly declare, at the center of debates on declining birthrates is an anxiety about not having enough of the "right" babies born, a problem connected to the growing presence of migrants and minorities of non-European origin. Indeed in Britain, Brown and Ferrees's research on the print media of the early 2000s demonstrates that newspapers on all sides of the political spectrum have pronatalist articles, most of which connect the issue to migration and the increasing multiethnicity of British society, considered either as threats or as possible remedies to declining birthrates.[11]

Children of Men insightfully captures these anxieties of security and declining birthrates, as it opens with a bomb explosion and places at its center the threat of human infertility. Appropriately, at the core of the action is the government chasing a non-British citizen, a black refugee woman Kee (Clare-Hope Ashitey) who holds the key to the resolution of the world's biggest problem, as she is miraculously pregnant after eighteen years of human infertility. The action of the film centers around Theo's goal to save Kee from the hands of the police state that "hunts down refugees like cockroaches" as well as from the Fishes—a resistance group that intends to use Kee's baby to instigate an uprising against the government.

The centrality of a refugee character who needs medical and humanitarian protection gives voice to yet another European anxiety represented in the film, that of so-called bogus refugees, the politically ubiquitous blaming of refugees as potential frauds for attempting to profit from Europe's social welfare systems, which include free health care, child support, and unemployment benefits. This anxiety appears frequently in British tabloid press with headlines such as "Open Door for Bogus Refugees; Home Office Caves in to Let 55,000 Asylum Seekers Stay in Britain,"[12] "Britain Is Top Asylum Haven"[13] "Asylum: Time to Pull Down the Shutters,"[14] or in radical-right political campaigns that instigate a fake emergency: "Every day of every year, swarms of illegal immigrants and bogus asylum seekers invade Britain by any means available to them. . . . Why? They are only seeking the easy comforts and free benefits in Soft Touch Britain. All funded by you—The British Taxpayer!"[15] While the so-called crisis of asylum is surely overdramatized, since the majority of refugees remain in other countries of the Global South,[16] the figure of the asylum seeker is constructed more and more as a significant economic burden on the rarefying resources of European welfare states. In that sense it is not a coincidence that in *Children of Men* the central character is a refugee who is in constant need of medical care and assistance.

Children of Men perceptively reflects the social anxieties about security, birthrates, and refugees that the alarmist discourse of some politicians and mainstream mass media in Europe reinforces. In order to provide a comprehensive picture of these contemporary and urgent anxieties that extend from London to continental Europe and even to the United States, the film makes numerous references to political crises that concern ethnic and racial Others of the Global South (ranging from the London bombing to Abu Ghraib and Guantánamo). As in the opening scene of the film, these abundant references to the political emergencies of the twentieth and twenty-first centuries are often presented in the film's background. As opposed to many mainstream Hollywood genre films, the background is not a decor for the characters in the foreground of the action. In *Children of Men* the background shows the quotidian dystopia that the spectators inhabit, focusing particularly on discriminations and xenophobia to which ethnic and racial Others are subject to.

The near future is rendered more immediately dystopic by placing recognizable political emergencies in the film's background. *Children of Men* underscores the political urgency of these historical crises further through blending science fiction, disaster, and action genre conventions. The narrative conventions of biological disaster films and the stylistic conventions of action (mobile long takes) bring the dystopia closer to the human body. In other words, the recognizable disasters of the film are all the more immediate and catastrophic as they target the human body, rendered fragile under invisible biological threats and sudden corporeal attacks captured fortuitously in mobile long takes. The most precarious human bodies in the film, those that are most vulnerable to government violence and in most need for security and medical care, are the refugees.

This chapter explores how *Children of Men* on the one hand acutely exposes certain social anxieties that relate to ethnic and racial Others in Europe, and on the other hand adopts a historicity of emergency and crisis that, to some extent, reinforces these anxieties in the first place. Within the historicity of the film defined by perpetual state of crisis the portrayal of refugees plays a central role in presenting the ongoing misery of the contemporary world. In response to this permanent state of crisis, the film promotes the urgency of embracing a humanitarian conscience. Gearing toward such moral economy, I argue, the film is symptomatic of the frequent ways that refugees in films produced in Europe become symbolic victims whose silent and suffering bodies are thrown into the catastrophic world in urgent need of ethical politics characterized by humanitarian aid.

The Present as Chaotic and Catastrophic

In the foreground of *Children of Men* is an action film with a continuous movement toward the goal of saving Kee, the pregnant refugee. In the background of the film there is an ongoing string of references presented through recognizable iconography and sounds—references to the instances of global suffering, poverty, wars, genocides, prisons, detentions centers, human rights abuses, and environmental disasters of the twentieth and twenty-first centuries. Alfonso Cuarón explains his choice of iconography as follows: "I brought in my files. It was about Iraq, Somalia, Sri Lanka, Northern Ireland, the Balkans, Chernobyl and I said this is the movie we are doing. The rule I set is this movie is not about imagination, it is about reference."[17] In his interviews about the film the director often makes a point to emphasize that in this science fiction there is no alternative reality; the dystopia is that of our world as the film documents the disasters and political crises of the present and of the recent past.

When talking about production design, Cuarón contrasts his film and distinguishes it from one of the most profound examples of dystopian science fiction—Ridley Scott's *Blade Runner* (1982). Cuarón explains that "rule number one is recognizability. The goal is not to be *Blade Runner*, we'd like to be *anti-Blade Runner* . . . I told art department . . . I would like references of iconography, contemporary iconography that is already engraved in human consciousness."[18] By bringing up *Blade Runner*, Cuarón on the one hand sets the bar of comparison for his film, and on the other hand implies his film's originality within the science fiction genre—its uniqueness for its emphasis on the documentation of the dystopias of the present via its use of contemporary iconography. Cuarón's claim that *Children of Men* is unique in its focus on the present as a dystopic future needs to be taken with a grain of salt. The treatment of temporality in the science fiction genre has often been metaphorical and anachronic, representing the future to make a claim about the present.[19] The manner in which the film historicizes the present, however, is quite unique. The film does not aim for cognitive distancing—a common thread in Marxist or Marxian readings that valorize science fiction[20]—but engages with the affectual proximity of the recognizable present, inciting the spectators' imminent anxieties about this present. It interweaves science fiction with disaster genre conventions to construct a present/future defined by numerous recognizable and imminent catastrophes, emergencies, humanitarian crises, and disasters.[21]

Vivian Sobchack suggests that science fiction before the atomic bomb was predominantly utopian, but after the bomb it became nightmarish.[22] A similar claim can be made about disaster films after September 11 as the relationship between the spectator's perception of image and reality has changed. Films such as *Deep Impact* (1993), *Independence Day* (1996), *Godzilla* (1998), and *The Siege* (1998) had already imagined a postapocalyptic New York before September 11. After the event, the hypermediated image turned into lived experience, and the experience eerily resembled the spectacle: "The image entered and shattered our reality,"[23] which eventually resulted in an alteration of the relationship between the spectacle and reality in dystopian fiction. September 11 and to an extent bombings in London and Spain that followed September 11 changed the perception of the relationship between the aesthetic object and experience of disastrous reality in the Global North. A certain sobriety in accounting the historicity of the catastrophic experience, with its causes and aftereffects dawned upon the image.

Children of Men reflects a post–September 11 shift in disaster films. Subsequent disaster movies have become more concerned in the representation of plausible causes and in reflecting the immediate consequences of disasters on the individuals going through them. In post-9/11 genre films, the threats are more immediate; they are in the present tense, in familiar spaces, rendered less otherworldly, more human.[24] In *Children of Men* the dystopia that hits London is all too familiar; it is reflected through the iconography that the spectators can easily recognize, frequently connected to the aftereffects of September 11 (Guantánamo, Abu Ghraib) but also other twentieth-century human cruelties. The urgency of the present as a temporality of crisis is conveyed in the form of daily newspaper headlines or hourly news broadcasts that announce numerous global disasters in the film.

The opening scene already draws the spectator's attention to a dystopic present saturated with political states of emergency such as sieges, occupations, border controls and infertility all around the world. Soon the antigovernment resistance group the Fishes captures Theo to demand his help in transporting Kee to the Human Project, a group of scientists dedicated to preserving humanity. The small container where the Fishes take the protagonist is fully covered with newspapers that carry headlines of crises and apocalyptic events that took place in the recent diegetic past. As Theo is interrogated in the foreground, in the background the headlines show "extremist explosion," "Africa devastated by nuclear fallout," "Kazakhstan annihilated." Throughout the film, the background frequently contains an abundance of newspaper clippings as well as headlines that appear on TV screens and news tickers. The public sphere, from the streets to trains and buses, is flooded with news announcing the apocalypse in the everyday.

Although considered "the most obvious" the everyday is also "the best hidden," Henri Lefebvre suggests, especially because it tends to be disguised by the catastrophic: "Images, the cinema and television divert the everyday by . . . the spectacle of the distinctly noneveryday; violence, death, catastrophe."[25] At the heart of *Children of Men*'s dystopia is this very merging of everyday with the noneveryday; the present becomes a part of "the spectacle of the distinctly noneveryday"; the temporality of the present becomes associated with that of chaos, emergency, and crises. In this sense the film reflects the conception of historicity established in the post–Cold War era and furthered after September 11, "the end of history" that became an eternal present detached from its future and its past.[26] Even though there are not many more disasters happening in the world compared to the last century or the beginning of this century, within this contemporary "ambulance philosophy"[27] of history, the most meaningful historical movement and experience is considered to be the rupture of disasters, as "the rhythm of life . . . is punctuated by disaster. Images of catastrophe form part of our everyday surroundings, evoking private and public responses of compassion and solidarity."[28]

Children of Men adopts, with its advantages and shortcomings, this contemporary bankruptcy in the conception of historicity or the understanding of history as predominantly "infertile," traumatic, and catastrophic: "True infertility [in the film] is the very lack of meaningful historical experience."[29] Cuarón's film captures what Jacques Rancière calls the post-1989 "ethical turn" in politics and aesthetics. *Children of Men* "mourn[s] for the world"[30] as it witnesses one that is shaped by catastrophes and police order and one in which the possibility of transformation is dim. According to Rancière two features characterize the ethical turn: "The first is a reversal of the flow of time: the time turned towards an end to be accomplished—progress, emancipation, or the Other—is replaced by that turned towards the catastrophe behind us. But it is also a leveling out of the very forms of catastrophe."[31] The film is in a sense true to the contemporary perception of history that Rancière articulates—history not perceived as progress or emancipation or any end to be realized but history and historical experience as past catastrophes and their aftereffects. In the film, the movement toward the future coincides with a reconsideration of past disastrous event—be it the Holocaust, the London bombings or Yugoslav wars—in such a manner that the abundance of catastrophic references, to an extent, eliminates their historical specificity.

The violent events and political issues portrayed in *Children of Men* are historically linked to each other within the globalized world of capital: the environmental degradation that we see toward the edges of the frame on the roadsides that the characters travel is connected to global warming and environmental disasters, which are also linked to immigration and the creation of ghettos.[32] Despite this global connectedness, however, historicity is fleeting in the film in the vertigo of references and saturation of signs. Joshua Rowin observes, "*Children of Men* must accede to the demands of its mass audience for recognizable structures and character arcs—by stripping substantive issues of all but their iconography, the film's spectacles function as politics, its politics as spectacles."[33] In this sense, the room with newspaper clippings, as well as the film's background images that range from the Yugoslav wars to Abu Ghraib, are markers of a collage that at times plays into "politics as spectacle." This spectacle is not a problem in itself, as one may consider all politics as spectacular and performative. The spectacle becomes problematic when it moves between different historical periods and in the meantime levels historical specificity into an endless repetition of evil.

Within the abundance of references a particular element furthers both the affective potency and the sense of timeless repetition of historical disasters in the film: the references to well-known artworks that represent traumatic events. The last image of the opening scene is a screaming victim who comes out of the coffee shop holding her detached arm. For those who are familiar with the July 7 London bombings the scene brings to mind Kira Mason, a victim of the London bombing who had her arm amputated at the elbow. This precise documentation of a grotesque detail from the historical event also draws a careful connection with Pablo

Picasso's *Guernica*, a painting that we later encounter in the film, a painting that is abundant with fragments of arms stretched with open hands. While it was made in response to yet another historical bombing–that of the Basque village by the German and Italian forces—*Guernica* itself is devoid of any specifics about the time and space of the historical bombing. The context is indeterminate, while at the core of its representation lies the abstract and timeless body in pain rendered even more powerful in its affect by its scale, a giant canvas reminding of a film screen.[34] Hence, the imminent and time-specific documentary reference to the London bombing is carried to an atemporal scale with a reference to Picasso's iconography of war and catastrophe.[35]

Works such as Picasso's *Guernica* and Polish composer Krzysztof Penderecki's musical composition *Threnody for the Victims of Hiroshima* that appear in the film form an intermediality that allows an affective multisensory perception of catastrophes and their human costs. These references also carry the past violence to the present and vice versa; we hear the Libertines song "Arbeit macht Frei" in the camp where the treatment of refugees recalls images from Guantánamo and Abu Ghraib, or *Threnody for Victims of Hiroshima* during the escape from the Bexhill refugee camp. Hence, the Holocaust is connected to the U.S. "war on terror," while the Hiroshima bombing is linked to the refugees' situation. The film's intermediality renders the cruelty and suffering of mankind as phenomena that link and level different temporalities and geographies.

The director emphasizes the significance of the intended *mise en abyme* effect that includes many intermedial subtexts that mirror each other and the film itself:[36]

> You see . . . this woman wailing, holding the body of her son in her arms. This was a reference to a real photograph of a woman holding the body of her son in the Balkans, crying with the corpse of her son. It's very obvious that when the photographer captured that photograph, he was referencing *La Pieta*, the Michelangelo sculpture of Mary holding the corpse of Jesus. . . . At the same time, we use *The Sculpture of David* early on, which is also by Michelangelo, and we have of course the whole reference to the Nativity. And so everything was referencing and cross-referencing, as much as we could.[37]

The filmic reality references an artwork (the detached limb of the bombing victim, a mother crying over the dead body of her son, and burning corpses of horses in the rural landscape are all figures in *Guernica*) while the artwork references both another artwork (the mother figure crying over her son's body on the left middle part of *Guernica* references Michelangelo's *Pietà*) and then war photography (a photograph taken during the Yugoslav wars). As the fiction becomes real and the real becomes part of the fiction, the filmic references maintain several layers of mediations of the historical experience. The film itself becomes an impressive piece of art that witnesses, documents, and records the numerous catastrophes of the present and recent past.[38] Historical references are multiplied endlessly through the mirrors of mediation.

The background images of the film move back and forth between "an archive of the past" in art that shows historical violence such as the Guernica bombing, and recent history that shows "contemporary off-screen narratives of xenophobia, detention camps and racial conflict."[39] The collage of disasters lose their polemical meaning as they work in consensus to build a community for a more humanitarian world, like the utopian promise at the end of the film. As Rancière explains, "[Collages in contemporary art] tend towards social mediation, becoming the testimonies, or the symbols, of participation in a non-descript community construed as the restoration of the social bond or the common world . . . yesterday's polemical violence tends to take on a new figure; it gets radicalized as a testimony to the unrepresentable, to endless evil and catastrophe."[40] Rancière emphasizes that the changing nature of collage from confrontation to collaboration marks an era of artistic representation limited to an ethical conception of witnessing. This witnessing renders the catastrophic event as universal, constantly repetitious and timeless. The multiple back-and-forth references and references within references to historical events and to art in the film create a collage that gives a glimpse of the history of the present in snapshots. The film's collage of images flattens historical specificity of various events and imagines historicity as that of disastrous eventfulness.

Mobility under Disaster: Fragile Bodies in the Catastrophic Present

In the film Theo's cousin Nigel, the founder of the Ark of the Arts—the fictional museum that collects the disappearing world's cultural heritage, arranges transit papers for Kee. The fact that the minister of art secures flexible movement for an illegal refugee pokes an ironic finger at the schizophrenic regime of mobility in Europe. On the one hand, in most European states, especially in the UK, flexible mobility is promoted to facilitate the profitable heritage and cultural tourism.[41] On the other hand, mobility of economic migrants and refugees is tightly controlled through strict border security policies.[42]

As a subtle reference to this differential and clashing regime of mobilities in Europe, the mobility of the camera in *Children of Men*'s fluid long takes clashes with the disrupted mobility of the characters, especially that of the refugees. The refugees who often appear in background of the frame are either put in cages, packed in a bus to be carried to a camp, or live inside decrepit buses that provide a makeshift shelter for them rather than facilitate their mobility.[43] While refugee bodies are fragile and their movement is difficult and stunted, the disembodied eye of the camera remains fluid and mobile, which renders more chaotic the context that the refugees try to survive in.

The boundless mobility of the camera even during the long shots reinforces the sense of chaos and the affective power of apocalyptic dystopia in the film. The mobile long take that is the predominant aesthetic structure in the action scenes of the film gives an immediacy and urgency to the image. As opposed to fast-paced impact editing encountered frequently in the action genre, Cuarón uses minimal editing in the action scenes.[44] The camera's mobility transcends and shows the limits of the body. It conveys memorable scenes of chaos and catastrophe especially during the longest take, about eight minutes, at the refugee camp. As bodies fall and die, the camera moves on. It gets so close to action and to the fragile bodies of refugees that a splash of blood is spattered on its screen; regardless, it carries on capturing the revolt in Bexhill refugee camp and the characters' struggle to remain alive under constant gunfire. While Cuarón prides himself in the absence of futuristic technology in his science fiction, the way the camera is used in these long shots subtly gives the sense of superior technology over human fallacy, showing the human bodies as even more vulnerable in their attempt to escape the chaotic surrounding.

The mobile long take is chaotic as it provides a wealth of details that the spectator finds hard to keep up with. As the spectator searches for meaning and for something to hold onto, *Children of Men* conveys the anxiety of the movement within an unknown and dangerous territory, within the chaotic world of the present/future. As Joshua Clover states: "There's no order because there's no cause, just as there's no cause offered for the biological crisis; it's all simply become a way-things-are, some endgame of imperial decline. The camera, red smear on lens, shifting subtly between over-the-shoulder and POV, doesn't know where to look. Everyone's shooting at everyone."[45] While reinforcing the sense of chaos in its frantic mobility, the camera becomes an independent and superior eye, which exceeds that of the characters and the spectators, lingering behind, or panning around, revealing the unseen or ignored.

Due to these wealth of details it provides, the long take is often associated with realist narration, assumed to give a sense of unmediated immediacy of the event along with the ambiguity of meaning as the details within the image remain unfocused and indeterminate.[46] Cuarón stresses that he and his cinematographer aimed to give the film the look of a documentary, in terms of both the events that are represented in the background and the style of the film, which stays away from close-ups and montage, especially in the action scenes: "character is as important as social environment. That means that there are no close-ups, everything is seen from a distance and also we are trying to avoid editing seeking for an effect. Rather than that we tried to create moments of truthfulness and to have the camera registering that moment of truthfulness."[47] Hence, along with the effect of immediacy and chaos, the long takes in *Children of Men* aim to promote the director's stated goal of increasing the sense of verisimilitude.[48]

While the camera is extremely mobile in capturing the chaotic "moments of truthfulness," the humans in the film are constrained not only because of state violence that chases them or hunts them down but also their own biological limits and feeble nature.[49] Infertility in the film shows the limits of the body and its weakness against a virus that attacked one of its core functions. The threats appear in the form of viruses, and the government claims to respond to these threats by a permanent state of war to protect its borders and limited resources. The dystopia is concerned with imminent biological disasters and biopolitical regimes, the limits of our bodies and their malfunctioning. The body's limits are tested with disease (which killed Theo and Julian's child, for instance) including one that seems to have caused the decline of reproduction in *Children of Men.*[50]

Vulnerable Refugees and the Ascent of Humanitarianism

Despite the fact that a refugee character, Kee, defeats this death of reproduction and represents survival of the human body, it is again her body that is the weakest and needs the most protection throughout the film. Along with Kee all refugees in the film become epitomes of the fragility of the body facing the chaotic and catastrophic present. They ask for food in sign language, sob hysterically in fear, cough their lungs out, are locked in cages, speak or protest in languages other than English, are stripped naked, wear hoods like those of the Abu Ghraib victims, and mourn over the dead bodies of their children. The refugees are often portrayed as silent bodies, as very few of them ever voice their wishes or discontent through a manner of speech comprehensible to the spectators. The speech of the refugees is hampered in multiple ways in the film. A case in point is the scenes that take place in the Bexhill refugee camp. where we see graffiti on the wall that says *Intifada* in Latin script and in Arabic, only misspelled in Arabic. In fact, the graffiti written all over the refugee camp are misspelled repeatedly and everywhere.[51] In another scene Theo imitates a refugee's fragmented speech to divert the attention of an immigration cop: "Caca. Caca. Piss. Piss. Smell. Girl." "You people disgust me," says the cop. The message may be that the cruelty of camp conditions renders refugees speechless and inhuman, but the film perpetuates the inhumanity by making it a background spectacle that the characters have limited interaction with as they pursue their goal of saving humanity.

As opposed to the common notion about the inflation of TV images of suffering, Jacques Rancière suggests that it is not the excess of images that is the problem, it is the method by which they are presented and their always being "deciphered" by "speaking and reasoning beings." He explains: "we do not see too many suffering bodies on screen. But we do see too many *nameless* bodies that are an *object* of speech without themselves having a chance to speak. . . . The politics specific to its images consists in teaching us that not just anyone is capable of seeing and speaking."[52] In *Children of Men,* rather than hearing a refugee speak, we hear Theo's former activist friend Jasper (Michael Caine) interpreting a scene for us. As a string of faces in an overflowing "Homeland Security" bus looks toward the horizon behind the iron wires, Jasper explains and renders the situation comprehensible for the spectator: "Illegal immigrants, taking them to Bexhill. Poor fugees. After escaping the worst atrocities in the world and finally making it to England, our government hunts them down like cockroaches."[53]

As the central refugee character in the film, the representation of Kee contradicts the general invisibility and inaudibility of refugees in the film. One of the main differences between P. D. James's dystopian novel (1992)—which the film script is loosely based on—and Cuarón's film is the racial and ethnic Otherness of the pregnant woman, the mother of future humanity. P. D. James's novel *Children of Men* shares very little with the film except for the general premise of a dystopia that describes a childless world. In P. D. James's novel the questions of race and nationality are evoked but not fully developed, while Cuarón's film brings these issues to the foreground.[54]

P. D. James's mother-to-be character is a white British citizen with a minor disability. Cuarón's adaptation of her as a precarious black refugee shows the director's gesture toward a consideration of the racist anxieties involved in security concerns, border controls, and reproduction in Europe, as discussed in the introduction of this chapter. Before analyzing further the representation of Kee, the kind of promise and the alternative of political activism in Cuarón's film—particularly with regard to refugees who remain the central cause of the film's activism—beg for further investigation. In this sense, a survey of the various differences between P. D. James's novel and Cuarón's film provides insights not only into the film's approach to political activism but also into the changing landscape of activism for racial and ethnic Others who reside in Europe as noncitizens—reflecting a gradual shift from the fight for labor rights to humanitarian rights from the 1990s into this century.

In the book, James describes an aging authoritarian state in which the Warden of England, who happens to be Theo's cousin, has ultimate control. Among the aging population the order is preserved by forced deaths of the elderly who are incapable of taking care of themselves, the establishment of a distant "Penal Colony" (where a state of anarchy and rule of the strongest reigns) for all prisoners, routine reproductive controls of healthy bodies, and a labor system in which immigrants provide services for the population, only to be deported once they age and are unable to work. James's dystopia responds to the dismantling of the welfare state and the neoliberal turn of the Thatcherite era in British politics.[55] The political discussions in the novel remain relatively rhetorical, and the activism of an extremely small group of dissidents (The Fishes) seems to be limited to distributing flyers that oppose the Warden's authoritarian policies. Regarding the question of labor migrants (named "sojourners"), the Fishes in the novel are critical of their exploitation and maltreatment: "We import [sojourners] from less affluent countries to do our dirty work, clean the sewers, clear away the rubbish, look after the incontinent, the aged. . . . We take the best and then chuck them back when they're no longer wanted. . . . They work for a pittance and they live in camps, the women separate from men. We don't even give them citizenship; it's a form of legalized slavery."[56] The activists in P. D.

James's novel demand citizenship rights for "the sojourners," a right given as remuneration for the labor they provide: "full civil rights including the right to live in their own homes, to send for their families and to remain in Britain at the end of their contract of service."[57]

Though an oppressed group with marginal existence in the novel, the "sojourners" are one of the causes for political activism, a cause that is articulated as much in terms of labor rights and social welfare as humanitarian concerns. In the film, however, while the refugees have taken a more central role, the issue of labor is almost entirely eliminated. For instance, a scene in the script that shows refugees in the background collecting potatoes from the fields at the Bexhill camp is omitted from the film.[58] The world is in chaos, undermaintained, and lives tend to continue between a state of hedonistic preservation (Theo's cousin Nigel and his Ark of the Arts), a slow death (Theo drinking and gambling), and imprisonment (refugees in the camp). As Jasper describes, refugees come to England to "escape from the worst atrocities in the world" to find a safe haven in the only country that supposedly "soldiers on" as the world collapses. Cuarón and other scriptwriters turned labor migrants in the novel into refugees and shifted the ultimate dystopia in the film from prison camps for criminals to refugee camps.

Such changes in the adaptation of the novel into the film are indicative of the ways that political activism regarding ethnic and racial Others has gradually changed in the Global North from activism for civil rights and labor to humanitarianism. Craig Calhoun observes that the disillusionment of 1960s left-wing activists with more conventional agendas of political and economic change and their turn toward humanitarianism retained "the emotional urgency of 1960s politics, but in a form not dependent on any political party, movement, or state."[59] It is no coincidence that in the film one of the central characters who helps Kee is Theo's best friend Jasper (a retired Oxford professor who remains a marginal character in P. D. James's novel), a former activist, currently a disillusioned organic farmer, portrayed as an old hippie by Michael Caine, who admits to emulating John Lennon.[60] When Theo visits Jasper, the first images of his farmhouse are newspaper clippings on a wall, clippings that portray the history of an activist couple who took a stance against issues such as the Iraq War and the ban of immigration. As the world is conditioned by disasters, political activism is hampered, a paralysis symbolized by Jasper's speechless and motionless wife, Janice (Phillipa Urquhart), a former photojournalist who became paralyzed after government-involved torture. Theo himself is a former activist disillusioned by the unviable political movements in the extremes of religious spiritualism and terrorist violence—until he gets back into action for the humanitarian cause of saving Kee and her baby. While Kee is a central character in the film, most strategic debates take place between Miriam (a midwife, a health expert that is a common figure in humanitarian activism) and Theo, the two white saviors of Kee from the hands of the government and from the Fishes, the resistance group that wants to make Kee a flag for their cause and whose radical stance and unethical acts—such as killing their own leader Julian (Julianne Moore), make it yet another unviable political alternative. Within this framework, the only hope for the future is Kee's safety and the birth of her baby, a hope that is merely biological and formulated on a humanitarian basis.

It is crucial that at the crossroads of the struggle between the government, the resistance group, and the humanitarian activists are the body and the well-being of a refugee. While catastrophes are considered the movers of history and humanitarianism has become the dominant form of political action, the refugees have become the primary figures to bring home, especially in Europe, both the political crisis and opportunities for political activism, for "refugees are the prototypical face of the emergency, strangers in their new lands as well as to those distant people who may try to send help."[61] Humanitarianism moves people (especially in the Global North) into action on the basis of compassion for strangers, while the central criterion for political action has become a solidarity based on common humanity. Yet the conceptualization of humanity is human existence taken down to its biological minimum, which is "below the real minimum of the truly human, the capacity for speech and shaping social life."[62] Refugees are the ultimate personifications of this "bare life" in Giorgio Agamben's words, and they remain outside the zone of politics so long as their lives are administered within the zone of humanitarianism: "The 'imploring eyes' of the Rwandan child, whose photograph is shown to obtain money but who 'is now becoming more and more difficult to find alive,' may well be the most telling contemporary cipher of the bare life that humanitarian organizations, in perfect symmetry with state power, need."[63] Agamben suggests that the refugee, as long as he is associated with humanitarianism outside politics, human rights outside citizen rights,[64] becomes the ultimate political nonentity. By leaving refugees outside the realm of politics in a permanent "state of exception," humanitarianism excludes them from the realm of politics.

Kee's Body as Spectacle of "Truthfulness"

Kee, the first pregnant woman in eighteen years, is a refugee who is considered worthy of protection not due to her political or social identity as a refugee, but as a result of her basic attachment to humanity as bare life, as a mother of the much-awaited baby that will save humanity from perishing. She is the future mother of humanity; yet, devoid of her social character, she is reduced to bare life or her biological function that needs to be protected. What moves Theo is the fragility of the pregnant body. Kee reveals her pregnancy to Theo in a barn, a reference to the nativity scene.[65] Until that very moment Theo did not seem to care for the concerns and safety of this or any other refugee, or for the political cause of the Fishes for that matter. Only once the pregnancy is revealed and he sees her naked pregnant body does he become determined to help her out. Inside the barn Kee starts the conversation by talking about cows, how farmers cut a cow's tits so they fit into milking machines, forming a symbolic link between the cruel biopolitical order that deforms the bodies of the cows and her own situation as a refugee. When Theo questions Kee about the reason for meeting in the barn and the meaning of this conversation, she slowly reveals her pregnant body for the eyes of the spectators and for the main character.

Zahid Chaudhary notes that seeing a pregnant naked black body in a farm among cows uncomfortably brings to mind racial stereotypes about excessive black fertility. Chaudhary suggests that although the pregnant black body recalls stereotypes, this image needs to be thought of as an allegory, along with Abu Ghraib and Michelangelo's *Pietà*, that "challenges us to read race and biopolitics more broadly" in temporal and spatial terms.[66] Chaudhary considers allegory a tool that allows the text to assume several meanings through time and space, and this ambiguity makes race in the film elusive, as it evades any hermeneutic certainty.[67] As the camera strives to represent the absolute alterity of race, all signs become cipher, and allegory presents an infinite richness that continuously evades meaning.

Such a focus on the unassimilability of absolute alterity and allegory's multiplicity of meanings or its "transhistorical" nature has the potential to undermine the connotations of body as timely and historical marker of truth, or in director's own words, as a marker of "truthfulness," in this image. While the allegorical frenzy that appears in intermedial forms in the film diffuses historical reference into a homogeneous category of the catastrophic, the film does not lack a certain historicity in its approach as it conveys how the status of alterity is imagined in relation to refugees today. Hence, the representation of alterity in the film is not so much about an overproduction of signs and their ambiguation; on the contrary, alterity is either underrepresented as a silent flow of bodies or displayed as alterity revealing itself through a wounded or fragile body that needs urgent health care and humanitarian aid. So if we consider "biopolitics as a kind of traumatic sign that persists across history,"[68] as Chaudhary describes, we would miss the historicity of allegory in the scene of revealed pregnancy and the particular historicity of biopolitics it unfolds. The revealing of pregnancy scene gives a hint as to the contemporary regime of treatment of refugee bodies: the bodies of refugees are required to *reveal* themselves for truth.

The body has become the new bearer of reality for refugees. In his research on the asylum applicants in France, anthropologist Didier Fassin points out that while in the 1970s refugee status connoted political dissidence in the country of origin and a refugee's narrative was sufficient for claiming political asylum, in the 1980s narratives of trauma and violence certified by reports of psychiatric experts became required evidence for asylum applicants. These reports, often shaped by the demands for objectivity from asylum-giving agencies, gradually started to avoid the accounts and narratives of the refugees, "depriving the voiceless of their voice. Thus they bear witness—sometimes effectively, in terms of the hoped-for result of winning refugee status—without expressing anything of the asylum seeker's truth."[69] Since the late 1990s even psychiatric expert certificates of trauma have lost their validity in asylum applications. Instead, medical certificates that validate corporeal evidence of abuse and torture have become a necessity to strengthen the refugee's asylum application. That is, the refugee who applies for a political asylum has to show torture wounds or evidence of sickness, such as a medical report of AIDS that might be the result of rape, which supposedly prove his or her eligibility for humanitarian medical aid and asylum. Undocumented immigrants in France, in order to benefit from the "illness clause" and gain the right to stay in France and receive treatment, often look for ways to infect themselves with AIDS or other serious illnesses.[70] The political choices for refugees or undocumented migrants are limited to poverty, exploitation, or illness, choices that would display a particular moral economy that attracts the compassion of the humanitarian donor, be it a state, an NGO, or a benevolent individual: "With humanitarianism as the driving logic, only the suffering or sick body is seen as a legitimate manifestation of a common humanity, worthy of recognition in the form of rights; the view is based on a belief in the legitimacy, fixity, and universality of biology."[71]

In *Children of Men* the center of focus is the fragile body of the pregnant refugee who needs medical care. When Kee asks Theo's opinion about what to do after Julian's death and their confrontation with the police, the first thing Theo says is "You need proper medical care," and that's the reason, in the end, why the Human Project is chosen as the main destination; they have doctors to give Kee proper care. This is how the ultimate utopia is imagined in the film—a humanitarian group of doctors whose main goal is to provide health care to the needy. Like the boat full of health care professionals who do not represent a country in *Children of Men*, the medical profession becomes the new realm for sovereign power. Medical humanitarianism (such as that of Médecins sans Frontières, which won the Nobel Peace Prize in the 1999) has been playing a more and more prominent role in the global politics with the power to decide who can be included within the realm of humanity, along with the rights that designation would bring, such as citizenship and the right to live and work in a country, "intervening in the name of basic human life in ways that neither human rights organizations nor development projects are allowed to do."[72]

In cases of traumatic silence, the body, the wound, and then the medical report of the trauma speak for the victim who remains silent, who finds it hard to relate his or her experience of violence. But what does it mean to take the body as the sole source of evidence and not take into consideration the voice and testimonies of refugees? Fassin draws some larger conclusions about the status of Other bodies in the eyes of Western countries that are receivers of refugees and donors of humanitarian aid. The role of the body in the West, Fassin claims, has moved away from being evidence of political power; the state does not torture the body to prove its power and might. But the state still desires to see bodies, sometimes wounded or tortured or in pain, as the evidence for truth.[73] The refugee needs to show a wound to make his pain believable. The wound is proof of how full life with social value turns into bare life with no value other than its mere existence. Both Didier Fassin and Miriam Ticktin's anthropological work show how the status of refugee has moved from a political right to a humanitarian status, hence how the regime of power in the way it deals with human bodies, refugee bodies in particular, gives certain meanings to them that change in time. Cuarón's film both shows, but also is conditioned by, the treatment of voiceless refugee bodies as evidence of "truthfulness." Kee, knowing her testimony will not be proof enough, shows her naked, defenseless, pregnant body to make Theo believe that she needs to be protected and be given asylum by the Human Project. Only after the truth is revealed to Theo's surprised gaze in the barn does he decide to take up the cause of defending Kee and help her escape the possible horrors she would face as a refugee in an England that closed its borders to noncitizens.

A tortured body or a medically sick body and Kee's pregnant body revealed for truth cannot be considered the same, although drawing parallels is not entirely impossible. The lack of reproduction in the film is treated as an epidemic, and when Kee talks about how she experienced her pregnancy, she describes it as an illness: "When I started puking I thought I catch the pest." Kee is doubly fragile and doubly reduced to her bodily function, as she is pregnant and a refugee. In her study of the abundance of images of pregnant motherhood in America of the 1990s Lauren Berlant argues that "fetal motherhood" "has taken over the representational space of public dignity and value that used to be reserved as a utopian promise for women."[74] Thus, while pregnancy becomes a woman's right and privilege, women's power is both tied to and limited by the fetus and rendered apolitical in the civil sense. On the one hand, the pregnant woman is "a vehicle for the production of national culture."[75] Hence, as a nonwhite noncitizen Kee is a source of anxiety bringing to the imagination the hyper-reproductive body of the ethnic and racial Other. On the other hand, she presents a form of humanity that is degraded to its basic biological function. Cuarón's film, by presenting a pregnant refugee woman, confronts and attacks the fears and anxieties of the changing composition of the British and European population, and yet the film considers pregnancy and refugee status in such a way that in both categories bare life is valued over social experience. Although Kee's image goes against the ideal white British mother, her body is still imagined as one with no more value than a biological one. In conjunction with that, Kee's baby or fetus represents an imaginary and unmarked utopian Other that promises a world not corrupted by catastrophes, a nostalgic vision of a new world based on common humanity—the very idea behind humanitarianism.

Conclusion

For Slavoj Žižek what makes *Children of Men* a politically powerful film is the way it presents all meaningful action in the background, making space and context as important as the characters in the foreground. Žižek explains that this method is effective in attracting the audience's attention because it is "the paradox of . . . anamorphosis: if you look at the thing too directly, the oppressive social dimension, you don't see it. You can see it in an oblique way only if it remains in the background."[76] In the opening scene, for instance, the explosion occurs in the background, which forces the spectator to pay more attention to what is taking place beyond the center of the frame and implies that the real heart of the action remains toward the edges of the frame. Throughout the film the camera's point of view often exceeds what Theo sees or cares about by capturing the state of future London independently from his gaze; the camera ventures out to display landscapes and situations that Theo avoids. The film calls for an awareness of the background images and sounds as it maintains a critique of the televisual flow of images, perhaps situated and consumed in the background of a spectator's dinner table.[77] In *Children of Men*, the images and sounds that are at the margins of the frame, not quite registered or cared for, are highlighted in an effort to debanalize mediated horrors and disclose the spectator's potential proclivity to treat violence, discrimination, racism, and misery in the world as distant and marginal spectacles.

Anamorphosis, which Žižek praises, however, has been no secret to Hollywood, as the background has long been used for product placements.[78] While *Children of Men* insightfully captures the present anxieties of contemporary Europe, the director's method of anamorphosis at times treats political events and disasters as product placements that appear in quick consequent flashes of image. This method does indeed ingrain these images in the spectator's memory but also approaches these images as products that quickly emerge and disappear one after another to be consumed in urgency. As the references to historical events and timeless art flicker in the background, watching the film becomes a trivia exercise in late twentieth- and early twenty-first-century political history, one underpinned by catastrophes, wars, and human rights abuses. As the film itself becomes a spectacle through its representation of the future/present in a permanent state of war in the critically praised shooting technique relying on mobile long takes, what ultimately remains in the background are racial and ethnic Others, refugees as voiceless epitomes of global suffering and victimhood. Hence, along with and even beyond the question of *what* is in the film's background—a question that has overly concerned many critics of the film—one shall also ask *who* is in the film's background and *how* is he or she represented. In this disastrous landscape refugees are the ones with no speech, no means to talk but the use of sign language or foreign languages. They become part and parcel of the landscape.

The spectator is shown a dystopic terrain of the late twentieth century and early twenty-first century defined by violent events—a history depicted as a string of catastrophes that threatens the fragile human body. The affective power of this collage of images is achieved by integrating the most urgent European anxieties over terrorism, reproduction, and migration, interweaving the aesthetics of science fiction with disaster and action genres, and the use of the mobile long take over impact editing. The director seeks an impact of "truthfulness" by bringing together a documentary sensibility and fantastic narrative. For this impact the portrayal of refugees, their silent bodies and destroyed lives as voiceless objects of misery in the background, is central, as they become the epitome of victimhood in constant need of humanitarian aid in an apocalyptic world.

Children of Men is certainly not the only film in which refugees are part of the background picture, portrayed as the ultimate victims of globalization, whose voiceless and suffocated bodies become bare symbols of the "misery of the world"[79] that moves from one catastrophe to another. The representation of refugees in contemporary European cinema, including films representing Europe by non-European directors such as Cuarón, is frequently inflected by concerns with humanitarian crises. Refugees and migrants are portrayed as the victims of human trafficking in border spaces or of exploitation as undocumented workers in the destination countries. The filmic representations of refugees in Europe use tropes such as suffocation and voicelessness. In Damjan Kozole's *Spare Parts* (2003), a film that focuses on the lives of human traffickers, for instance, one of the most memorable scenes is when three African migrants are forced into the trunk of a car, where they suffocate; their corpses are thrown into a river. In Alejandro González Iñárritu's *Biutiful* (2010) undocumented Chinese workers at a sweatshop in Barcelona die in their sleep from the toxic gas from a heater, and their bodies are thrown into the Mediterranean, symbolizing double suffocation through the drowning of the corpses. In both cases the deaths of voiceless migrants disturb the main characters as they face the ethical dilemma of bearing the guilt of these deaths.

There are, however, some other films that place refugees at the center of their narratives, giving voice to these characters. Films such as Michael Winterbottom's *In This World* (2002) and Phillip Lioret's *Welcome* (2009) are different, as they treat refugees as central characters who struggle to make their way to the UK. The spectator hears the migrant or refugee characters' voices and perspectives, as their dreams, stories, and goals are at the crux of these two films. Both characters are political refugees; while Jamal, the main character of *In This World*, is an Afghan traveling from one of the many refugee camps in Pakistan to England, Bilal in *Welcome* is a Kurd from Turkey who seems to have left the country after having been tortured by the army, a torture he describes briefly in the film. While these political issues form the background, the main focus of both films is the vulnerability of the refugee bodies who face closed borders, become stuck in a container for days, and lose a best friend (*In this World*), or try to cross the English Channel by swimming, only to be drowned (*Welcome*). The refugee characters are represented primarily through the challenges that their bodies are forced to face, ultimately revealing their vulnerability or their survival. The refugee bodies in both cases face extreme situations of humanitarian crises happening under the noses of European spectators. In these films, the challenge always emerges from nature, rather than the bureaucratic mazes that asylum seekers go through, which are more frequently the causes of their hardships. In the end Jamal and Bilal become identifiable and rather epic heroes as they deal with and try to defeat natural conditions that test their bodies. Bare life, survival, and continuation of life are central categories that the refugee lives are considered to be within the bounds of.

Soon after Lioret released his film *Welcome* he told reporters: "What is happening here [in Calais] reminds me of 1943. Except that this is happening today, not in 1943. And it's 200 kilometers from Paris."[80] The debates around the director's statement escalated as Eric Besson, the minister for immigration, integration, national identity, and mutually supportive development,[81] criticized Lioret for comparing the fate of *sans papiers* to that of Jews during World War II and the current French immigration office to the Vichy regime. Finally, the issue was taken to the streets of Paris with a demonstration in support of the French citizens who were punished by the immigration law for the humanitarian help they offered to the *sans papiers*. The fact that the riots initiated by Lioret's film supported the rights of the humanitarian French citizens to help the *sans papiers* rather than the rights of the *sans papiers*[82] shows that at times "the victim identity imposed on so many [migrants] in the name of helping them makes helpers themselves disturbingly important figures."[83] In the end, *Children of Men* resolves that the safety of Kee and her baby, hence the continuity of mankind, comes to depend on the individual heroism of ordinary white men and women (Jasper, Julian, Miriam, and Theo), who sacrifice their lives to save humanity.

With the rise of humanitarian discourse while such heroism of ordinary white men and women becomes the model for activism, the absence of action and reaction to the misery of the world gets to be the target of critique. In *Children of Men,* Theo's earlier absence of care and effort for self-preservation, his cousin Nigel's negligence and hedonism as he collects disaster art, and all the background images of suffering that the film's characters pass by without noticing reflect the problems with watching and observing from a distance without taking action. Such a critique of white men's negligence and hedonistic living in a state of blissful forgetfulness and guilt are central to Michael Haneke's representation of his main character in *Hidden,* which I will explore in the next chapter. In *Children of Men* the remedy offered against catastrophism and eruptive crises is individual conscience and reaction rather than collective activism, as collective action for refugee rights is associated with terrorism and explosive events such as riots and rebellion that lack any care for the bare life. The next chapter will examine Haneke's approach to the possibility and validity of individual action and conscience in relation to the suffering Other. Haneke places the suffering of the ethnic and racial Other beyond the intensity of the present by tracing "hidden" histories of violence against minorities. Haneke's film deepens the historicity of discrimination against minorities through exploring a violent historical event (the massacre of Algerian protesters in October 1961), its silencing, and the affect of thrill that this suppression raises today among the nonminority population in fear of a sudden eruption of vengeance.

TWO

The Thrill of French Colonial History

Michael Haneke's Hidden

> The propaganda of far-right parties . . . is often deemed as "irrational". . . . In fact, the force of this political strategy is precisely that it does not appeal to reason but, instead, addresses the "subconscious" . . . xenophobic discourse plays on fantasies such as fear and exoticism. What matters here is not so much its content as its form. By constantly hammering on the same subjects, xenophobic discourse seeks to create associations of ideas and, especially, of images.
>
> —GERARD NOIRIEL, *The French Melting Pot,* 211

On October 27, 2005, the most intense and widespread riots since May 1968 broke out in Paris. The riots started in the Parisian *banlieue* Clichy-sous-Bois following the electrocution of two teenagers, Bouna Traore (age fifteen) and Zyed Benna (seventeen), who died instantly, and severe injuries suffered by a third, Muhittin Altun (seventeen). All three had run to hide in a power substation while being chased by the police. The riots lasted three weeks and spread to most major cities in France, from eastern Dijon to northern Rouen. Thousands of cars were burned and numerous public buildings, including schools, churches, mosques, synagogues, police stations, and city halls, were vandalized. Over five thousand people were arrested and the estimated financial damage was over 300 million euros. Discussions in the media focused on the damage caused and the spectacular displays of irrational violence rather than the deaths of the two teenagers and the responsibility of the police that precipitated the riots.[1] What did the rioters want? Why were they burning their own cars and public buildings in a nihilistic manner rather than making viable political demands? These questions brought violence to the core of the so-called "irreconcilable . . . differences between the French (*us*) and 'them,'" the *banlieue* youth, most of them minorities origins whose traced to former French colonies.[2]

Preceding the riots, then interior minister Nicolas Sarkozy had provocatively announced his intention to "fire-hose" areas of delinquency and called the young residents of *banlieue*s "scum."[3] Such Othering of *banlieue* youth was crystallized in President Jacques Chirac's declaration of a state of emergency in the *banlieues* one week into the riots. This repressive extension of state control over the suburban neighborhoods has a loaded colonial history and shows the persistence of the colonial heritage in the administrative mechanism. Years ago, when such a state of emergency was enforced in Paris, it was aimed again at "the Other within," the migrant population of Paris who lived in the *banlieues*, and it produced the disastrous outcome of the October massacre. In 1961, toward the end of the Algerian war of independence, the Front de Libération Nationale (FLN) organized a peaceful demonstration opposing the emergency laws and curfews against North Africans in Paris. The demonstrations resulted in two hundred deaths, two hundred missing persons, and twelve thousand arrests, of whom two thousand were deported to the Beni Messous prison camp in Algeria.[4] The media, at the time, misrepresented and concealed the event: the official number of deaths reported was three. Despite the increased public interest in remembering the event, the government's investigation in 1998 did not result in bringing the perpetrators of the massacre to justice. Nor has the government paid any reparations to the victims' families.[5]

Michael Haneke's psychological thriller *Caché* (*Hidden*) prophetically entwined these two historical junctures, the events in 1961 and in 2005. It is a film about the resurfacing of the October 1961 massacre, and it was released in October 5, 2005, only a few weeks before the riots began. The film's protagonists, Georges and Anne—the stereotypical bourgeois couple who appear under the same names in all Haneke films—are "terrorized" by surveillance videotapes left on their porch, videos that capture their quotidian lives. Gradually the videotapes lead the way to the revelation of Georges' secret childhood guilt: in their family farm Georges's parents employed an Algerian couple who disappeared after attending the demonstrations in October 1961, leaving their son Majid behind. Georges told lies about the couple's son, the orphaned Majid, to dissuade his parents from adopting the boy, which leads to the carting off of Majid to an orphanage. Following the clues in the videotapes, Georges hastily concludes that Majid is responsible for shooting the tapes in an act of revenge. Georges's refusal to communicate with Majid perpetrates more violence, leading eventually to Majid's visceral suicide, the climactic scene of the thriller. Despite having experienced the traumatic suicide, Georges denies any guilt for Majid's destitution when confronted by the latter's son. The film ends with Georges going to bed after taking some *cachet*'s, sleeping pills, to help him seal off both his past and his present guilt.

Michael Haneke explains that his French-produced *Hidden* is "a tale of morality dealing with how one lives with guilt. Do I accept it? And if I don't, what do I do? And if I do, what do I do?"[6] Haneke evokes issues of colonial guilt and responsibility by revealing "hidden" territories of individual and collective memory in France. Guilt, both of the main character and, by extension, of the audience, builds in tandem with the fear of terror, or terrifying repercussions of the colonial past, a fear similar to the one that resurfaced in France during the 2005 riots. The audience continuously becomes guilty by identifying with Georges's fear of revenge, while the director repeatedly challenges this racially conditioned victim-perpetrator dynamic. Haneke's skillful use of thriller conventions is central in mobilizing certain expectations and fears of the film's French and, to some extent, European audience. These anxieties emerge within the broader context of political tensions that result from Europe's uneasy relationship with its colonial past and multicultural present.

The 2005 riots instigated the worst kinds of racial and ethnic fears. The riots were seen as justifying the clichéd representations of the *banlieue* as a seedbed for violence and the stigmatization of its young residents as the "imaginary other"[7]—a discourse that has moved from extreme right wing of Jean-Marie Le Pen's Front National to the populist center-right of Nicolas Sarkozy's Union pour un Mouvement Populaire (UMP). This discourse is further stimulated by allusions to colonial history. What I mean is, references to the memory of colonial history are not only made by the Left to point out the roots of contemporary social tensions and racism in France. This repressed history is used regressively by the Right in order to address and instigate fears of its repercussions.

Sarkozy's much-debated 2007 campaign speech in Toulon is a good illustration of this appropriation of memory by the Right's discriminatory discourse. In Toulon, then presidential candidate Sarkozy raised concerns with his blunt disavowal of the crimes against humanity committed during the colonial period. Implicitly addressing the minorities of former colonial origin, he asked, "By what right do you ask the sons to repent for faults that often weren't committed by their fathers other than in the imagination of those who profess repentance!"[8] Sarkozy's denial of colonial crimes repositioned "the Algerian, Moroccan or Tunisian" outside the French national body and suggested that, in order to become "French," "he has to accept that the country to which he comes is an old country that started to exist long before him." Sarkozy's speech evoked an ancient and "authentic" French past and identity that exist separately from France's colonial heritage and its contemporary vestiges. Through an ironic repositioning of perpetrators and victims, Sarkozy held France's minority population accountable for the contemporary social tensions: "To all the people of the Mediterranean who spend their time dwelling on the past and the age-old hatreds, I want to say that the time has come to look toward the future."

Sarkozy's speech and politics utilize colonial history not only to otherize ethnic minorities but also to convey an underlying message for the "majorities" that "age-old hatreds" and possible desire for "vengeance" may have violent repercussions: "Our children are not condemned to vengeance and to hatred for eternity . . . the time has come not to reclaim vengeance one more time, but to simply love life." Beyond the message of "loving life" lies the dangerous possibility of a stubborn historical vengeance. This abuse of memory politics, revisionist, exclusionary, and abundant with embedded pointers to potential violence and revenge of the ex-colonial minorities, is part and parcel of the populist fear-mongering ingrained in Sarkozy's campaign and later presidency.

Conventions of the psychological thriller serve Haneke well in this larger French context of fear-mongering that mobilizes the affective dimensions of historical memory. Sarkozy's reference to colonial history not only excludes minority communities from proper citizenship because of their supposed hatred for the Republic, but also conveniently locates the root of the present political and social problems of the *banlieues* in the past, as the potentially explosive repercussions of history. The epigraph from historian Gerard Noiriel observes: racism works through fear and the unconscious rather than rationality, an element that Haneke embeds in *Hidden*, a thriller in which the form of the discourse takes precedence over the content. *Hidden*'s employment of the affective potentials of the thriller genre is an understudied yet crucial element of the film's social and political commentary. The film, in its representation of the eruptions of repressed history, both anticipates riots and depicts the tense emotional landscape surrounding the events.

Gaze in Haneke's Thriller

In an interview with *Indiewire* Haneke explains, "As a European filmmaker, you cannot make a genre film seriously. You can only make a parody. . . . Because the genre film, by definition, is a lie. And a film is trying to be art, and therefore must try to deal with reality."[9] While Haneke considers the genre film synonymous with Hollywood filmmaking, which distorts or at best ignores reality, he suggests that European art cinema tackles reality as an ethical position. Rosalind Galt succinctly observes the director's position underlying this claim: "It is haunted by a series of binaries that have structured European cinema since 1945: Europe versus America, authorship versus genre, seriousness versus superficiality, truth versus lies, meaning versus profit, art versus commodity."[10] Haneke distinguishes himself as a European director not only through his filmmaking that adopts urgent political themes (such as historical guilt, consumer capitalism, and transnational migration), but also through his counter-Hollywood stance maintained both in interviews and in the accelerating critical literature on his ethical approach to the spectatorship of violence and his media-critical stance.

Partly as a result of Haneke's stance on Hollywood and genre cinema that confirms his legitimacy as a European filmmaker, and partly due to the traditional approach to film genre defined in opposition to auteur originality, Haneke's use of genre conventions remains understudied. In one of the rare analyses of *Funny Games* in its treatment of thriller conventions, Catherine Wheatley acknowledges that the director's approach to genre is more complicated than what "parody" may surmise: "Haneke's genre based films . . . ironize generic conventions, but at the same time they use these conventions to place the spectator in a more immediately responsive position than the counter-cinematic principles of pure negation of mainstream convention allow."[11] Haneke does not simply reject genres. He draws from genre conventions and expectations, which serve to mobilize certain affective responses and identifications, which are to be challenged and overturned.[12]

A number of narrative elements place *Hidden* within the thriller genre: the emphasis on guilt and confronting the hidden past, the metaphorical chase (Georges being chased by his past), danger conceived as a life-and-death threat, Georges's fear of intrusion and losing the comforts of a cultured bourgeois life, the invasion of the household from within through Georges and Majid's sons' probable relationship that is hinted at the final scene, prophetic markers such as the joke involving a neck injury told at the dinner party, which creates shock and laughter, or a racial confrontation with a biker.[13] In terms of camerawork and mise-en-scène *Hidden* distinguishes itself as a thriller with elements such as careful use of shadows and lights (truth revealed in a dark room, the camera and probably Georges hiding in the barn at the flashback scene when Majid is taken away to the orphanage), the camera's tight framing of Georges, the protagonist's multiple entrapments (in a police van with Majid and his son, in the room with Majid's dead body, in a crowded elevator with the possibly vengeful son of Majid, then in the bathroom with Majid's son), and the use of tight, claustrophobic space such as the dark corridors leading to Majid's apartment with suspenseful sound of footsteps. As in all good thrillers, *Hidden* does not have a resolution.[14] Haneke withholds the resolution of the mystery and tilts the focus toward presenting the social and historical dilemmas.

In a generic realm of unlimited possibilities, why did Haneke choose surveillance videocassettes as the element of thrill? What is so terrorizing about being watched and filmed for a TV presenter accustomed to being televised and taped? Surveillance and voyeurism have been central to the genre of the thriller.[15] In their 1957 book on Hitchcock, *nouvelle vague* directors Eric Rohmer and Claude Chabrol point out that "the primary importance of Hitchcock to the thriller genre, and indeed to cinema in general, derives from his obsession with voyeurism."[16] As Rohmer and Chabrol point out, voyeurism and the ubiquitous gaze make Hitchcock's work a metanarrative commentary on the link between power, affect (be it thrill or desire), and spectatorship: a connection central to the critical literature on Hitchcock with important repercussions for feminist and postcolonial film studies.[17]

Critics have similarly interpreted the thrill of the surveillant gaze in *Hidden* through its affinity with power and control: Georges is terrorized by the ubiquitous gaze of the videotapes because he fears the loss of control in the realm of media over which he has assumed full control via his occupation.[18] Ranjana Khanna's postcolonial reading emphasizes that surveillance in *Hidden* connotes the shifting control over images and the power dynamic between the former colonizer and the colonized: "a narrative of revenge in which a camera gaze is returned in an oppositional structure. . . . *Hidden* is ultimately a film about anxiety in relation to a history of colonial violence and the technology associated with it."[19] Surveillance technology signifies the reappropriation of the gaze and the power associated with it, especially considering the censorship of the images associated with the 1961 massacre of Algerians until the 1980s. Along similar lines, Ara Osterweil points out that in the film the ex-colonial subject looks back to stigmatize the privileged white subject, the original master of surveillance.[20]

These reviews from a postcolonial angle, however, disregard the ambiguous role that the spectator of the film (an art house audience that is possibly closer to Georges in class and race position) takes in the process of overturning the gaze from the former colonizer to the colonized. Hence, who looks back and returns the gaze, as well as the nature of this gaze, is more complicated than it seems. Thomas Levin points out that surveillance videos in *Hidden* and their power is problematic since they gradually gain "a truth function," from which emerges an unprecedented disciplinary role for the audience, who starts policing and interrogating the protagonist. For Levin, this panopticism grows in contradiction to Haneke's much-emphasized media-critical stance: "instead of being a source of anxiety, [surveillance] now increasingly functions as a welcome locus of disambiguating omniscience."[21]

While Khanna's approach ignores the questionable role that the film's spectator takes via the surveillance videos, Levin's emphasis on the audience's power of the gaze is equally limited as he associates videos with the control embedded in voyeurism, a one-sided power dynamic. This established notion of "seeing as a form of power and being seen as a form of powerlessness"[22] only partially explains the thrill of the surveillance images both for the protagonist Georges and, by extension, for the audience. While acknowledging the connotations of power and control embedded in the gaze, I suggest an additionally productive route to elucidate the politics of the surveillant gaze in *Hidden*: the gaze as a trigger for memory and for an affective relationship with the past. In *Hidden* the surveillance videos propel the thrill of colonial history.

Deleuze articulates such links between gaze, temporality, and memory in his approach to Hitchcock spectatorship. He detaches the Hitchcockian gaze from the pleasure that arises from identification or control. For Deleuze the gaze enables a different affective experience: the inclusion of audience into the labor of forming mental relations. These mental relations establish links between different temporalities within and outside the film; they are stimulations of memory. Adopting Bergson's philosophy, Deleuze articulates the dilemma of temporality that shapes film and spectatorship as the existence of the past in the filmic present that dynamically moves toward the future: "The past co-exists with the present . . . at each moment time splits itself into present and past, present that passes and past which is preserved."[23] This operation of time is visualized in "crystal-image," which is the image of duration that enables a perception that links the three temporalities—the past, the present, and the future: "mobile mirror which endlessly reflects perception in recollection."[24] The crystal-image connects the gaze to mental images through constantly referring to the audience's memory, facilitates connections between the past and the present of the image as well as its outside, audience's memory. The past survives in the present as it moves toward the future, and this preservation and stimulation of memory is key to spectatorship for Deleuze.

Patricia Pisters reads Deleuze's contribution to the literature on Hitchcock as the possible route to a new definition of subjectivity in spectatorship: the gaze is not only defined through pleasure, control, and power but also as a negotiation between different temporalities as well as the film and the spectator; "The self/subject is no longer dependent on the supposed desire of the other . . . but has to negotiate between the images presented to his mind and the memories induced by his own body."[25] The subject/ spectator gains new agency in the process: as an alternative to being a desiring consumer of images, she is involved in an active perception process that does not necessarily involve the pleasure of control. In Jacques Rancière's terms, this "emancipated spectator" is an "active interpreter" of the film who translates the image into his own realm of experience and memory, be it personal or collective.[26]

In line with Pisters's reading of Deleuze, I argue that in *Hidden* the thrill of surveillance videos does not emerge from the pleasure of the gaze but from an uneasiness that these videos create through stimulation of memory, both of Georges and of the audience. This feeling of uneasiness is reinforced by the fact that surveillance videos do not only watch and are watched but also break the narrative time and instigate first personal and then collective memory. Videos articulate a complicated affective experience: a potential pleasure of voyeurism is interrupted by the thrill of memory and the affective link between the present and past. As Thomas Elsaesser explains, in *Hidden* the surveillance videos produce metaleptic shifts that are "radically disturbing our sense of chronology and temporal hierarchies of past, present, future . . . it is these moments of metalepsis that give [Haneke's] films their seeming power . . . to invade the spectator's psychic and emotional life."[27] The surveillance videotapes raise mental images both through instigating memory and affecting thrill through this memory—for both the protagonist and for the audience. The affective relationship between the thriller and its audience is pursued not only by the mobilization of a repressed colonial history but also through connecting this history with its present, overwhelmed with anxieties and tensions of multicultural postcolonial France.

Memory, Temporality, and the Tapes

Hidden opens with a long and wide shot of a peaceful Parisian house captured from across the street. After watching this static shot for over two minutes, we hear a man's voice in the background: "Well?" A woman replies, "Nothing." The man questions further: "Where was it?" "In a plastic bag on the porch." The cut to a closer shot of the house as a man leaves and then the rewinding of the image reveal that the earlier static shot of the house was from a surveillance videotape received by the owners of the house, the literary talk show host Georges and his editor wife Anne. Both the film itself and the surveillance video are shot with a high-definition digital camera, and hence the transitions between the two kinds of images are seamless, distorting the spectator's sense of space. While spectators believe that they are looking at the house from its outside, they are in fact watching a video image of the house from inside that same house, along with the two protagonists. The videotape puts the spectators immediately in the position of voyeur, along with the characters under surveillance. In opposition to this proximity with the film's characters, the spectator is distanced from the image by the invisible presence of another camera, which shoots the tape. Thus, the spectator is closer to the film's characters than he had perceived, while more distant from the image itself. This spatial disorientation is complemented by a confused sense of time. The image of the house in the video belongs to the film's past, the past of the diegesis. While the spectator thinks he is situated in the present time of the narrative, he is, in fact, watching the past as if it were the present. What is seen is a previously recorded scene on a videotape within the film, a rupture in temporality perceived as continuity.

The second tape the couple receives also shows their house, this time shot at night, and it is accompanied by a disturbing childish drawing of a rooster whose throat is cut and bleeding. Then, Pierrot, their son, receives a card at school with a similarly childish image of a boy gushing blood from his mouth; Georges receives the same card at his office. The suspense is augmented not only by the decentering and spatial expansion of the threat posed by images, but also temporally: the violent childish drawings aim to unveil the darker territories of childhood. The third tape reveals personal information about Georges, showing a car driving to the family farm where he spent his childhood. Thus, the tape points to Georges as the target: it is his past, his childhood that the tape tracks. The tape directs him to follow its clues, which lead Georges to visit his mother to provoke her memory about Majid, the Algerian orphan, a topic Georges's mother refuses to think and talk about. Next, the fourth tape shows a run-down apartment in a Parisian suburb. Tracing the clues on this tape, Georges finds his childhood foe, Majid. Thus, the surveillance videotapes gradually change function, from capturing the protagonist's present to traveling to his past, from stalking him to forcing him to visit the places shown on the videos. The tapes start to foreshadow his movements. The video images simultaneously target the past, the present, and the future: they are intended both to provoke memories of Georges's past actions and to direct his future movements. The tapes' triple trajectory—provoking the past, leading the present, and foreshadowing the future—continues to rupture the diegetic continuity to recall other temporalities that are experienced simultaneously with the filmic present.

The final videotape records the confrontation between Georges and Majid, which the spectator has already witnessed. The surveillance camera records the meeting and its traumatic effect on Majid, which has remained, until then, unknown to the audience. Moreover, the surveillance videotape informs Anne of Georges's confrontation with Majid, a fact that her husband had spared her, and thus it enforces the unveiling of the protagonist's past: Georges is obliged to confess to Anne (and the spectator) about Majid's parents' death in the 1961 massacre, his own parents' subsequent willingness to adopt the orphaned boy, and his own lies about Majid to dissuade his parents from adoption.

The confrontation scene, which contains a rare verbal interaction between Majid and Georges, is symbolically located at the center of the film, halfway through the script.

> GEORGES: Who has been terrorizing my family?
> MAJID: I don't know. Why do you talk like we're strangers? . . . How did you wind up on TV? You didn't take over the estate?
> GEORGES: Tell me what you want.

Majid gestures to the past, while Georges wants to keep their exchange in the present. As the conversation proceeds, Georges and Majid are gradually distanced from each other and placed into separate frames. The camera is tighter on Georges, framing him in medium close-up—a camera perspective rarely used by Haneke, who prefers to draw his camera away from his characters. Conversely, Majid is captured in a long shot situating him in his surroundings, shot from Georges's point of view. The camera's distance from Majid emphasizes his destitution and provides material for comparison between his house and that of Georges, his would-be brother. The different camera perspectives on the two also reveal Georges's anxiety and childish incommunicativeness in opposition to Majid's visibly calm disposition, a representation that builds itself against mainstream cinema's depiction of the victim-perpetrator dynamic in racially informed confrontations.[28] The interrogator (Georges) gradually becomes interrogated by the camera, and he makes a tepid confession that delves into their common past: "You were older and stronger than me. I had no choice."

Georges leaves the house after threatening Majid. He calls Anne but hides his confrontation with Majid: "I went round, nobody was in. . . . No, it was just one in a row of doors, it was locked. . . . I did, he said it was unoccupied, it must be a storeroom or something like that." Georges' desire to "lock" up this confrontation, the memory of Majid, and his past in "an unoccupied storeroom" proves to be impossible when the videotape of this meeting reaches Anne. The video footage of Georges's confrontation with Majid produces a flashback that reiterates the reality of the meeting, reproducing the film through the video. This forced flashback not only refreshes Georges's memory of the meeting and of his past but also displays a previously invisible perspective: it extends Majid's side of the story. This extended perception adds a critical function to the surveillance videos: that of witnessing the concealed future of the lived experience.

In the beginning, surveillance is presented as the source of the thrill that disorients the audience in spatial and temporal terms, pointing to ruptures in space and time, from the past to the present. Surveillance videos, then, instigate memory to lead the story and the characters in their search for a solution to the mystery. The tapes take the protagonist to his parents' house and then to the suburbs of Paris, two rides that force him to confront his past. And, finally, the surveillance tapes acquire the function of chronicling the unseen future of the experienced confrontation, providing a perspective that differs from the protagonist's point of view. The mediating videos provide mental images that stimulate a repressed memory for the protagonist and gesture toward what he and the spectators fail to see: multiple temporalities lived in the present.

Kristin Ross explains that "history as rupture" has shaped French official discourse on the colonial era: "France's denial of the ways in which it was and is formed by colonialism, its insistence on separating itself off from what it views as an extraneous period irrelevant to its true national heritage, forms the basis of the neo-racist consensus today."[29] Compartmentalization of colonial history as an "extraneous period" and its derivative historical revisionism effectively suppress continuities of colonial mentality and structures in contemporary France. The historical event, its concealment, and the contemporary repercussions of such violence (both of the event and its silencing) are central to *Hidden*'s structure. The film's temporal index suggests that Haneke blends film and video images to evoke multitemporality in the present, and also to evoke the history of injustice as continuity presented to us as rupture.

The media-critical stance Haneke takes shall be considered within the context of a further dilemma: the rupture that is created through the absence and repression of violent images of the 1961 massacre is compensated with the oversaturation of violent images that portray the minorities today. Colonial memory shapes both left- and right-wing politics, though in radically different ways. The former delineates historical legacies of racism in France today, while the latter revives an "extraneous period" to instigate fear of its consequences. For Georges and in extension for the film's French audience, the raising of a suppressed and undocumented colonial history has very immediate repercussions in today's multiethnic France. The videotapes witness, track, force out the memory of the violent past within the film, and consequently, the film itself becomes a witness to the violent suicide initiated by the traumas of the silenced past.

The tapes thus have two interconnected functions: they accuse Georges of telling his past lies and of his present ignorance, and they threaten his comfortable life and career. Therefore, Haneke accomplishes two goals simultaneously when he inserts surveillance images within the film. On the one hand, he affirms the validity of the filmic reality and its witnessing of an invisible history by benefiting from the more reliable indexicality of the video images and their "truth function."[30] On the other hand, he unsettles the perception of his protagonist and the audience through the temporal disturbance of a memory that potentially threatens the stability of the present. Haneke's appropriation of the temporal indexicality of surveillance video enables Deleuzian "mental relations" in the present (not-so) perfect tense, showing a past whose effects stretch into the present. Haneke both shows us that historical injustice is a continuity presented to us as ruptures, and mobilizes the memory of colonial history to point to the thrill of its potentially explosive (the potential revenge of Majid and his son) repercussions in the present. Hence, it was all the more timely when the film's premier coincided with the 2005 riots.

The Thrill: Guilt and Sensationalism

Establishing guilt in the audience is an essential convention of the thriller genre. The identification with the victim and the desire for the victim to overcome the threat blends with the contradictory identification with the villain's success, the guilt of desiring to see the spectacle and to feel the thrill of an ongoing threat or on-screen violence. Regarding *Hidden*, Haneke confesses that he appeals to the conventions of thriller genre in order to produce guilt: "It basically develops like a classic thriller. Thrillers always work with fear. . . . I used this format principally to ask one question: how do we deal with our guilty consciences?"[31] Embedded in the thrill is the relationship of guilt between Majid and Georges, and by extension, between Majid and the audience.

The induced guilt is also the political core of the film's message, a thriller that centers on a French family "terrorized" by its colonial past and Algerian half-brother. The film continuously challenges the expected racial dynamics of culprit-victim. The suicide scene—in which the potential victimizer becomes the ultimate double victim—is crucial to this challenge. Despite the death of Majid, however, the director keeps the suspense alive until the end of the film. The continuing threat of a revenge act by Majid's son either on Georges or on his son Pierrot keeps the audience on his toes even in the very final scene, where we see an inaudible interaction between the two sons. The director promotes the idea of Majid's son as a potential threat by the latter's uninvited "invasion" of Georges's "respectable" workspace. The camera captures them together in a claustrophobic, long, and suspenseful elevator ride, after which Majid's son calls him out of his office in front of his colleagues, furthering the discomfort. Georges himself makes the situation worse by rudely trying to avoid Majid's son and taking the conversation to yet another claustrophobic space, the men's bathroom, a possible allusion to the fact that he wants to flush down the disturbing memory and assumed threat. The ongoing potential of a threat is never fulfilled despite Georges's visible anxiety and fear. The protagonist's ongoing anxiety promotes repeated identification that becomes the instigator of guilt again and again for the audience. Yet a major fraction of the audience's guilt may also emerge from having secretly expected the unfulfilled genre convention: the victimized white French protagonist and vengeful Algerian victimizer, the racially conditioned expectation of terror and irruption of violence.

Haneke depends strongly on the shocking power of the suicide scene to generate guilt in his spectator. *Hidden* is advertised on a poster that shows a plain white surface slashed with a stain of blood that represents the climactic scene of a suicide. Georges accuses his Algerian childhood acquaintance (Majid) of "terrorizing" his family with surveillance videos of their private lives. Majid invites Georges to his house, where he calmly denies this charge saying, "I called you because I wanted you to be present." He takes out a razor and slits his own throat in a split second. The camera shooting from behind Georges situates the spectator and the protagonist side by side while they watch the shocking act. The long, static shot emphasizes the unsettling nature of the suicide. We, along with Georges, are forced to remain in the room with the bloody corpse blocking the way out.

The director admits that "This is the most important shot of the film: if the suicide scene is not plausible, then the entire film is spoiled . . . a static and fast-paced, terribly realist shot. . . . We can even consider this suicide a special effect!"[32] Haneke connects the reality effect of the film to its shock value, its ability to raise intense audience affect and reaction. This bloody and disturbing physical violence is made central to the film—as the film poster implies and the director admits. The suicide's thrilling effect is crucial as it extends to the audience like a surrealist painting that aims to reach out, grab, and shake its viewer so as to revoke the history of violence that has, until recently, been repressed in the French collective unconscious. Haneke establishes links between the personal and the collective conscience, the private and the public forgetting, the protagonist's denial and the French state's refusal to admit to the perpetration of colonial violence.

The manner in which this suicide is performed and shot aims to violate both the protagonist's and the spectator's vision with an explosive virtual accusation: "You are all my murderers!" In a way, Haneke (and Majid) assaults the spectator to attain affect, which the director believes stimulates mental processes and propels thinking on violence. Brigitte Peucker, in her analysis of Haneke's work, detects two interrelated tendencies in the director's films: disturbing acts of violence and the tableaux of bourgeois melodrama. Against the common affiliation of Haneke's cinema, mainly asserted by the director himself but also by his critics, with Brechtian distanciation and intellectual provocation, Peucker suggests that Haneke's films force the audience "into the realm of programmed emotion and creates melodramas obsessed with heightened emotions, guilt, and fears."[33] Peucker's implicit association of melodrama with "programmed emotion" is debatable, but her analysis observes a significant and understudied element in Haneke's cinema: its strong appeal to audience affect.

The shock value that Haneke attributes to the suicide scene recalls an age-old modernist technique, *épater le bourgeois.* However, the modernist thrill that strives to take the middle class out of its comfort zone can hardly be seen through the same interpretive lenses and considered to have the political edge it had in the late 1920s. At its time, Luis Buñuel's eye-cutting scene in *Un Chien Andalou* (1929) shocked the audience with obscenities and shook them into new ways of seeing. Violence in art cinema today, however, has become a convention in itself, a convenient way to fulfill the expectations of the art house audience that is ready to be provoked by an art film. New Extreme French cinema of the late 1990s and early 2000s, for instance, turned gruesome corporeal violence into a trend.[34] Art cinema today frequently appropriates emotional structures of what Linda Williams calls "body genres" or "genres of excess" such as horror, porn, and the "weepie," for which the measure of success is the extent of the bodily reaction or sensation on the audience.[35] One needs to acknowledge Martine Beugnet's insightful analysis on the rise of corporal violence in cinema as a call for a different epistemology, an attempt to create a multisensory relationship and bodily identification between the image and its audience, which gets the audience closer to borderline experiences such as physical violence.[36] However, it is impossible to avoid such films' cult commodity value within festival and art film audience circles. Violence and shock tactics, previously limited to popular genres such as horror or porn, become a way to profit and enter into international film circulation by way of a bodily "affect economy": "something that persists after the viewing is over, something that makes you want to talk about."[37]

Admittedly, Haneke's philosophical stance on violence is more nuanced than, for instance, some New French Extreme filmmakers. Haneke's frequently stated political agenda intends to make audiences think critically about the senseless flood of violent images in mass media and in the film industry. There is an inherent dilemma, however, in Haneke's use of violence in his cinema, as Thomas Elsaesser underlines: "violence is bad for you, says the director who inflicts violence on me."[38] This dilemma becomes apparent in the director's desire to make the audience more sensitive to violence and the alternative methods he resorts to for securing such an effect. Haneke claims, for instance, that in representing violence the appeal to the spectator's ears is more effective than addressing his eyes. That is, to hear a victim's cry or scream creates more intense affect than to see the act of violence or the victim's wounds.[39] In *White Ribbon* (2009), for example, one of the most violent scenes is the flogging of a child, we hear the whip and the boy's muffled sighs from a camera that remains unmoved in front of the closed white door. Haneke's intention to evoke reaction and leave a stronger and memorable impression on the viewer invades less explored and exploited spaces of the audience's body, in this case the aural realm. This fresher pathway to memory and attention is disturbingly close to the techniques of provocation that cash in on the memorability of visceral effect. As film scholar Jonathan Beller explains, "in a fully globalized situation, capital expands not outward, spatially and geographically, but *into* the body, mining it of value."[40] The memorability of the film is inherently linked to its circulation and commodity value, and in art cinema the horizon is more and more defined through the affective influence that circulates through the audience's body. This, at times, brings art cinema closer to "body genres," porn, melodrama, and horror, in its parallel aspiration for affective excess, not, however, for a temporary instigation of pleasure but for long-lasting effect and memorability.

In *Hidden,* the director's intention to thrill and provoke guilt in its bourgeois audience inherently limits this very possibility since it pushes the director to the limit of sacrificing the victim to force out affective excess. The irony in the way the director deals with his obsessive themes (bourgeoisie and violence) is that he not only denounces violence by representing violence, but similarly, his films denounce the bourgeoisie to produce representations of bourgeoisie for the bourgeois art house audience. With the focus on French bourgeois guilt and affect, the Algerian Other becomes an inaccessible text, or a pretext to contemplate guilt, a guilt whose very existence is void in the illusion of presence of a subject that is inherently incapable of raising audience empathy and responsibility. Majid and his unnamed son become incommunicable absent presences. Majid's limited psychological depth makes it especially impossible to rationalize his actions and hence increases the suicide's "terrible realism," its shocking and thrilling effect on the audience. Beyond the valid and important question of the lack of political use of guilt,[41] do shock and a rather cheap thrill have the potential to extract guilt in the first place? More significantly, is it necessary to produce one more Algerian victim, one more death to commemorate the October 1961 victims?

Majid's suicide becomes an inaccessible act whose meaning is closed to the audience. Sociologist Maurice Halbwachs indicates that a suicide becomes less impressive if we cannot perceive the motivation or formulated thought behind it. Halbwachs argues that most suicides have a societal basis, and points out that there are close analogies between a suicide and a sacrifice. Especially when "the desperate person seems to wish to provoke a scandal by the outrageous or unexpected nature of his act to terrify and torture his survivors, to crush them beneath the weight of remorse, to project on to them clearly the responsibility for his death,"[42] he commits suicide in front of a particular person who, in his eyes, represents society at large. Such a suicide, according to Halbwachs, recalls "certain forms of sacrifice of imprecation and vengeance."[43] Halbwachs's description illuminates the function of Majid's suicide: Haneke sacrifices Majid to imprecate the audience with guilt by staging a public self-prosecution with a mute but vengeful accusation: "You all are my murderers." Majid exists in his death and suffering (dying on the film, crying on the videotape after the confrontation), which create "programmed emotion" to provoke guilt in Georges, and possibly in viewers as well. Majid's act is incommunicable, as it lacks more viable visual and textual language. His story is closed and removed from the film as a passive-aggressive death whose only meaning is the imposition of affect and guilt through Haneke's "special effect," if not recognition of his innocence by the audience and a possible spark for a future threat by Majid's more reactive son. Majid's more reactive son, too, is incapable of telling his father's story, or his own. The nameless son, in his confrontation with Georges after Majid's death, seems to approach Georges only because he "wondered how it feels, [to have] a man's life on [his] conscience. That's all."

Majid's violent suicide places him in the position of masochist, while both Georges and the spectators, in a mediated sense, become sadists. A Deleuzean reading of Majid's masochism, like Jean Ma's analysis of Erika Kohut's self-mutilation and masochistic fantasies in Haneke's *The Piano Teacher* (2001), would separate this masochism and sadism as fundamentally different positions, since "while sadism draws out the violence of the world in order to multiply it . . . masochism reflects the excess of violence in order to reconstruct it in a different format that nonetheless still preserves this excess."[44] Ma mentions the difficulty of disregarding the power dynamics in play when it is a female victim whose body is objectified in the masochistic aesthetic. There are problematic connotations of representing the female in *The Piano Teacher*, and the postcolonial minority in *Hidden*, as bodies that are assigned to "preserve" the "excess of violence." In some sense, Haneke confers upon the bourgeois art house audience the right "to draw out the violence of the world to multiply it"[45] and, in turn, to map the position of already subordinated subjects as doomed to containing violence within themselves.

In Jean-Paul Sartre's terms, the guilt-inducing suicide as a masochistic act is "a perpetual effort to annihilate subjectivity by causing it to be assimilated by the Other,"[46] while it produces spectator sadists who are entitled to "treat the Other as an instrumental object, seek[ing] to utilize the Other's body as a tool to make the Other realize an incarnated existence."[47] Eventually, both masochism and sadism are merely "assumptions of guilt." The position of the masochist is a self-deception, a futile effort that fails to eliminate the subject position and to turn oneself into an object: "The more [the masochist] tries to taste his objectivity, the more he will be submerged by the consciousness of his subjectivity."[48] Thus, Majid's masochism may potentially produce an inert, enclosed, self-centered, subjective conception of guilt but does not necessarily exert an existential guilt that emerges from reciprocal human recognition since: "It is before the Other that I am *guilty*."[49] Majid's suicide rejects a feeling of guilt that opens one's heart and eyes to the Other's pain by enclosing violence in the antagonist himself.

Even if Majid's character was more accessible, the complexities of representing the Other are never easily solved—hence the last videotape that shows the voiceless, suffering, crying Other. My critique does not suggest that the film lacks a progressive political agenda. I intend to present the inconsistencies that undermine its progressive agenda. As Paul Gilroy's brief analysis of *Hidden* sums up: "When the Majids of this world are allowed to develop into deeper, rounded characters endowed with all the psychological gravity and complexity that is taken for granted in ciphers like Georges, we will know that substantive progress has been made towards breaking the white, bourgeois monopoly on dramatizing the stresses of lived experience in this modernity."[50] Majid becomes the object of the thrill, a "special effect," the suicidal Arab (yet another thrilling stereotype that recalls terror and eruption) who becomes one with the razor that cuts his throat. The film's "terrible realism" brings about a narrative closure that buries what it successfully captures—the perpetuation of historical injustice in present-day France—once again, in the dusty archives. The potential threat that comes from the past, to the relief of the protagonist and the spectators, is buried in that past again.

Conclusion

The quotidian lives of *banlieue* youth and how they are perceived as potential threats even in simple interactions with the white French bourgeoisie are depicted in colorful comical snapshots in the animated television series *Les Lascars* (2000 and 2007). One of the episodes shows a husky minority youth asking for a cigarette from a white businessman in a suit who replies, "There's a tobacco shop over there!" The young man responds calmly, "Oh yes, but I didn't ask for directions, I only asked for a cigarette." The Parisian businessman starts to get nervous: "You guys from the *banlieue* never know when to stop," which annoys the young man, who replies, "Why do you bring up the *banlieue*, you fool, I live in Châtelet," a neighborhood in central Paris. The former looks visibly alarmed, threatening the latter: "I'll call the police." The latter is taken aback, "Why? No one stole anything. I only asked for a cigarette." Finally, the businessman takes out a pack of cigarettes and offers them with shaky hands, and when the young man finds out that they are ultralights, he rejects the offer and walks away.[51] The video provides insight into the unreasonable feeling of threat, fear, and stereotyping of minority youth in France, a picture of affects crucial to the political landscape of everyday life. Haneke's psychological thriller perceptively reflects on the roots of such everyday xenophobia, the fear and the thrill that underlies stereotypical perception of minorities in today's France. While fears incite the need for security—the security of white French citizen overtaking and making invisible the fragility of minority lives and various threats they face—the thrill feeds itself with memory politics.[52]

Anne Donadey suggests that, when dealing with colonial history in postcolonial France, guilt-induced mourning for the dead or asking for forgiveness is not enough. She claims that simultaneous with memorialization one should always be aware that "at least at the unconscious level, [today's] racist acts can be seen as a continuation of the repressed, lost colonial war."[53] Such appeal to memory politics is not solely an affair of the left. Populist right-wing politics intentionally recalls the repressed history of colonial war, not to acknowledge the past but to raise the fears of history repeating itself within the mainland postcolonial, multicultural France. Such populist politics is, of course, highly selective in its choice of focus and approach to history, at times taking the revisionist approach (as in Sarkozy's talk in Toulon), often neglecting the historicity of events altogether.

In the attempt to find the causes of French riots in 2005 (as if the causes were not visible) the center-right government authorities decidedly ignored both the near and far past of the events and provided various superficial cultural explanations such as the growth of radical Islam, African practices of polygamy, and the violence incited by rap music. Media sources such as *Le Monde* focused on more credible economic reasons such as systematic unemployment that leads to crime and delinquency in the *banlieues.* Although significantly different, both approaches stressed the crisis in the *banlieues* and the violence of the minority youth, and to an extent ignored the violence that preceded the riots. Despite the fact that police brutality lies at the root of the 2005 riots and almost all riots in the *banlieue*s since the 1980s, and despite the statistics that show systematic police violence—between 1977 and 2002 175 young people, most of them of African and North African descent, were killed by police abuse— police abuse has rarely been discussed as the main cause of the 2005 riot, and no police officer has ever served time for any hate crime.[54] In fact, the roots of racist police violence date back to interwar period, when special police brigades were formed to control migrant workers,[55] an institutional violence that powerfully displayed itself in the 1961 massacres of peaceful Algerian protesters. In a context of selective appeal to history when the activist group Les indigènes de la république, formed in January 2005 soon before the riots, identified themselves as "descendants of slaves and African deportees, daughters and sons of the colonized and the immigrants, militants involved in the battle against oppression and discrimination produced by the postcolonial republic," that is, they claimed a direct connection between French colonial and postcolonial practices and policies, they were heavily criticized on different fronts.[56] Their founding statement was also indicative of the context that prepared the riots soon to take place: "the banlieues are labeled as zones of disorder that the Republic sets out to conquer all over again. Identity checks based on profiling, and various provocations and persecutions, continue to multiply. Meanwhile, police brutality, sometimes extreme, has become acceptable in a two-track system of justice."[57]

Within this significant conjuncture, that is, when a deeper consideration of the thick historicity the 2005 riots was most crucial, Michael

Haneke's thriller was premiered. *Hidden*'s treatment of the rupture between France's colonial past and its postcolonial present provides surveillance images as the contemporary repercussions of repressed images of the past. The film ponders the politics of memory and forgetting, and it appeals to the emotional structures that are connected to these politics: fear, threat, and guilt. Regarding the representation of race in new brutality films in Hollywood, Paul Gormley writes: "The white cultural imagination is often a state of paranoia, anxiety and desire generated by the threat of black violence when confronted with images of blackness. It is also the condition where those fears of black violence are experienced as immediate and affective even though they are produced."[58] Playing on similar affective construction of threatening minority as the potential source of violence, *Hidden* overturns the conditioned racial expectations by placing a white body as the cause of historical and contemporary violence. With a template voyeuristic gaze, *Hidden* engages with the absence of visibility of a certain violent episode in colonial history, appropriating the narrative tools of objectivity (surveillance videos) in order to scrutinize the ethics and politics of media realism and to point to the incomplete nature of our vision, instigating the spectator's memory. As a thriller that is set to establish a certain affective relationship with its audience, the film reaches out beyond itself to grab the cool-headed spectator, as if to say: your continuing allegiance with and sympathy for the (seeming victim) perpetrator makes you an accomplice. On the one hand, genre conventions of the thriller remind the audience that fear and thrill are at the heart of contemporary minority politics and right-wing memorialization of colonial histories. On the other hand, however, the sensationalized thrill of the suicide eliminates the Algerian and his story to turn memorialization of violence into a self-centered flagellation.

The film represents the repression of colonial violence in French collective memory and its transfer to postcolonial subjects as the inheritors of this repressed violence. This history becomes the core of the thrill that may potentially haunt the present in vengeance. But eventually the pursuit of affective excess reproduces the original repression and the consequent explosion of images. Evoking the eruptiveness of suppressed history and memory is crucial to Haneke's thrill. The director changes the signification of eruption through embedding the thrill in surveillance technologies that break the narrative time, refer to different temporalities, and instigate both personal and collective memory. However, the eruption in the suicide scene eventually reverses the effect of the multitemporal videos and makes it again about the thrill of the present. In that sense, the urgent and catastrophic immediacy of Majid's suicide, just as does the dystopic and eventful present depicted in Alfonso Cuarón's *Children of Men* analyzed in the previous chapter, undermines the power of *Hidden*'s historicity. Majid's suicide turns a minority citizen into an eternally suffering, silent victim, who needs to destroy his body to ensure the recognition of his suffering and to prove his innocence from the charges of "terrorism."[59]

As the Algerian characters seem to be obsessed with the recognition of their suffering, their identity is established as one that emerges from this very suffering. Their ontology is constructed on and around "the wound" that creates a foreclosure of identity to the "eternal repetition of its pain."[60] Wendy Brown suggests that minority identity based on injury may be recuperated by inserting "I want," the moment of desire in the formulation of identity, a desire that is not fixed and fixated on the wound but changing and not assuming the "wound," the injury as its defining feature. The only minority desire in Haneke's film is framed within the limits of displaying the consequences of the wound, as Majid explains before his suicide: "I called you because I wanted you to be present," or when his son visits Georges because he wants to see "how it feels, [to have] a man's life on [Georges's] conscience. That's all." The desires of minority Others in *Hidden* are directly linked to their injury and are not independent from the person who caused this injury (Georges); hence the basis of the ethnic and racially Other's identity is once again a sense of woundedness and potentially explosive revenge. The audiences who feel equally threatened by the possible consequences of the wound, initially identify with the bourgeois couple, and then at times feel guilty for their alliance; at still other times, they feel morally superior to Georges for being able to recognize and fulfill their "duty of memory."[61] Watching the film is in itself a cathartic experience, evidence of being the good liberal postcolonial French citizen capable of remembrance and repentance. Funding, producing, awarding, and seeing the historical injustice now makes up for not having seen it in the past and not seeing the continuing legacy of this injustice. The film offers an arbitrary narrative solution to active social contradiction since it remembers the dead safely: without bringing them out of silence, reminding of the explosive threat of their repressed wound, the narrative closes on the French-Algerian victims.

While the agency of the protagonists, the white men, of the films explored in the previous and the current chapter move between humanitarian death and conformist denial of guilt, the ethnic and racial Others in both films are equally voiceless. Just as the pregnant refugee Kee has to reveal her body to prove that she is in need of humanitarian aid in *Children of Men,* Majid becomes the bearer of truth who needs to reveal his suffering and trauma through corporeal means. Both films show ethnic and racial Others as objects rather than subjects of their tragic fate, while biology and bare life rather than an active political involvement for their social, political, and historical rights define their existence.

The following chapter shows a migrant who tries to get out of this dilemma of silent victimology in a narrative that places him at the center of action as the noble protagonist of a Greek tragedy. Similar to Haneke's *Hidden,* Giannaris's *Hostage* explores what has been left out from the mainstream media's narrative, the deeper historicity of a migrant-related violent event beyond the claims of an eruption, this time of Balkan violence into European space. Giannaris's film expands the geographical boundaries of the event, connecting multiple locales, hence questioning the assumed borders that separate the Europe of emigration and the Balkans of immigration. As the next chapter moves from the center to the edges of Europe, the continent's borders become central to debates on ethnicity and race.

THREE

Balkan Borders and Transgressions

Constantinos Giannaris's Hostage

> The border . . . is not a metaphor of subversive transgression and radical hybridity, as some cultural critics have suggested, but rather a site of policing and discipline, control and violence.[1]
>
> —ALI BEHAD, *A Forgetful Nation,* 144

On May 29, 1999, Albanian migrant worker Flamur Pisli hijacked a bus with nine hostages in a Greek village near Thessaloniki. He was armed with a Kalashnikov and two grenades. The hijacker contacted the media and security forces with a hostage's cell phone. On the phone he accused some locals and the police of setting him up and sending him to jail on a false charge of weapons possession. Pisli claimed he was beaten and sexually harassed in jail. He told the Greek public: "I am innocent. They charged me unjustly . . . I want to recover my honor. I don't want to do anything bad to the passengers on the bus."[2] Pisli demanded 50 million drachma (approximately $160,000), the three Kalashnikovs that were allegedly planted in his house by the police, and free passage to Albania.

Greek media, ambulances, and police vehicles followed the hijacked bus to the Greek-Albanian border. Once the bus crossed the border, the Albanian police killed the hijacker and, mistakenly, one of the hostages, Yorgos Koulouris. Albanian authorities and the state news agency ATA declared that it was the hijacker who shot the hostage, even as Reuters coverage showed an Albanian sniper shooting both Pisli and Koulouris. The controversy created tension between the Greek and Albanian governments; the former emphasized "the very foolish behavior on the part of the Albanian police" in carrying out the rescue operation.[3] In the aftermath of the hijacking, Greek prime minister Costas Simitis guaranteed reinforcements to the border police and declared a *skoupa*, or "sweep-up" operation, of illegal migrants. Massive deportations of Albanians took place as "security measure."

Though criminologists have repeatedly demonstrated that the majority of migrant and Albanian crimes are in fact violations of migration laws or offenses related to the illegal status of migrants, Greek government officials often use "symbolic language, metaphors, exaggerations, inaccuracies" that create anxiety and fear against migrants.[4] The Pisli hijacking seemed to validate the prevalent government and media discourses that associate migration, primarily high rates of post-1989 Albanian migration, with criminal activity.[5] The hijacking was uninterruptedly covered by Greek television. The mainstream Greek news media presented the event in a histrionic manner. *Ta Nea*, for instance, described the hijacker as a criminal associated with a network of Albanian mafia and sensationalized the story further in an entangled soap-opera-like narration that found the motive behind Pisli's act in an adulterous love affair, "an illicit love affair, rivals, vendetta, and social outcry in which almost all residents of the small village community are involved."[6] The majority of the media sources focused on the death of a Greek hostage and national security concerns over an imminent threat of migrant crime while neglecting any responsibility on the part of the Greek government. There was no official or journalistic investigation regarding Pisli's public claim about trading guns with the police and the violence he experienced in jail. The government officers pathologized Pisli, declaring his acts those of a "disturbed personality" in an otherwise safe country.[7] The hijacking was considered to be an event that signified an eruption of exterior Albanian violence into the peaceful Greek space, a disruption from without.

Six years later, Greek director Constantinos Giannaris made a documentary drama on the hijacking: *Hostage* (2005). The film's story line is true to the event, but the director presents the pieces of the puzzle that were missing in the media coverage. Exploring the hijacker's claims about gun trading and police violence, Giannaris constructs the background story through the hostages' accounts and his research in Albania. The film confronts the media images of the hijacking—images that assume migrant crime to be the manifestation of a pathological condition or of an inborn primitive nature. The documentary drama blends narrative tools of media "objectivity" with dramatic enactment to reconstruct an event from the "subjective" point of view of an underrepresented protagonist. To add further to the element of drama and to the discontent of its native spectators, Giannaris puts the experience of an Albanian migrant into public space by borrowing from an "authentically" Greek genre: ancient tragedy. In contradiction to a general trend of migration films that show migrant characters as defenseless victims of quotidian tragedies, hence intending to raise spectators' empathy, *Hostage* provocatively inquires into the experience of a criminal migrant and promotes an alternative conception of "migrant tragedy" and of a tragic hero. The tragedy opens a public space, not for cathartic compassion, but a space in which violence committed by a migrant is considered within a larger socioeconomic framework.

The construction of space as in a road film in *Hostage* renders the complex politics of transnational migration, which involves an uneven exchange between the country of immigration and that of emigration. The film's border crossing conveys the hierarchies implied in transnational migration in ways that a number of travel and migration films in contemporary European cinema neglect. *Hostage* reveals the systematic sites of violence that remain invisible in the media's representation of the event, such sites as forced illegalization of work, state violence directed through the police, and the deportation office. In that sense, the film demonstrates the thickness of a historical event (the hijacking) as violence with complex political connotations, an event that is not simply an eruption of Albanian (foreign) violence in a peaceful Greek space, but one that is historically situated in regional social, political, and economic dynamics: Greece's post–Cold War migration politics and relations with Albania. Through blurring the relationship between documentary and tragedy, blending two modes of representation that signify different temporalities and aesthetic frames of visibility (documentary mode is often associated with the underprivileged of the world,[8] while ancient Greek tragedy attributed to noble heroes), the film renders the hijacker's act of violence, which has been isolated as a singular event, as a larger situation of violence with multiple affective, political, and economic repercussions. Before the analysis of film in detail, the following section considers the film's unique place within the extensive corpus of migration films produced in Greece.

As soon as journalists and critics entered the movie theater for *Hostage*'s press premiere in Salonika (March 2005) they met the father of the deceased hostage Koulouris, who was protesting the film: "You are paying to see what? How they killed my son? . . . Everybody forgot about him and now they make a film to earn money out of his death."[9] Soon the police interrupted the premiere, barging into the Olimpion movie theater and asking the audience to vacate the building because of a bomb threat. When *Hostage* was finally released, the public reception in Greece was not favorable. The number of tickets sold (11,000) was significantly lower than that of Giannaris's previous film, *One Day in August* (95,000).[10] The forum at *Hostage*'s official website carried extensive debates with thousands of comments on the film and the political issues it raises.[11] The discussion topics ranged from criticism of the film to pro- and anti-immigration debates, racist comments against Albanians, replies from Albanian migrants, and comparisons of immigrants in Greece to emigrants from Greece. Most of the commentators admitted that they had not even seen the film, which they boycotted for its representation of an Albanian criminal in a favorable manner:

- I feel ashamed. A true Greek lies dead and a director tries to make money out of this. Humanitarian conscience and the memory of the dead are violated in the name of art. The question is reasonable: Why should I see this film, what will it offer to me? Only pain, suffering and hatred. *Madrid,* March 4, 2005
- Giannaris my friend, we don't want the harmful Albanians and we don't excuse them at all. . . . It is not simply racism, it is adversity with Albania, here and years now. The same thing doesn't happen with all foreigners. We have all kinds of races here. The Albanians however, we don't assimilate them, no way! *Vrasidas,* March 29, 2005
- I haven't seen the film and nor will I see it. *Makis,* March 30, 2005

As these comments show, even the idea of making a film on this topic was disturbing for a certain segment of its Greek audience and the film created heated debates on Albanian migration and integration into Greek society. The larger topic of the film, however, the treatment of migration in Greek cinema, was not at all rare or peculiar to Giannaris's film. A year after *Hostage*'s debut, the Forty-Seventh Thessaloniki Film Festival (2006) had a retrospective on migration in Greek cinema, screening an abundant number of productions on the topic since the 1960s. The retrospective attested both to the flourishing post–Cold War trend of immigration films and to the longer tradition of Greek cinema on emigration (the former often considered an extension of the later), with famous examples such as Elia Kazan's *America America* (1963) to Nikos Papatakis's *The Photograph* (1987) and more recent major productions such as Pantelis Voulgaris's *Brides* (2004).

Post–Cold War migration to Greece shifted many coordinates of Greek society, initiating demographic, social, and cultural changes as well as redefining the country's place within the Balkans and its relation to the new and expanded Europe. The Greek cinema of the 1990s often thematized this post-1989 confrontation with the migrant Other, particularly revealing the literal and metaphorical borders that reinforce an unequal encounter between the migrant from the Balkans and the Greek host. Katherina Zacharia describes the 1990s as a decade in which Greek cinema repositioned itself as its filmmakers responded to the challenges and anxieties associated with the increasing migrant presence in Greece: "Greek cinema is attuned with the global fascination with cultural flows and circulations, syncretism and migrancy, engaging in the post-colonial discourses of multilayered identities and deterritorializations, and deconstructing dominant national discourses."[12] Wendy Everett highlights Theo Angelopoulos's leading role in the articulation of the path for both Greek and European cinema during this period when themes of immigration, borders, and shifting identities became predominant. Everett describes Angelopoulos's films in the 1990s as "key illustrations of the move from autobiography to journey narratives that marked films across Europe in the 1990s."[13] Indeed, immediately after the collapse of the communist regime in neighboring Albania, Angelopoulos shot *Suspended Step of the Stork* (1991) and later *Eternity and A Day* (1998), among the first works to depict the then recent phenomenon of migration to Greece and the Greek-Albanian border. These films contemplated the solitude of humanity divided by borders. During the 1990s and early in the next decade Greek directors explored migration and borders from a range of different perspectives. Among the well-known examples, Giorgos Korras and Hristos Voupouras's *See You* (1997) threw a critical glance at the leftist politics of migration, while Sotiris Goritsas's *From the Snow* (1993) showed the hardships faced by illegal migrants on their way to Greece, and Kyriakos Katzourakis's *The Way to the West* (2003) focused on the victims of sex trafficking. These works addressed the exacerbated identitarian anxieties of Greeks and introduced migrant characters that were, at the time, marginal to Greek cinema, in ways that revealed the exploitation, social exclusion, and xenophobia they faced in Greece.

Giannaris himself directed several other films on migration before *Hostage. From the Edge of the City* (1998), initially a documentary project that evolved into a narrative film, portrays Russian-Greek youth residing in the ghettos of Athens, where their relations with Greeks is strictly on the basis of contract labor for illegal or low-paying jobs: pimping, prostitution, or construction jobs. The film carries influences of the prevailing realism in the works of young European filmmakers of the mid-1980s and 1990s—such as Mehdi Charef's *Tea in the Harem* (1985), Mathieu Kassovitz's *Le Haine* (1995), Kutluğ Ataman's *Lola+Billidikid* (1998), and Fatih Akın's *Short Sharp Shock* (1998). Giannaris's next feature film, *One Day in August* (2001), was a philosophical engagement with issues of death, disease, and reproduction. In the film, the two migrants and their petty crimes are instrumental in providing an opening to the enclosed life of the Greek bourgeoisie. It was both a national success, winning the Best Film Award in the Thessaloniki International Film Festival, and recognized in the European festival circles by making official selection for the Berlin International Film Festival (2002).

Hence, the question that needs to be addressed is this: what distinguishes *Hostage* from these previous films by Giannaris and other Greek films that depict migrants and even migrant criminals without raising such protests in online forums or in front of movie theaters? *Hostage* is the first film in Greek cinema to prioritize narration from an Albanian protagonist's point of view. In an interview Giannaris admits: "*Hostage* had a personal cost. My longtime relationships with friends and coworkers dissolved because they could not confront the theme with the earnestness I expected. They told me disdainfully: "C'mon, you will make a film about an Albanian?" . . . And we are talking about progressive, intellectual people."[14] The majority of the more recent Greek films on migration portray the experiences of migrants from distant lands (e.g., Bangladesh, Kurdistan, a former Soviet republic) with few historical connections to Greece or ethnic Greek migrants from Albania and the former Soviet republics, characters who raise more sympathy because of their Greek heritage. But even compared to other Greek films with Albanian characters *Hostage* received much harsher criticism and inspired more passionate anti-immigration debates.[15]

Most of the people who reacted to the film protested the representation of an Albanian criminal as a tragic hero. *Hostage* focuses on a criminal character as a tragic protagonist, thereby focusing on his agency and the fatal action he has chosen to undertake. The protagonist of *Hostage* is neither clueless nor innocent, nor an ideal, honest migrant worker. The film rejects a certain progressive cultural and political discourse in Europe that produces yet another cliché against the media representations of migrant criminality: the honest and innocent migrant. In the film, the protagonist trades Albanian Kalashnikovs to the Greek police from across the border, and he hijacks a bus with nine hostages. The hijacker is someone who tries to survive within the system that is always already corrupted and exploitative, first by forming a privileged relationship with the police in gun trading, then by hijacking a bus to return to Albania with honor and money. The question remains: despite the privileged perspective of the protagonist, isn't the film limited to the realm of criminal migrant paradigm repeatedly pronounced in the media and official discourses? Why produce yet another migrant crime narrative?

Analyzing migrant crimes and their narratives in their historical and geographical depth goes against the grain of scholarship, fiction, film, and political activism that aim to disassociate migrant figures from criminality and violence, and that seek out positive models of migrants in Europe.[16] However, these positive models do not inhibit discrimination against migrants. For after all, such discrimination legitimates itself primarily through events and narratives of criminality, terrorism, and acts of violence that "prove" migrants' "inassimilability to the Western democracy."[17] Critical thinking on migrant violence and its representation is an issue that remains untouched in most narratives and discourses on migration. This is not simply finding legitimization of such violence. Inquiring into the larger forces that are involved gives clues about the migration politics and tensions that involve the host society. As anthropological literature suggests, an alternative approach to the study of violence is to explore criminality and victimhood, "not as exceptional moments and crises . . . but as integral parts of a social fabric already fragmented in innumerable ways."[18]

Stuart Hall analyzes racial stereotypes of blacks in the British media and popular culture to inquire into how power functions in the process of circulation or exchange of (primarily visual) representation as an intervention to fix meaning. In his analysis of the strategies against racialized "regimes of representation," Hall explains that confronting a negative stereotype with a positive one is not an effective strategy for overturning the stereotype: "adding positive images to the largely negative repertoire of the dominant regime of representation increases the diversity of the ways in which 'being black' is represented, but does not *necessarily* displace the negative. Since the binaries remain in place, the meaning continues to be framed by them."[19] What needs to be done instead, Hall claims, is to reconsider the negative stereotype to make it "work against itself." This strategy "locates itself *within* the complexities and ambivalences of representation itself, and tries to *contest it from within.* It is more concerned with the *forms* of racial representation than with introducing a new *content.*"[20] Giannaris's *Hostage* is a crime narrative that pursues this latter strategy to reveal "the complexities and ambivalences" in the representations of migrant-as-criminal that frequent the media and official discourses. In his migrant crime narrative Giannaris both provides the underrepresented point of view (of the Albanian migrant to Greece) and confronts that which is overrepresented in the media (racist discourses that associate Albanians' crime with their so-called temporal backwardness).

Focusing on the Criminal Migrant: Between Documentary and Fiction

In *Hostage*, Giannaris's handheld camera and lightweight mobile equipment capture events fortuitously the way they appear in newsreels. His insistence on location shooting (in a hot and claustrophobic moving bus) and the use of documentary style grainy shots follows neorealist conventions. However, the director intentionally manipulates documentary stylistics. He argues for the need to take the camera *closer* to the event than any journalist would go, zooming into the hijacked bus and the hijacker's past in flashbacks. In an interview with the newspaper *Ta Nea*, Giannaris stresses that in order to reconstruct the hijacking, he did archival research of media sources, but his narrative was primarily influenced by the chronicles of two hostages in the bus. As both the director and the screenwriter, Giannaris states that he intended to show what was missing in the media reality, and attempted to reconstruct the story from *inside* the bus. He blames the journalists for mechanically reflecting the event as a sensational instant with no human element rather than as a longer process with a background story and motivations that precede the event, and the hostages' trauma that follows the event:

> Outside the bus there is television, the sensational, big news. The humanistic detail, however, is inside. . . . But actually that detail was lost. We never understood why this event took place. And it wasn't so dif-

ficult to find out what was concealed inside. We reached the point of saying, "There's something flimsy here." But no one moved beyond that. Not a single journalist. Damn it, why?[21]

While loyal to the details of the event, the director does not use footage of the event from television news. Yet the color scheme of the mise-en-scène, the hijacker's and hostages' statures, ages, and physical characteristics recall the media images of the event. The filmic image differs from the journalistic images in respect to the location of the camera and its focus. In the film the stylized camera is almost always placed *inside* the bus, reflecting the director's prioritized space of attention, as he underlines in the interview. This spatial priority is emphasized with deep-focus shots, which suggest the feeling of proximity to the hostages and the hijacker and clarity of vision inside the bus. The lighting alters according to whether the camera is shooting inside or outside the bus. Giannaris uses documentary-style photography with grainy texture (16 mm film blown up to 35 mm) that gives the film a news image effect when the camera is located outside the bus, where he uses natural light. Inside the bus, however, the lighting is manipulated in order to enhance illumination and gives the images relatively sharper definition. The selective use of artificial lighting increases the ironic sense of a dual reality: outside the bus is the realm of obscure media-reality, while inside the bus is the realm of clear dramatic-reality.

As a docudrama *Hostage* benefits from both fiction's "imaginative relationship" with the audience and the documentary's "inferential relationship" between the represented events and the viewer. Keith Beattie explains that the two narrative forms have different priorities when constructing an event: "Fictional narrative rests on a relationship of cause and effect: an event or action (cause) sets in train a series of actions (effect)" while "documentaries often replace cause and effect with a simple problem-solution structure: a problem is posed, the historical background to the problem is examined and current dimensions of the problem are explained. A solution or solutions to the problem (or ways to find a solution) are outlined or suggested."[22] The documentary narrative of *Hostage* takes migrant crime as its problem. This narrative style outlines the crime's background and dimensions that suggest corruption at the institutional level, corruption in how migration and criminality are being treated at the state level. The documentary becomes limited when the solution to the migrant crime problem appears to perpetrate it; the solution becomes the problem itself. The fictional narrative at this point builds the cause-effect relationship around "the problem." It reconstructs the past and the hidden motives behind the hijacking, since evidence cannot be found in official sources and is only hinted at in the newspapers. Fictional aspects provide the director the dramatic freedom to explore larger social and economic structures behind the migrant crime, forces that are not readily documentable.

In the beginning of the film the protagonist, Elion (Stathis Papadopoulos), takes the intercity bus and sits in the backseat, looking around anxiously. As the bus moves, the camera captures the dichotomy: predominantly Greek passengers inside chat and sing while the workers outside, probably Albanian, pick crops under the burning sun. The protagonist takes out a gun and a grenade and orders the driver to stop the bus. In Thessaloniki the hijacker makes his demands to the Greek police. A parallel narrative in Albania shows the police urging Elion's mother Francesca (Rajmonda Bulku) to convince her son to surrender. A third narrative displays the protagonist's past in flashbacks. Though the Greek audience is already familiar with the hijacking and its consequences, an event exclusively covered in the media only five years before the film was produced, Giannaris further underlines the semidocumentary nature of his film by asking viewers to refresh their memory of the event through the epigraph that opens the film: "This film is inspired by a real event in northern Greece in 1999. The characters and action in the film, however, are entirely fictional." The epigraph has contradictory emphases: a "real event" with specified date and time is confronted with an "entirely fictional" world. The composition of the cast, comprising mainly established actors, gives the audience a sense of dramatized reality. The documentary-like shots outside the bus and documentary-drama inside the bus are juxtaposed with dreamlike flashbacks of the hijacker's past in Greece (with darker lighting) and in Tirana (with brighter lighting) that personalize the narrative. The lighting in the flashback scenes reflects Elion's psychological mood. The camera emphasizes *his* perspective on the reality.

The title of the film suggests that in opposition to the media narrative, this is the hijacker's story, as the film privileges the experience of a single "hostage" (όμηρος), not that of "hostages" (όμηροι) plural. The focus, camera movements, and at times lighting intentionally recall realist conventions and simultaneously diverge from them in order to stress the centrality of the hijacker within the film narrative. The focus on the Albanian protagonist's reality begins in the opening sequence of *Hostage*. With realist artfulness, we are introduced to the protagonist's psychological state before he takes action. Extreme close-ups capture Elion's face and body only in fragments, never in full. Tight framing of his body parts suggest his state of imprisonment and fragmentation. Later, the shots in the limited space of the bus perpetuate the camera's focus on and framing of the protagonist. The claustrophobic setting of the bus itself forces close-up shots and brings our attention to the minute details in the interaction between the protagonist and the hostages. Even at instances when the hostages are placed on the foreground and in focus, Elion's presence is always ensured by placing him out of focus in the background. The audience is introduced to the background story of the hijacker in conjunction with the foreground story on the hijacking from the contemplative eyes of the hostages from inside the bus.

The director refers to the incomplete nature of the purportedly "objective" news coverage, and thus the need for a subjective personal story in the climactic scene when Elion is raped in the detention center, the final flashback in the film placed before Elion's execution in southern Albania. The setting of the interrogation scene—a clean, spacious, and bright warehouse rather than a small, crammed, and dark basement commonly used as torture chambers—gives the sense of a public interrogation. The officers ask Elion questions about the Kalashnikovs and he claims that a policeman, his boss, set him up. When they ask why the police would bother to do such a thing, he confesses he had a relationship with the policeman's wife. One of the interrogators says, "You see, pretty bad all around. Nothing good can come of it. Fucking a guy's wife is bad enough. But fucking his wife and being a foreigner and all, it's like . . ." The other officer completes the sentence: "Like cutting the guy's dick off in his own home [Pause. Two officers look at each other meaningfully] Thirsty? Want a soft drink? Regular or light?" They leave the room to take a bottle, the instrument of rape.

The spectators are first provided an aerial shot of the rape. The two guards force Elion down on the interrogation table from a distance above the table, such that the audience is in the uneasy position of detached but omniscient viewer. The camera quickly focuses on Elion's face in an extreme close-up as he struggles and finally undergoes violation. In this rape scene, the focus being on Elion's face rather than on the act or the area of violation protects the privacy of Elion's body. Furthermore, the reaction shot that focuses on the face and Elion's cry of pain puts the emphasis on the subjective pain. The affective power of the scene is augmented and the pain is rendered more immediate for the audience by the fact that the instrument of rape, a bottle, is presented to the audience and the protagonist before the act. As Elaine Scarry suggests, regarding one of Amnesty International's most influential brochures on torture that was published in newspapers in 1963, displaying the image of a torture weapon communicates the physical pain and suffering "by the greatest possible tact . . . and by the greatest possible immediacy."[23] The viewer, disturbed by the explicitness of suffering and violence materialized in the torture instrument, is reminded again that this is exclusively Elion's tragedy that eventually reflects on the public sphere and becomes a social tragedy.

The scene violates our vision with its disturbing explicitness: not simply demanding sympathy or the right of the protagonist to act violently, it forces the audience to confront what is only implied in the media coverage of the hijacking. The rape scene amplifies how the violence that the hijacker perpetrates does not eliminate or make invisible the violence that was done to him. The director visualizes the physical consequences of the nationalistic hysteria in the media discourses on border crossing that, on the state level, exercise themselves upon the migrant's body. The officers decide to rape him when they realize that he has not only physically crossed the border and traded guns but that he has symbolically violated the national border through having sex with a married Greek woman who is, above all, the wife of their colleague, who is a representative of state authority. The physical boundaries of the nation are supported with "symbolic borders (criminality, deviance, dirt, disease), a fictional preservation of racial purity against 'alien contamination."[24]

A Contemporary Greek Tragedy: Initiating Public Debate

Most media sources described the Pisli hijacking as tragic, depicting the father of the deceased hostage as the primary protagonist of the tragedy. To confront and complement the mediatic image of the suffering Greek father, *Hostage* introduces the "tragic figure" (described as such in the film) on the other side of the border—the Albanian mother, the hijacker's mother. The film begins and ends with the voice of Elion's mother, speaking to her son, first through the voice-over of her letter, then from outside the bus encircled by the police in Albania. Her voice is a prophetic reminder of her son's tragic destiny: "in your own land people will exploit you to the bone. In a strange land they will devour your bones as well." Giannaris expands the conception of *who* would qualify as a tragic character, from the hostages to the hijacker, and from the Greek father to the Albanian mother.

From the first minute into *Hostage*, with a second epigraph the director forces the Greek audience to identify the story of an Albanian criminal with the tragic end or fatal choice of the Greek hero Ajax: "One must live with honor like a man or die with honor. Yes. There's the rub (Sophocles)." The film follows certain tragic conventions, such narrating events that take place in twenty-four hours, the presence of chorus-like hostages in a bus, a prophetess figure foretelling the future, and an audience expected to be familiar with the story. The epigraph taken from Sophocles is presented in a Modern Greek translation rather than the ancient Greek original in order to have a more direct appeal to the film's national audience. The allusion to Hamlet ("there's the rub") in the English subtitles further highlights the reference to tragedy for the international audience. What was the director's social and aesthetic agenda in insisting that the film is an ancient Greek tragedy? What does tragedy offer to a filmmaker who pursues the dramatization of a violent media event?

Tragedy provides conventions and stylistic tools to represent the complexity of the violent act at the intersection of the individual, societal, and institutional levels. Two factors make tragedy suitable for thinking of and representing violence. First, the ethics of tragedy precludes the reduction of the individual's violent action and its consequence to moral judgments on character. Second, the tragic hero's action and agency is not considered an end in itself; instead it opens the path for public discussion. Violent action, then, extends from the individual to the society and the state and vice versa. Violence is brought into the collective sphere of discussion rather than being dismissed as erratic eruption. By insisting that the film is a tragedy Giannaris not only invites the Greek audience to think about what is and can be tragic, but also portrays how an individual, whether a foreigner or not (in fact, all the more so when a foreigner), is implicated in the Greek social and political body.

Elion's mother's tragic soliloquy in the final scene underscores how larger structures of violence have shaped Elion's violent act: "You were never bad. How did you end up like this? So heartless, like a wild animal. I know they hurt you, they beat you. Cruel people, they dirtied your life. Don't become like them." Elion's character, feelings, and past are developed only to the extent that would make his actions meaningful within their particular context and symbolic significance. We see him having sexual intercourse with his boss's wife with no sign of love or further information on their affair; we hear his mother's praise of Elion's personality and their warm relationship, but we do not see their relationship developed on the screen. The sympathy for the protagonist emerges not necessarily as a result of the flashbacks to his past or his mother's plea, but mainly because of his relationship with the hostages and the community spirit created in the bus toward the end of the film. As in a classical Greek tragedy, although Elion is the center in focus as the tragic agent, his character and feelings are intentionally distanced. This distancing places the emphasis on his actions, a series of illicit border crossings (having sex with a Greek policeman's wife, crossing and trading guns illegally across the border) and their public significance. Rather than emphasizing character traits, tragedy concerns itself with action interpreted in relation to its social meaning and consequences. Giannaris, on the one hand, provokes the Greek audience with an Albanian tragic hero; on the other hand, he uses the political potential of ancient Greek tragedy to think about a violent act without preconceived judgment about the character. As Raymond Williams suggests: "We think of tragedy as what happens to the hero, but the ordinary tragic action is what happens through the hero. . . . The life that is continued is informed by [his] death."[25]

It is no coincidence that Giannaris chose to juxtapose his protagonist's story with that of Sophocles's *Ajax* in the epigraph. In mythology the great hero of the Trojan War, Ajax, ends up dead and disgraced, and almost unburied as he attempts to slaughter his own people in a spur of anger. After realizing what he has done, he rejects continuing to live in such dishonor and commits suicide. Sophocles's version of the play has an unusual point of climax, as Ajax's suicide is located in the middle rather than the end and a long diminuendo follows this climax. After the hero's death, there is a long debate that focuses on whether or not Ajax should be honored with a burial despite his violent and dishonorable act against the public. This unusual and extended debate reevaluates the hero's actions by bringing them into the collective sphere of discussion. Ajax's violence is not an end in itself; it is a means to open a discussion that brings in different views of society. Sophocles's treatment of Ajax provides a guide for Giannaris's representation of an equally debatable hero and his violent act in *Hostage*. Giannaris similarly intends to open the protagonist's action and motive to a discussion in the Greek public space. Individual violence in both tragedies requires exegesis in the form of public interpretation and is discussed as the hero's desire for justice in the face of humiliation.

Hostage reveals multiple sites of violence and competing decadences for further debate: that of the hijackers, that of the police, and that of the society, which takes the form of discrimination against minorities. One of the hostages, Orpheus (Antonis Ntourakis), who happens to be a junkie, goes through a fit in the bus and draws Elion into a quarrel. The scene demonstrates how the tragic hero initiates a public debate through his violent action:

ORPHEUS: What do you call an Albanian with no hands?

ELION: Tell me . . .

ORPHEUS: Trustworthy, you asshole! Trustworthy!

(Camera captures tense and worried looks of the other hostages.)

GRIGORIS (YANNIS STANKOGLOU): Why don't you shut it?

ORPHEUS: Oh, come on you are so touchy!

ELION: And what is the Albanian doing inside the theater?

ORPHEUS: Tell me . . .

ELION: Stealing the show, asshole!

JACK (MANOLIS AFOLIANO): That's real funny. (Other hostages smile in relief.)

ORPEHUS: (With a tone of irony) Real funny! I pissed myself laughing. What do you know about theater? Us, the Greeks, we invented theater. What does your lot know? Goatfuckers. Hicks. The nigger over there, he knows how to dress. He's got music in him, rhythm. The nigger is a fucking cool dude. Hey, seen the shoes the assholes walk around in? They want to act all tall and strong. (Elion looks at his shoes.) For years they starved in their own country like gypsies. Now they come and throw their weight around in our country. Am I wrong?

ELION: Everyone liked me in my town!

ORPHEUS: Oh, I'm gonna cry!

ELION: Like a son!

ORPHEUS: They adopted you?

ELION: I worked hard.

ORPHEUS: You want a medal?

ELION: If there was work I was first in line.

ORPHEUS: And now, I'm out of a job!

ELION: We do jobs you wouldn't touch!

ORPHEUS: Oh, come on, Superman.

ELION: You are only good for partying. The foreigners do all the work and you treat them like animals. (Lifts his shirt to show the marks of torture on his chest) They had me for a month in there, dying of thirst. Locked up with the niggers, the junkies, the whores. Drowning in my own shit. No one heard me cry. Not even allowed a lousy phone call. (stuttering) What they dddd . . . did to mmmm . . . me you don't do to a mmmm . . . man!

(Orpheus silently looks the other way. Elion withdraws to the backseat.)

The metanarrative gives an idea of what the film itself intends to do within the Greek public space. The hero's suffering and his violent acts are made public to initiate a discussion around them, a debate that was stifled in the mass media. The scene begins with two racist jokes, commonplace stereotypes on Albanian criminality that point to a quotidian racism and public anxiety about migrants. Each joke conceives the criminal stereotype differently: the former assumes a criminal Albanian who has to be turned into a victim of violence or an incapacitated person so that the native society accepts him. The latter joke, on the other hand, describes a criminal Albanian who wants to be visible, or be a part of "the show," the tragedy.

The junkie dislikes the second joke, which puts the Albanian in the position of an agent, an actor on the tragic stage. He confronts Elion again, with a claim that an Albanian's "show" can never be genuine or artful. Elion counters the junkie this time by claiming that he has in fact been an honest, hardworking migrant—trying to subvert a negative stereotype with a positive one. The junkie is not convinced until he sees the marks of torture on Elion's body. At that point the wounds are no surprise to the film's viewers—who are made well aware of the torture through prior implications as to what has provoked Elion to hijack the bus. With the torture marks Elion finally proves his point, publicly shows the visible sign of the state violence to which he was subjected. By the time the bus crosses the Albanian border a chorus-like community is formed. Yet this is nothing close to a utopian community, as hierarchies work among the passengers. While the junkie places the African migrant hierarchically above the Albanian, the Albanian feels disgraced to be considered equal to "the niggers, the junkies, the whores," perpetrating the racism directed toward him. Nevertheless, the forced proximity of this group of marginals creates room for discussion and the visibility of Elion's tragedy along with that of his hostages in a public space.

Giannaris's allusion to tragedy must be considered in the light of Raymond Williams's commentary on how to perpetuate the affective and political power of ancient Greek tragedy today: the tragic in life must correspond to the tragic in art by giving agency to the ordinary hero at times of corruption and disorder, agency that unfolds through an exploration of the violent event. Williams explains that Hegel's emphasis on the nobility of the tragic act and its perpetrator is debilitating not only because it excludes ordinary people's suffering or victimization but also because it denies the human agency that may emerge from the suffering of common people:

> There is the exclusion, already evident in the language of Hegel, of ordinary suffering and this is surely the unconscious attachment of significant suffering to (social) nobility. But there is also the related and deeper exclusion of all that suffering which is part of our social and political world, and its actual human relations. The real key, to the modern separation of tragedy from "mere suffering," is the separation of ethical control and, more critically, human agency from our understanding of social and political life.[26]

What Williams refers to in the last sentence is the ignored and forgotten role of tragedy as a political commentary that reflects the times when the order dissolves. It is an art form that dramatizes "a particular and grievous disorder and its resolution" by telling what happens through the hero, or the agent of action.[27] Violent events in tragedy and in *Hostage* are not an eruption that present themselves for easy reading, but thick events produced in relation to the social and institutional forces around them.

Spatial Coordinates of a Historical Event

Hostage's appeal to tragedy establishes a link between the private and the public drama. Through the suffering and the agency of an Albanian migrant the tragedy opens a debate about xenophobia as well as illegal or "gray areas" of migration politics in Greece. *Hostage* starts with a close-up on the tragic Albanian character enclosed in his bare house and ends with a wide, panoramic angle in southern Albania, opening the camera and the problematic to the world, to the socioeconomic relations and hierarchies between Albania and Greece.[28] After the climactic rape scene, a sound bridge connects Elion's cry in the detention center to the final scene of his shooting in southern Albania. This sequence ironically demonstrates that the very same border whose transgression is heavily penalized in the rape scene proves to be extremely porous in the institutional level: Elion crosses the border only to be trapped and killed in his home country at the hands of his compatriots, who are subcontracted by the

Greek police.[29] The migrant's return becomes a move from the zone of transnational to national state violence—a violence that unrestrainedly exercises its right on the life of its citizen. The "friendly" conversation between two colleagues, Greek and Albanian police officers on the eve of Elion's murder, shows what the border and passage from Greece to Albania means in their terms: transgression to a violence-free zone.

GREEK OFFICER (MINAS HATZISAVVAS): (laughs and slaps the Albanian officer on the cheek in a friendly, paternal manner) Smell that air. I bet there is good hunting here.

ALBANIAN OFFICER (LAERTIS VASILIOU): Anything your heart desires.

GREEK OFFICER: Can't understand all those hell-bent on outlawing hunting . . . when it's in our very nature.

ALBANIAN OFFICER: We don't have that problem here.

GREEK OFFICER: I fear it's only a matter of time.

The dialogue refers to the subsequent "hunting" of the hijacker. It shows the dynamics of the division of labor in this transnational exchange of relations. Albanian territory serves as the Greek backyard where certain laws and humanitarian concerns can be bent. The dialogue displays how the Greek area of influence stretches across borders, and how the Greek police force subcontracts Albanian police for cleaning up a cancerous product of transnational migration. The camera captures the asymmetrical socioeconomic and political relationship between Greece and Albania.

The space-time relationship in the film allows for situating the event (the hijacking) in its multiple histories and geographies, Albania and Greece. What makes Giannaris's film unique among migration films in Greece and in Europe is the very opening that brings in the questions of uneven and combined development in the region. *Hostage* reflects on the transnational division and hierarchy of labor between democratic European Greece and postcommunist Balkan Albania. The film's border crossing raises certain issues that are often neglected in theories, policies, fiction, and films on migration. First, the politics and policies of global transnationalism—allowing the bus with endangered Greek hostages to go over the Albanian border—have to be considered along with their economics—subcontracting Albanians to resolve a breach of law that primarily affects Greek citizens—and vice versa. The subcontracting of the Albanian police force enables the bypassing of Greek criminal laws, just like the consequences of subcontracting in labor laws,[30] and makes less visible the Greek government's potential accountability in the murders that end the hijacking.

Then, the connection evoked between Greece and Albania suggests that the process of *immigration* can never be explained separately from the parallel process of *emigration.* The film takes place in three different locations that include both individual and institutional relations: the geography of immigration at the level of individual immigrant and the Greek state (Elion's love affair, beating and torture at the hands of officials); that of emigration at the level of the immigrant's relatives and the life he left behind (his fiancée, the rejection of her family) and the Albanian state (bargaining with Elion's mother, subcontracting Albanian security forces); and the liminal transit space (the bus of misfits, the stereotypes and hierarchies between them) that moves from the zone of immigration to that of emigration. This spatial scheme breaks what sociologist Abdelmalek Sayad, in his work on Algerian migration to France, calls "the caesura" between immigration and emigration:

> The caesura is introduced by a division of competences, interests and political stakes between political partners who are situated, with respect to one another, in a fundamentally asymmetrical relationship. . . . It is as though we had, on the one hand, a (relatively) surplus labour force—with no questions asked as to the reasons for that surplus available (for emigration)—and on the other hand, jobs that are available—with no questions asked about the mechanisms that make these jobs available for immigrants.[31]

Clearly the history of French colonialism gives Algerian emigration a historical background different from that of Albanian migration to Greece. Nevertheless, some parallels in the link between forces of immigration and those of emigration can be drawn, considering the role of Greece in the 1990s and early 2000s as a major source of foreign direct investment for the transition economies of the Balkans.[32]

Economist Michel Chossudovsky defines the role of Western powers, especially that of neighboring Greece and Italy, in the politics of post-communist Albania as "criminalization," since both of these countries have undeniably profited from the economic impoverishment of Albania and supported its oppressive neoliberal regime in the 1990s. Greeks together with Italians were the first to send armed forces to suppress the 1997 rebellions against corruption in the Albanian government, rebellions that were depicted in the Western media as "spontaneous street rioting . . . the misdeeds of armed gangs and the looting of state property," and thus, "political dissent by civilians . . . was depicted as sabotaging the 'transition' to a 'free market' society."[33] Between 1992 and 1999, Italy and Greece were the largest source of foreign direct investments in Albania.[34] In those years, Greece was one of the major receivers of Albanian exports of garment and footwear sweatshops and food exports, and had the highest number of private construction companies in Albania that ran infrastructural programs.[35] Remittances by emigrating workers were an indispensable financial source for the Albanian economy, especially those coming from Greece (over 80 percent of all remittances in the initial years of immigration 1991–92) and formed a large part of GNP.[36] The Greek state frequently used massive deportations of Albanian immigrants as a means of pressuring Albania regarding bilateral issues during the period 1991–99. When considering Albanian emigration to Greece in the 1990s and early 2000s, one must take into account how Greek economic interests influence and at times regulate the internal politics of this country of emigration.

Filming Migration, Filming Albania

Problematizing the border and uneven relations between Albania and Greece, mobility in *Hostage* places the film generically within the broader category of European travel cinema in addition to being a cinematic work on migration. Film scholar Dina Iordanova points to the domination of a wide range of films that focus on movement in world cinema, "the growing number of films that explore diasporas-in-the-making, the processes of migration and changing places, as well as itinerants and journeying."[37] In conjunction with this global trend, the road film became a predominant form of narrative in post–Cold War Europe because of increasing population movements and the growing idea of a united Europe beyond individual nationalities.[38] Travel films such as Wim Wenders's *Lisbon Story* (1994) and Aki Kaurismäki's *Leningrad Cowboys Go To America* (1989) present flexibility of borders and identities, and mobility of European populations along the lines of road movies as Hollywood genre that generally "offer audiences a glimpse at an ecstatic freedom. . . . On the road anything appears possible because nothing seems fixed, the journey itself represents a degree of seduction as the protagonists leave the confines of their world and see the geographical expense of their future before them."[39]

Films that represent economic emigration to Europe, however, frequently associate the idea of transnational mobility with claustrophobia and suffocation rather than an expression of freedom in an outstretching geography. As Yosefa Loshitzsky succinctly observes, two themes have dominated cinema of migration and films that represent minorities in Europe: narratives of the hardships during the "journeys of hope," and those on the difficulties of life "in the promised land."[40] The latter frequently reflect a sense of claustrophobia and suffocation due to entrapment in an urban ghetto. Mehdi Charef shows stifling concrete blocks in *Tea in the Harem* (1985); *La Haine* depicts the city center symbolized by the Eiffel Tower as always distant and unapproachable; Giannaris's earlier film *From the Edge of the City* shows enclosed lives of migrants in Athenian suburbs; *40 Square Meters of Germany* (1986) by Tevfik Başer films a Turkish woman migrant imprisoned by her husband in their house in Germany.[41] Hamid Naficy suggests that the iconography of claustrophobic spaces is characteristic of exilic cinema.[42] The "journeys of hope," on the other hand, reflect the road as an alienating source of unknown, frequently leading to death by suffocation at the hands of traffickers or through the wildness of nature (cold or storms at sea); as in films such as Xavier Koller's *Journey of Hope* (1990), Michael Winterbottom's *In this World*, Philippe Lioret's *Welcome*, and *From the Snow* in Greek cinema.

Hostage shows no "journey of hope" to a distant destination forced upon the migrant by abstract forces of globalization; it shows instead a return journey that is forced by the migrant. His death shows that the road does not necessarily connote an expanding space of unknown: the road does not expand to Albania; it contracts back to Greece. As the Ali Behdad quotation in the epigraph suggests, the economic migrant's perspective on transnationalism is not fluid; it is defined by conditions of fixity, control, and multiple forms of violence. Most importantly, for the migrant, there is no utopian land of immigration to go to, but more importantly, there is no isolated utopian land of emigration to return to.

Hostage's exploration of border crossing to Albania can be compared to another film that similarly explores the Albanian border, travels between the center and the periphery, and problematizes Western democracy and capital's exploitation of the peripheral Balkan neighbor Albania. Italian director Gianni Amelio's *Lamerica* (1994) is the story of two fraudulent Italian businessmen, Fiore (Michele Placido) and his young assistant Gino (Enrico Lo Verso), who go to Albania after its "democratization," ostensibly to privatize a shoe factory, but in reality to get EU funds, and then go bankrupt to retain the money without providing production or services. Gino's job is to find a figurehead Albanian partner, and he decides to use Spiro (Carmelo Di Mazzarelli), a mentally ill former political prisoner. Soon Gino discovers that Spiro is his compatriot, a Sicilian imprisoned by the Hoxha regime after the Second World War. When Spiro escapes on the day of the business deal, Gino travels after him to desolate inner Albania. Upon his return to Tirana with Spiro he gets arrested by the Albanian government and charged with corruption. The police take his passport. The film ends with a silent Gino on board a ship overwhelmed with Albanians hoping to get to Italy, sharing the same conditions with people he looked down on when he first entered the country. He is stripped of his Western standing and privileges, "Albanized" like his compatriot Spiro, and becomes a migrant on the road to a dream country.

The film received criticism from a group of Albanian intellectuals including writer Ismail Kadare, for "a hostile, damaging and harmful" depiction of Albania[43] and representation of Albanian people "as so desperate as to be virtually servile."[44] Amelio defended his work by saying that this in fact is a film about contemporary Italy, a criticism of its neoliberal politics and its Western gaze on the Balkans, of Italy's forgetfulness of its own history of fascism, destitution, and emigration. Albania is his source of inspiration, Amelio explains: "When I went to Albania it felt like returning to the home of my childhood. I've experienced misery and poverty. . . . I'm very familiar with the Italy of that period. That's why I love Albanians the way I do, because they resemble Italians so much."[45] Thus, in Amelio's film Albania serves both as a metaphor for old Italian poverty and as an unsullied victim of new Italian finance.

Regardless of Amelio's claim that the film is a metaphor for Italy, *Lamerica* was received as a film that portrays the destitution of postcommunist Albania, and most critics failed to see its subversive critique of Italy. This reception has partly been conditioned by *Lamerica*'s neorealist representation of Albania, its use of nonexperienced Albanian actors, location shooting, and cinemascope[46] to give a panoramic view of desolate mountains, scarce, dusty, gray buildings, restaurants with no food but lots of alcohol and Italian television, and hungry desolate people everywhere on the run to some promised land. Albania is "ambivalently characterized as a virgin land to conquer and as a place of entrapment for Italian characters."[47] *Lamerica*, recalling nineteenth-century adventure fiction and travelogues on the Balkans, and then journalism during the war in former Yugoslavia in the 1990s, depicts a Balkan country as "dangerous, unstable, a war zone,"[48] a zone of "dehumanization, deaesthetization, destruction of civilization."[49]

How would a film that claims to be a critique of the Western gaze upon the Other end up reproducing the gaze upon the "Albanian reality"? Amelio said, "No matter how I might have tried I could not become Albanian. I couldn't have become invisible. Nor could I have their purity of gaze."[50] Beyond the problems involved in this nostalgic search for "purity of gaze," this wish contradicts the construction of the film narrative. Although the film has visually crossed the border to Albania, it stays focused on Italy, and thus on the Italian gaze in the symbolic sense. Travel to the margin is not really going there but rather returning to oneself in nostalgia; therefore "the Albanian other remains raw material of representation and self-knowledge."[51] Amelio's film reflects a major problem that Ien Ang observes in European cinema of the 1990s: the inability to "come to terms with the complexities of its present without resorting to idealized images of either the past or the future," the inability to go beyond the centrality of Europe "to marginalize itself, to see its present in its historical particularity."[52]

Similar to *Lamerica*, *Hostage* focuses on Europe via Greece and criticizes the Greek capital and state for neoliberal violence against the migrant body, but in its criticism of contemporary Greece the Albanian gaze is central. Giannaris's film does not claim to "discover" or display Albania, a country closed to the foreign gaze (as well as capital) since World War II. It does not attempt to present what is unknown, exotic to the curious Western eye; it rather shows what is known but not talked about. Amelio's Albania is static, and temporally and spatially distant from contemporary Italy. Giannaris' Albania does not live in a different time zone and constricted space, it is in the domain of the contemporary Balkans where power differentials determine borders, exclusions and movements. The difference between Amelio and Giannaris' capturing of Albanian reality in relation to Italian or Greek reality is a matter of self-conscious narration, the awareness that "to use the other as material is a matter of privilege,"[53] which determines the matter of focus: while the former intends to reflect a country that remains temporally distant (be it Italy or Albania), the latter focuses on the question of border and mobility which allows to elide the reifications of uneven development on a regional basis.

Conclusion

Hostage treats a sensational media event involving a criminal migrant and places its marginalized protagonist at the center of migration debates in Greece. The film is an overt criticism of the "grey areas" of Greek transnational migration politics. *Hostage* places the "immigration problem" at the very heart of the state institutions rather than pushing it away to the metropolitan ghettos. Giannaris displays a viable web of corruption that was left invisible through the eyes of a protagonist who is expected to be silent and voiceless. The film shows corruption and exploitation in state institutions in the manner they deal with migration: whether fictional or real, it shows the possible connections of an Albanian migrant-criminal with illegal guns trade involving the police, and overtly displays what is only hinted in the media—the state violence applied on the hijacker's body in graphic detail. Moreover, the film suggests the Greek government's involvement in the fiasco that ends the hijacking in Albania with two murders. Hence, *Hostage* situates a historical event disregarded as an incidental eruption of migrant violence within its larger context, post-Cold War economics and politics in the Balkans.

Hostage makes the event and a criminal Albanian central through its appeal to tragedy—a particularly Greek genre—with an Albanian hero. Tragedy brings the violent event and migrant crime into the public space for a deeper consideration of its historical and geographical span. Moreover, the intervention of tragedy sidetracks the neorealist aesthetics that commonly frames migrants and minorities in Europe. Migrant and Diaspora communities have become, in Rey Chow's words, the new "primitive" of filmmakers: the oppressed classes or the underprivileged that provide a creative source of fascination for European and diasporic filmmakers alike who in turn produce ethnographic or auto-ethnographic representations.[54] Especially in the case of diasporic filmmakers it is not only a question of whether or not they intend to accomplish auto-ethnographic representation but a question of reception that tends to frame their films and characters through sociological readings, a dilemma I will discuss extensively in the next chapter on Fatih Akın's *Head-On*.

Giorgio Amelio's attempt to recreate the Italian past through the Albanian present in *Lamerica* becomes both an auto-ethnography of the post–World War II Italy and an ethnography of today's Albania. The "epistemological hierarchy" assigns the European or Italian as the temporal norm (the Albanian present becomes the Italian past) and the aesthetic heart of the fictional metaphor behind the Balkan or Albanian ethnographic particular.[55] While the Italian past haunts the film narrative as a grounding metaphor (the element of fiction), the Albanian present remains outside the realm of fiction, within that of sociological, anthropological, and historical analysis. Here I do not suggest that the former realm surpasses the latter, but aim to point to a constricted politics of visibility that divides the world "between those who can and those who cannot afford the luxury of playing with words and images. Subversion begins when this division is contested."[56] The genre of tragedy in *Hostage* introduces the subversion of such division as it opens possibilities of thinking beyond the ethnography of multitude of nameless Others but also beyond the singularity of a migrant crime. The film, as it blurs the relationship between documentary and tragedy, calls upon the uneven politics of aesthetic visibility and opens a viable space in which a violent event can be discussed. Such critical consideration of violence in documentary-tragedy manifests something meaningful about subjectivity within and under certain social conditions of violence and breaks the common assumption that "a nonviolated phenomenological whole exists prior to the onset of violence."[57] The historical event of violence, the bus hijacking provides an outlet to connect an Albanian migrant's personal experience of violence and impersonal and continuous situations of violence that are embedded in the migration process in Greece.

In consideration of these various levels of violence manifested in the film I would like to go back to the instances and signs of physical violence, the previously discussed rape scene and the scene when Elion shows his torture wounds to the hostages. The director's aim to highlight the known but silenced forms of state violence so as to counter the visibility of the hijacker's acts of violence reproduces the idea of a migrant's eventual victimhood that needs to be presented to justify his violent actions. Although radically different in its approach and intent, the representation of violence in *Hostage* take a turn similar to that in Michael Haneke's *Caché,* as both films risk reinforcing the significance of eruptive violence that they initially set out to undermine. The sheer physicality of violence, the titillating display of bodily pain and victimhood, is a double-edged sword, as it conforms with the common definition of violence in the liberal imagination: "in a liberal democracy . . . the terrorists, muggers and murderers become the paradigms of violence, with the result that silent, noiseless, systematic and routinized violence is either not called violence or allowed to fall out of view."[58] Bhiktu Parekh observes that physical harm done to the individual haunts the liberal imagination, while psychic harms such as exploitation, manipulation, or denying one the opportunity for personal growth are easily neglected. The possibility of larger conceptualization of violence may require a move away from the established liberal focus on physical violence and its bodily connotations.[59] Bodily focus looks for a subject, an identifiable agent responsible for the act of violence.[60] So, on the one hand, Giannaris is concerned with the invisibility of systematic and routinized situations of violence—economic (workplace exploitation), political (random ID checks and detentions by the police), and social (discriminatory treatment due to xenophobic prejudices)—against the mediatic visibility of migrant and minority acts of violence. On the other hand, he resorts to the same sensationalism that emerges from the liberal conception of physical violence above other forms of violence. The sheer bodily violence of torture and rape titillates the audience's imagination while reaffirming the liberal emphasis on the priority of visible, physical, bodily violence over the invisible, systematic forms of violence implied in the neoliberal joke that precedes the rape: "Want a soft drink? Regular or light?" No matter which kind Elion chooses, the ultimate result is his violation.

Elion, just like Kee in *Children of Men* and Majid in *Caché*, needs to show his body, his scars of torture, his painful cry during the rape scene, to prove his pain and suffering that lead to his rage and kidnapping of passengers on the bus. Admittedly, Elion is represented as a much more active subject than are the ethnic and racial Other characters examined in the previous chapters. He takes his destiny into his hands, but the manner of his rebellion is still questionable, as the hijacking is suicidal. Hence the agency of the Other remains, as in the case of *Caché*, within the realm of self-destruction. No matter how much of Elion's agency is displayed in the film he needs to undergo bodily violence to prove his eventual innocence. Once again corporeal suffering and finally death render the migrant Other the ultimate victim of uncontrollable transnational forces, just like the string of nameless refugees crushed under multiple catastrophic events in *Children of Men* and the Algerian-French orphan of the 1961 massacre in *Hidden*. The next chapter will discuss further this question of victimhood and the suffering body of ethnic and racial Others of Europe, inquiring about the kinds of violent events that they are associated with, events that highlight a certain kind of victimhood that validates European liberal values and freedoms.

FOUR

Ethnicity and Melodrama in the German Media and Fatih Akın's *Head-On*

> DER SPIEGEL: In the film *Head-On* by Fatih Akın, there is a scene in which a group of Turkish men sit and play a board game. One of them asks: "Shall we go to the brothel?" The other says: "Don't you have your own wives that you can fuck?" Then the former smashes a bottle, holds it up to the latter's throat, and says: "Never again mention fucking when it comes to our wives." Is this, for you, a realistic scene?
>
> SEYRAN ATEŞ: Yes. The men talk about their sexual adventures in the coffeehouses but never those with their own wives. Your wife is holy. Married couples told me that sexuality in the marriage is more or less reduced to the compulsory.[1]

Der Spiegel's interview with Seyran Ateş, a lawyer and public intellectual known for her activism against the patriarchal oppression of Muslim women in Germany, reveals multiple problems in both party's approaches. Beyond the questionable set of assumptions that give Seyran Ateş the authority to be an informant on sexuality in Turkish and Turkish-German marriages, Fatih Akın's film *Head-On* (2004) is treated as a sociological document capable of providing a picture into a certain cultural realm. The irony of the question "Is this, for you, a realistic scene?" becomes more striking when one realizes that the interviewer misremembers the scene and exaggerates the level of violence involved:

in the film there is no bottle breaking or threat to the man's throat. In this scene, the distance between the two Turkish-German characters and their differing opinions on sexuality is maintained by the table in the middle and by the camera's separate framing. The interviewer not only conflates the two characters' points of view, he overdramatizes the scene by increasing the level of aggression among "a group of Turkish men." This emphatic dramatization reinforces binary opposites in the domestic picture portrayed in the background: the promiscuous and physically aggressive Turkish husband is juxtaposed with the "holy" wife who lives a compulsory sexual life in her marriage. As the villain and the victim are outlined, the scene is set for a familiar melodrama, one that has been playing repeatedly in the German mainstream media.

This chapter asks the following question: Is there any way to situate *Head-On* as a Turkish-German minority cultural production without sequestering it as mimetic or auto-ethnographic representation of minorities in Germany? I argue that Fatih Akın's film is a melodrama symptomatic of the limited frames of minority visibility in Germany. While going against easy readings of sociological accuracy, authenticity, ethnic allegory, or auto-ethnography, the film's address to the spectator through the melodramatic mode situates it historically as a symptom of and reaction to the ways that mainstream cultural outlets in Germany, from news media to a number of migrant literature and films, articulate ethnicity and Otherness. Akın uses the melodramatic mode as a tongue-in-cheek critique of the ways that the Turkish-German and Muslim communities are frequently represented in the media. By making a melodrama, Akın reveals the melodramatization of ethnic relations in Germany, the creation of villains (Turkish men), and victims (Turkish women) along gendered, religious, and ethnic frames. The moral legibility of melodrama enables a clear-cut separation of villain versus victim and transfers into the "racial legibility"[2]—the reading of Otherness through Manichaean dichotomies such as aggressive Turkish-German Muslim man and submissive Turkish-German Muslim woman. In a melodrama, the director also reveals the artificiality of the normative identification of German liberal subjectivity and agency. *Head-On* points to the performativity—the expected "imitation of [German] life"—that underlies the minority integration debates that focus on their so-called failure to integrate into German society.

This chapter explores the emotional and critical registers that the melodramatic mode provides the director. It explores the multisensory perception of *Head-On* where the visual, the aural, and the haptic act simultaneously in differing ways to complicate the spectators' understanding of the minority characters and their relationship. Vision is complemented and thickened and gains volume through other sensory perceptions such as sound and touch. Such multiplicity aims to complicate the unilateral melodramatic visibility of minorities in the German media as it introduces the possibility of a perceptual ambiguity in and through the affective excess of melodrama. The focus on the affective excesses in Akın's work follows Jane Shattuc's criticism of earlier theories on the melodrama. Shattuc urges a move beyond the Marxist tradition of melodrama studies that values the affective excess in the melodramatic mode only to the extent that it alienates the spectator ideologically. Shattuc's critique introduces the following question: how can we explore the affective excess in a melodrama in a manner that goes beyond the limits of a Brechtian ideological critique?[3] The answer to this question lies in the larger proposal of this chapter: when melodramatic mode is firmly embedded in the social realm of ethnic visibility, that is, when the mass media and other popular outlets of minority visibility repeatedly play out the melodramatic gendered and domestic victim-villain dichotomy, the supposed barrier between the ideological and the affective needs to be rethought. Akın does not use the affective excess to alienate but to reach out and to attract the spectator, and to challenge conventional perceptions from within. Hence, the chapter traces how *Head-On* shifts the meaning of melodrama in relation to minority subjectivity: from melodramas that visualize minorities as morally and racially legible victims and villains to melodramas of perceptive ambiguity where the spectators' embodied affect becomes a path to contradiction against legibility rather than a confirmation of it. Before a close analysis of the film that traces this shifting meaning of melodrama, the next section explores the aforementioned larger modes of melodramatic visibility surrounding ethnic and religious Others—Muslim minorities in German visual culture.

Melodramas in the Headlines: Visual Representations of Muslim Women in Germany

Further along into the interview mentioned in the prologue, Seyran Ateş talks about her (then forthcoming) book on the necessity of a sexual revolution in the Muslim world. Ateş explains that the original title she had in mind for the book was "I'll Fuck Whoever I Want!"—a phrase that references a widely publicized "honor" crime. Hatun Sürücü, a twenty-three-year-old woman of Kurdish decent, was murdered in Berlin by her youngest brother, Ayhan, in February 2005. The night of the murder Hatun allegedly told Ayhan, "I'll fuck whoever I want!" After the murder Ayhan explained his motives: "She lived too openly when it came to her relationships to men."[4] The murder, labeled an "honor" crime, became a media sensation; it inspired a narrative film, *When We Leave* (2010), by Feo Aladağ, and a thirty-three-minute documentary, *Two Sides of the Moon: The Honor Killing of Hatun Aynur Sürücü*, by David Gould (2011). The synopsis of Gould's documentary reads: "Had she not questioned her family and culture, she likely would have been kept safe," portraying Sürücü as a martyr of freedom against the bounds of patriarchal tradition.[5]

Hatun Sürücü grew up in Berlin, was taken out of high school at the age of fifteen, was forced into marriage in Turkey at the age of seventeen, and later ran away from her husband and returned to Germany with her son. At the time of her murder she was only twenty-three and was training to be an electrician. Hatun Sürücü quickly became and continues to be a media figure, as commentaries on her murder reappear in the media to this day. The murder became a symbol in the debates about Islam, patriarchy, tradition, and integration of minorities in Germany. After Sürücü's murder the media retroactively labeled other minority-related domestic murders "honor killings," isolating them from domestic violence in nonminority households in Germany.[6] The updated headlines that appear on every anniversary of Sürücü murder reanalyze the event as a cautionary tale and emphasize that the reason behind the killing was punishment for crossing the assumed line of tradition, for becoming too modern and Western, and for exercising sexual freedom. These headlines sexualize Sürücü, associating German femininity with an excessive sexuality: "Sürücü is seen as 'becoming' German through her sexual availability."[7] While the male members of the Sürücü family appear as patriarchal villains, Hatun Sürücü is labeled as the victim of her sexual desires, a desire equated with that of freedom.

Sürücü's murder reveals the foregrounding of a certain kind of violence against minority women in Germany: domestic violence, as opposed to, for instance, the racist violence involved in the murder of Marwa Sherbini in 2009. Sherbini was a Muslim minority woman of Egyptian origin who was verbally attacked by a neo-Nazi youth in a public park. She took this young man to court in Dresden for racist hate speech. At the court, before Sherbini could testify against him, the neo-Nazi youth attacked her with a knife and stabbed her to death. In the meanwhile, Sherbini's husband was trying to protect her, but, mistaking the husband for the attacker, the court police shot the husband, which hastened Sherbini's death. This incompetence of the police (hinting at racial profiling) and the racist murder of a minority Muslim woman pursuing her rights in a German court were significantly underrepresented in the German media in comparison to Sürücü's case.[8] Sherbini's murder lacked the melodramatic component of the domestic crime of passion featuring a victimized Muslim woman and a criminal male family member.

Taking a step back to look at the history of media and cultural representations of Turkish-German and Muslim minorities in Germany reveals a pattern culminating in the Sürücü case. Starting from the mid-1970s social science research, liberal feminist scholars and activists, literature, and especially images in mass media and film constructed Turkish and Muslim migrant and minority women in Germany as the primary victims of a patriarchal tradition. Studies of domestic abuse of minority Muslim women have flourished, while these women's participation in the work world is understudied.[9] Regardless of their antiracist activism in the 1990s, feminist movements in Germany have largely assumed a patronizing tone when contrasting "native" German women's emancipation to migrant and minority women's presumed oppression by patriarchal and Islamic tradition.[10] Toward the end of the 1990s and into the following decade, *Der Spiegel* repeatedly published issues that highlighted forced marriages and domestic violence against Turkish and Muslim women, with its covers titled "Allah's Daughters without Rights (2004), "The Headscarf Principle: Muslim Women in Germany (2003)," and "The Riddle of Islam (Special Issue 1998)."[11]

In the 1980s, a large number of fictions and films in Germany that explored migrant and minority women's lives were narratives of claustrophobia and imprisonment in the domestic sphere. Possibly the best-known example of such films is Tevfik Başer's *40 Square Meters of Germany* (1986), the story of a Turkish woman who comes to Germany after her wedding and is eternally confined in a small apartment by her husband. *Farewell to the False Paradise* (1988) by the same director, depicts a Turkish woman's path to emancipation, ironically taking place in a German prison through her interaction with the inmates after she has killed her husband. Another popular film of the same period, *Yasemin* (Hark Bohm, 1990), shows a young Turkish girl who lives a double life—the obedient Turkish daughter at home and a successfully integrated German student in school. She eventually escapes to freedom with her German lover. German characters in these films often lead the way to emancipation from the claustrophobic lives and spaces that the Turkish characters are confined to.[12]

This "paradigm of victimology" has been perpetuated by the authoritative voices of "native informant" women.[13] Autobiographies such as *We Are Your Daughters, Not Your Honor* (1999) by Serap Çileli, *The Foreign Bride* (2005) by Necla Kelek, and *The Great Journey into the Fire* (2003) by Seyran Ateş focus on the oppression that the Turkish-German and Kurdish-German authors suffer at the hands of their patriarchal Muslim migrant families in Germany.[14] Literary scholar Tom Cheesman describes these autobiographical and fictional works that promise to reveal the supposed horrors of the Muslim domestic sphere (forced marriages, imported brides, and "honor" killings) as "melodramatic social critique" since these works are "powerfully emotive, using techniques of melodrama: a simplified, Manichean moral schema, demonizing Muslims in general, and evoking shock, horror, pity and pathos in the reader."[15] Such works with moral legibility particular to melodramas have an easy market appeal. The publicized "honor" crimes and the parallel stigmatization of Muslim men[16] along with the former Muslim women's autobiographies of domestic oppression and violence set the scene for an ongoing melodramatization of ethnic Otherness along gender lines in Germany.

Fatih Akın: Transnational, Diasporic, and European

Head-On is a film about the failed love story of Sibel (Sibel Kekilli) and Cahit (Birol Ünel), Turkish-German minorities from Hamburg. Cahit, a middle-aged punk, meets Sibel, a young and spirited woman, at a mental clinic after their individual suicide attempts. Sibel proposes to Cahit a marriage of convenience, which will enable her to gain independence from her overbearing family. After a series of comical scenes of marriage arrangements, the wedding takes place, and Sibel starts enjoying a life of sex, drugs, and alcohol. The lighthearted comedy takes a tragic turn when the couple falls in love and Cahit accidentally kills one of Sibel's former lovers. While Cahit goes to jail, Sibel escapes to Istanbul for fear of her family's retaliation against her for shaming them. In Istanbul, Sibel takes up a job as a hotel maid, leading an alienated life dictated by work. Soon she quits her job and pursues a self-destructive path until she is eventually stabbed in a dark alley. While her fate is left unclear, in an ellipsis we see Cahit released from prison. He goes to Istanbul to look for Sibel and finds that she is now the mother of a small child and lives with another man. After spending a weekend together, Cahit invites her to Mersin, the homeland of his parents, to settle and build a new life as a family. At the end of the film, while Cahit takes the bus to Mersin, Sibel finds herself incapable of leaving Istanbul.

Upon its release, *Head-On* was immediately drawn into the realm of melodrama through the sensationalized debates about its female star in both Turkish and German media. The tabloid *Bild* newspaper quickly turned the focus of discussions on the film, shifting from the victory of *Head-On* as the first German film to win the Golden Bear in Berlin in eighteen years, to the life story of the leading minority actress. Sibel Kekilli's previous appearance in porn films made headlines, and interviews with Kekilli's father followed: "The disgrace is too great for the family. . . . I can never forgive her for it. I don't want to ever see her again."[17] The melodrama within the melodrama, a *mise-en-abime*, was reinforced by the shared names of the actress and the character.[18] Thanks to the pornographic images and videos of Kekilli disseminated across cyberspace the Turkish-German star was both further sexualized and established as a potential "honor" crime victim. Years later, Kekilli's leading role in *When We Leave* (2010) by Feo Aladağ, the film inspired by Hatun Sürücü's murder, has perpetuated her potential "honor" crime victim Turkish–German woman star image.

While the tabloid debates overwhelmed the mainstream media, film critics and scholars consider *Head-On* as one of the first works to bring contemporary Turkish-German diasporic cinema out of its ethnic niche toward larger frames of reference. Critics consider the main characters in *Head-On* global citizens, just as Akın describes himself as a "world citizen," rejecting the label of ethnic filmmaker.[19] Sibel and Cahit were described as "metropolitan elites" who deal with existential problems,[20] "abject heroes" of a transnational "double occupancy,"[21] "queer" identities that introduce androgyny into heteronormative frameworks,[22] characters who are looking for the redemptive promise of a return home in a rootless migratory film.[23] In other words, the critics of the film, partly as a response to the ethnic framing that has captivated both minority characters and filmmakers of Germany (and Europe for that matter), attribute to *Head-On* a postethnic and postnational framework.

The film has been considered transnational or diasporic, as it blends genres (from Fassbinder's melodramatic modes, Turkish style melodrama/*arabesk*[24] to the German romantic tradition[25]), languages, and shooting locations: "aesthetically hybrid, juxtaposing and fusing stylistic templates, generic conventions, narrative and musical traditions, languages and performance styles from more than one (film) culture."[26] The analyses of *Head-On* parallel other scholarship on Akın's oeuvre that highlights the director's use of multiple shooting locations and multilingualism, which situate him as the director of the New Europe (as Europe too defines itself through flexible borders and multilingualism),[27] as a transnational filmmaker "exploring the pleasures of hybridity,"[28] or as a diasporic filmmaker who foregrounds the migratory experience in a way that defies "notions of national belonging and identity, constructing instead alternative societies, based around transnational networks and connections."[29]

The declaration of Akın's work as transnational, diasporic, or European; and celebration of the mobility of his cinema, the hybridity of his approach (that appears through the use of multiple languages, cinematic styles, and shooting locations that all transcend national borders and traditions) suggest a trend in film criticism of minority directors in Europe. These correctives intend to overcome the ghettoization of minority cultural production and to go beyond the expectation from ethnic Others to mark their Otherness and produce familiar yet "authentic" narratives about themselves. In order to counter such clichéd framing of an "ethnic director," they trade an ethnic for a cosmopolitan identity.

Rey Chow observes that cultural studies and hybridity studies gear discussion on ethnic cultural productions toward "difference revolution," in which minority/ethnic subjects are celebrated both for their difference and their narrative's hybrid quality and mobility that goes beyond national borders. The fluent, dynamic, mobile, hybrid, and different is celebrated as the new radical transnational identity. For Chow, however, "the flip side of the difference revolution is its refusal of reference."[30] The cultural product becomes transnational or universal by losing reference to the context it emerges from.[31] The celebration of hybridity, difference, and mobility tends to dismiss the complex conditions, tensions, and contradictions from which the work draws. Along these lines, Mahmut Mutman explains that most critical analyses of Akın's oeuvre resort to a "culturalist pluralism" by which they explore and celebrate the different traces of Turkish and German cultural references in the director's films, only to describe the product as "happily multiple and multiply enabled."[32] A refusal of essentialist notions of identity is replaced by a celebratory approach to hybridity that may take away the historicity, or temporal and geographical situatedness, of the films. The following sections suggest that analyzing the use of melodrama conventions in *Head-On* is key to situating the film within its context, where media melodramas are the primary mode through which ethnicity and Otherness are articulated.

In terms of the narrative, *Head-On*'s exploration of emotional traumas of the protagonists in their self-destructive acts, the focus on the sentiments of love and loss, self-conscious use of cliché that depicts an oppressed Turkish-German woman and aggressive Turkish-German man, the Freudian overtones (sublimated passion, displaced aggression, sexual and gender ambiguity) and the ending that encapsulates its female character in a fatalistic circularity as the self-sacrificing mother all gesture toward the conventions of melodramatic mode. In terms of its formal aesthetics, *Head-On* is a melodrama thanks to its heavy deployment of music that conveys the emotional states of the characters, the excessive use of color (the dominant color being red, from splashing blood to red clothes, props, and lighting with red hues to mark the inflaming of desire and passion of the characters), extensive use of mirrors and reflection, the rhythm of the plot that has many ups and downs as comedy follows tragedy and emotions swing to extreme opposites (an emotionally touching cooking scene is followed by the disposal of food down the toilet, a friendly bar scene is tainted with a bloody suicide attempt). Following a staple generic convention of melodramas, time becomes the object of loss in the film as Sibel and Cahit's marriage comes too early, while falling in love and reunion in Istanbul come too late.[33]

Melodramatic conventions and significations in *Head-On* give the film both national (via Rainer W. Fassbinder) and global (Turkish *arabesk* tradition and melodrama as the quintessential Hollywood genre) qualities. Deniz Göktürk considers that melodramatic conventions in *Head-On* serve a dual purpose: they enable transnational legibility, and they take the film beyond the claims of mimetic representation, hence beyond the ethnic niche that potentially frames the film in sociological analyses. Göktürk argues that in *Head-On* Akın resorts to melodrama's "expressive excess" in order to detach his film from the social realist framework of reception for Turkish-German cultural productions, a mode of reception that collapses "actor and role, fiction and social reality, where staged and enacted representations tend to be read as mimetically representative of the experience of a disenfranchised group."[34] Göktürk's argument here suggests that melodramatic conventions mark the film as fiction and not a representation of social reality, while melodrama's formal excesses pose an alternative to social realist aesthetics.

The relationships between social reality and melodrama as well as realist aesthetics and melodrama are rarely those of mutually exclusive spheres, however. Thomas Elsaesser's seminal article on melodrama insists on the significance of the specific social context that the melodramas he explores emerge from: the 1940s postwar condition, along with anxieties about domesticity and gender relations.[35] Elsaesser describes family melodrama as a genre that exposes the tensions and contradictions that lie beneath the surface of the postwar suburban American life. Furthermore, the melodramatic mode frequently stands side by side with realist aesthetics and narrative in examples such as Pedro Almodovar's cinema and Lars von Trier's works, such as *Breaking the Waves* (1996) and *Dancer in the Dark* (2000). As Peter Brooks suggests, melodrama is a form born in conjunction with realist aesthetics and is dependent on realism as a style, fortifying its excesses but also depicting its limits of representation.[36] Melodrama has its particular way of articulating social reality, revealing the limits and inadequacies of realist aesthetics: "acknowledging the limitations of the conventions of language and representation, it proceeds to force into aesthetic presence identity, value and plenitude of meaning."[37]

As a contextual reference from which Akın draws, it is crucial that melodrama provides the primary narrative frame through which the debates on Muslim minorities are pursued in the German mass media. Linda Williams's work on the relationship between race and the melodramatic mode in the United States explains how the melodramatic mode extends from the cinematic into the media and vice versa. Williams insists that melodrama is not only a filmic genre but a mode that can be widely defined in its extension to popular culture: "It is a protean 'leaping fish' that flies from one spectacular manifestation to the next in popular culture generating novel objects of sympathy."[38] In the United States, Williams observes, melodrama is the main mode through which race relations become legible and are thought through. This can be observed in the incredible sales of the melodramatic novel *Uncle Tom's Cabin* and the high ratings of significant race-related media events such as the Rodney King beating and the O. J. Simpson trial, all three showing African-Americans as either victim or villain.[39] Williams reminds us that the question of moral legibility at the heart of the melodramatic mode is "intrinsically linked to a 'racial legibility' that habitually sees a Manichaean good or evil in the visual 'fact' of race itself."[40]

There is a parallel between the U.S. and German media melodramas in terms of transferring moral legibility to racial and ethnic legibility through emphasis on stories of victimized Turkish-German women and victimizer Turkish-German men. In turn, Akın's melodrama shows how social reality about minorities is often filtered through the melodramatic lens, hence the so-called minority reality is already thought through the framework of fiction that involves clichéd roles for ethnic Others. Through making a melodrama, Akın addresses the limitations of media's so-called objective reality and shows that it involves series of melodramatic plots; also, more fundamentally, he shows the inadequacy of realist aesthetics in making claims about minority lives and images. The melodrama undoes both the so-called objective minority reality and authentic minority fiction, showing the parallels between the two realms that produce stereotypical minority images. Melodrama shows that the fictional representation does not correspond to reality; instead, the assumed reality regarding ethnic or minority Others is always already filtered through melodramatic fiction. Hence, *Head-On* is a symptom of a discourse that envelops minority reality within a melodramatic frame.

Head-On's mediation on the politics of melodrama uses affective excess to disturb racial and ethnic legibility. The next section analyzes *Head-On*'s affective excess for its ambiguity rather than its dialectic legibility. The characters' alienatingly excessive emotions, as well as elements such as clichéd postcard-like musical interludes that divide *Head-On*'s sequences (and make the audience conscious of the ongoing spectacle), leave room for analyzing the film as one that blends Brechtian alienation devices with melodramatic techniques, as in Douglas Sirk and Rainer W. Fassbinder's melodramas.[41] But my interest lies in untangling the various affective constellations and excesses in the film rather than describing them uniformly as alienating. My question is this: how can we explore the film as "as an object with which we interact rather than an illusion into which we enter"?[42] The film invites its spectator to perceive differently, and suggests other ways of thinking and feeling ethnicity in Germany. *Head-On* reveals that the excess of affects and melodrama is the convention when it comes to the representation of ethnic and racial Others. It then taps into this convention to introduce a multisensory perception of ethnicity beyond the framework that specifies victim/villain protagonists versus empathetic spectators.

The close reading of the film in the following section discusses the multiple venues of perception that the film provides for its audience—the interaction of the aural, the visual, and at times the haptic to reveal the clichéd frames of legibility for minorities—and opens them up to discussion, going beyond these clichés by expanding the frames of perception. The meaning of each clichéd image in the film is altered by the auditory or the haptic, and vice versa. The film provides its spectator multiple stimuli in contact with each other, sometimes contradicting, other times complementing or deepening, the meaning of each stimulus. Claiming such sensory plurality is not necessarily an attempt to celebrate another multiplicity or hybridity in Akın's work and add to the criticism in a similar manner.[43] Multisensorality in melodrama shifts perception from conditioned empathy to open reception through the use of expansive stimuli and excessive affect. The techniques of "audiovisual contract,"[44] sonic border crossing, shock violence, and performative imitation question the frames of visibility of minorities and open these frames to further debate.

Against the Wall

After his car crash/suicide attempt, the therapist at the psychiatric clinic asks Cahit and hence brings the question to the attention of the spectators: "There are a thousand other ways to kill yourself. Why drive into a wall?" The therapist's question makes a reference to the original German title of the film, Gegen die Wand, literally toward or against the wall. The wall as the pre-1989 separation barrier has varied symbolic meanings in Germany. The fall of the wall, the rejoiced unification of the two Germanys, also marks the beginning of a violent history: the rise of neo-Nazism in the 1990s and numerous incidents of racial violence against refugees and ethnic minorities of non-European origin. Opening the film with a violent car crash against a wall may imply a reference to the wall that remains despite unification, the invisible wall of discrimination against minorities that has been fortified after the collapse of the physical wall. The use of such a symbolically dense marker is significant for the film's affective relationship with its audience in Germany, yet the wall and the crashing cannot be interpreted solely by their face value.[45] Karen Beckman argues that the collision of cars in cinema gives a visual form to anxieties concerning mobility and stasis, immunity and contamination, alterity and desire. The car crash makes the audience "consider the ethics of border, the line dividing self from other, the world of spectator from the world of image."[46] Indeed, in *Head-On*, the car crash into a wall brings into consideration a border: the confinement of the ethnic subject within certain bounds of visibility and knowability.

When I use the word "confinement" in relationship to *Head-On*, this is by no means a reference to a spatial limitation experienced as claustrophobia or agoraphobia that Hamid Naficy ascribes to exilic filmmaking.[47] The wall or the containment I refer to, against which the characters and the film crash, takes place on the metanarrative level rather than the spatial one. The wall is a metaphor for the containment within a particular form of social and institutional visibility, a visibility that becomes an entrapment.[48] This "visibility" is different from and broader than visuality. It is an epistemic construction of the ethnic subject that is "less a matter of becoming physically seen than a matter of attaining discursive attention and recognition"; hence it is an image constructed by a complex web of articulations beyond the visual.[49] Going against the wall in *Head-On* signifies the desire to go beyond the confinement within given terms of ethnic visibility; the desire to expand the limits of what is visible as ethnic. The film reveals the conditions of Turkish-German or minority forms of visibility and melodramatic legibility, as it attempts to enhance "the condition of possibility for what becomes visible."[50]

The terms of visibility for the minority woman and the minority gender relations are questioned from the very first scene in which Cahit and Sibel meet. The car crash becomes the catalyst for Cahit's transformative encounter with Sibel. The scene in the psychiatric clinic's waiting room where Sibel and Cahit meet follows the car crash sequence. A black screen directs our attention to the offscreen dialogue. An unfamiliar male voice speaking in German in an angry tone explains with fragmented sentences that he is in this institution because his wife claims to be afraid of him: "She tells Dr. Schiller: 'I'm afraid of my husband'. . . . What am I? . . . 'I'm afraid of my husband' . . . Lying cunt." As the speaker is left invisible to the spectator the camera moves jerkily in jump cuts to the closed doors and bleak fluorescent lights of the hospital waiting room. Point-of-view shots through Cahit's eye show the walls that contain contradictory signs of order and delirium.

The speaker's threatening offscreen voice continues to accompany Cahit's gaze: "But I got people, I'm telling you, I'll fucking show her." As another man's voice timidly asks, "What kind of people?" the camera lands on Sibel's bandaged wrists, the signs of self-inflicted violence, and moves to her face as she directly gazes at the camera and Cahit, breaking the fourth wall. While Cahit looks back we hear the man in the offscreen dialogue repeating his threat: "I'll show her, I tell you. She won't get away with it." Finally, the camera in narrow focus captures the two men in dialogue. Sibel remains in the background, out of focus, situated in the middle of the two men; she continues to look into the camera. In the crosscut Cahit is similarly seen situated between the two characters speaking, looking past them toward Sibel.

In this scene the voice whose source we cannot identify for quite a while—the voice without a body, or "the acousmatic voice" in film sound theorist Michel Chion's terms—takes on an omnipotent aura.[51] The elusive sound attaches itself to the bodies that the camera captures and contains the two protagonists' future relationship. The offscreen dialogue that suggests forthcoming domestic violence is visually attached to Sibel and Cahit; it hangs over their first encounter, establishing a narrative that frames their initial visibility. This frame of honor, shame, and potential domestic violence suggests the discourse for the gendered confrontation of minority subjects. The irony, of course, is that the domestic violence in the dialogue has a nonminority source. In the original script, the man who threatens his wife is named Ammer and described as looking like Michael Ammer, the so-called party-king of Hamburg, who among his other court cases came to the media's attention several times for sexual assault and violence against women.[52]

As soon as offscreen sound becomes onscreen we see that the men who speak are situated in the middle of the waiting room. The discussion on potential domestic violence and the speakers function as a barrier or a human wall upon which the mutual gazes of Sibel and Cahit crash. Cahit's and Sibel's meeting gazes are overburdened with the dialogue on potential domestic violence, but they also confront the dialogue as they hit the metaphorical wall with their direct gaze, which, in cinematic terms, breaks the fourth wall. Sibel and Cahit's mutual gaze raises awareness about watching, and in turn about being visible through the voice that hovers over them. The jump cuts and jerky handheld camera movements, along with the dissonant visual and aural stimuli, disorient the spectators and expand their perception at the same time.

The audiovisual dissonance, Michel Chion suggests, does not necessarily negate the image or contradict it. Rather, the aural encounters the vision to "carry the perception of the image to another level."[53] The gaze makes an "audiovisual contract" with the dialogue, sees through it, sees across it, and cuts right through it. The voice contains and contaminates the yet silent character (Sibel) but then the image equally contains the voice; Sibel's direct gaze overtakes the acousmatic voice and what the voice communicates. As Sibel and Cahit see each other in the space of the dialogue, framed by it but also going across and beyond the dialogue, their mutual gaze contaminates and breaks the wall of the dialogue. They reach out to the audience and convey the awareness of watching and being watched, and the limited conditions of minority visibility: that of domestic violence. It is no coincidence that Sibel's gaze in this scene becomes part of the official film poster of *Head-On*. The wall that Cahit and Sibel hit and break with their gazes is that of the melodramatic minority visibility that is imposed on them.

Starting from the car crash in the opening sequence, the film confronts its audience with the characters' desire to break the frame, to reach outward; the world of melodrama extends into the world of spectators. Borders, walls, and belonging to a preconstructed frame of visibility are revealed and continuously contested in the film through the use of sound that moves outside the allocated frame. Sound bridges break the sonic borders between sequential scenes, altering the meaning of the images as the sound grows excessive, expanding into the previous or following scene. This is well illustrated in the climactic moment before Cahit kills Niko, Sibel's ex-boyfriend. Sibel is at the amusement park, where the camera shows her in shallow focus, indicative of her being closed off in her own world and vision, unaware of the larger context and the looming danger in another space: Niko and Cahit's provocative conversation at the bar. While the lights in the amusement park become blurred and take on a dreamlike quality around Sibel, the nondiegetic soundtrack "After Laughter Comes Tears" foreshadows the grief that will follow and connects the amusement park to the next scene at the bar. Before Cahit kills Niko, Sibel is seen at home, lovingly placing on the bed a kitsch chocolate heart she bought for Cahit. The sound bridge carries Niko's voice over to Sibel's image by her bed, "What kind of fucked-up husband are you?" leading into the murder scene at the bar, where Sibel arrives too late. So while the soundtrack "After Laughter Comes Tears" carries over to the next scene, thereby connecting the two spaces (the amusement park and the bar), Niko's words cross over to the previous scene: overlaid on Sibel's loving preparation for Cahit. The dual sound bridges—the continuation of the soundtrack and the abrupt intervention of the voice that pulls Sibel's image into the climactic scene of murder—doubly break the sonic border and bring in the element of the unknown, the unfamiliar, the invisible background event. The resulting discrepancy between the sound and the vision increases the intensity of contradictions: the sadness that is bred in happy moments, the happiness in sad moments—an emotional disruption common to the melodramatic mode. In that mode, the disconnect and often unrealized connection between the characters always alludes to the possibility of the missing information, which again makes knowledge, rationale, or signification incomplete. Sound bridges in the film introduce a perceptive uncertainty as they oscillate between showing distance and proximity, continuity and abrupt change.

This perceptive uncertainty marks especially the final sequence of the film, leaving the melodrama open-ended. While in the opening sequence the characters confront the spectators with their direct gaze, in the closing shots they either turn their back against the camera or become invisible to it. As Cahit takes the ride to Mersin, his bus reflects the rays of the setting sun, and his wavering image becomes a silhouette inside the bus. The cinematic image becomes obscure and Cahit is wiped from the screen along with his past involving Sibel. We see Sibel left in her room with her back turned against us, her face hidden from visibility, her body curled up as she listens to the voice of her lover playing with her daughter in the next room. Once again the vision and the sound are separated, and this multisensory information implies a multiple sense of reality. What is visible is complicated with the aural, and perception is never complete, as ambiguities are omnipresent.

Breaking the Frame through Self-Destructive Violence

While the continuous tension between sound and image reinforces perceptive uncertainty, tactility of the film in the scenes of self-inflicted violence instigates perceptive disturbance in its uncalled-for proximity. The "wall breaking" in the film extend to multiple senses through the visceral images in which the characters attempt to move beyond the limits of their allotted narrative space and roles. Just as the characters' gazes venture outward to break the frame, their bodies in self-destructive acts—from car crash to gory wrist-slitting to glass-breaking with bare hands—expand beyond the cinematic frame to grab the spectator. The character's victimhood is not depicted in a manner that seeks distant empathy. As Lauren Berlant explains, "compassion is a term denoting privilege: the sufferer is over there."[54] In *Head-On* the affective excess leaves no room for the spectator to be "over there" in a distance.[55]

Before the bloody and visceral scene in which Sibel slashes her wrist in front of the camera, Cahit asks her why she wants to kill herself. She looks straight into his eyes and says, "Do you think my nose is nice? Touch it." Cahit runs his finger along her nose and Sibel explains: "My brother broke it because he caught me holding hands . . . Now touch my tits . . . You ever seen such great tits? I want to live, Cahit. I want to live, I want to dance, I want to fuck. And not only with one guy. Do you understand?" He answers, "I'm not deaf." Still Sibel is not convinced: "You don't understand shit! Will you marry me now, Cahit?" "Forget it!" She smashes the bottle and slits her wrist. The blood gushes out and spills on Cahit's face in a Tarantino-esque manner.

In the beginning of the dialogue Sibel's invitation and Cahit's touch on her nose are a flirtatious intimate contact between the couple. Yet Sibel's unchanging smile and her static image make her words about her brother's violence more haunting, as they change the signification of Cahit's touch so that the touched part of the face is now connected to a history of domestic violence. When Sibel asks Cahit to touch her breasts, the meaning of touch shifts yet again as the signification of tactility in the scene moves from intimacy to domestic violence then to sexual desire associated with the desire for freedom. Even more, the dialogue is rather melodramatic as it conveys the suppression of a woman's sexual desire within the patriarchal oppression of family. The shifting of significations between the touch as desire and the touch as violence refers to the vacillation between the two clichés of female minority subjectivity: the object of domestic violence and the subject of desire for sexual freedom.

The self-inflicted violence could be interpreted as an extension of domestic violence or the desire to break free from it. Yet the act of suicide is not peculiar to the "minority female," as both characters are equally suicidal. Furthermore, Sibel's awareness at every step of her action complicates her melodramatic victimhood. Her learning process makes this second suicide attempt more effective (she cuts her vein vertically rather than horizontally, following Cahit's earlier advice), and her purposefulness and consciousness (after the suicide attempt scene on the bus, she thinks of an elaborate explanation of how the marriage of convention would work) make the act of raw violence more than a pathological reaction. Sibel's actions ultimately guide the film narrative; she is the active character, while Cahit is reactive. Sibel puts a stamp on action. Akın establishes Sibel's guiding role precisely through her use of space in the mise-en-scène: in the initial scenes, when Cahit and Sibel first meet in the clinic, Sibel continuously moves from the edges toward the center of the frame, often taking the camera with her as she leaves the frame. Sibel's suicide attempt in the bar is a key move that draws Cahit into making a decision and persuades him into the marriage.

The suicide attempt on the screen is attached to the dialogue that precedes it. The effect of domestic violence takes on an embodied form through Cahit's touch, and then Sibel asks, "Do you understand?" and Cahit responds, "I'm not deaf." The shifting of sensory perception highlights the separation between hearing, touch, and gaze and implies the impossibility of a holistic perception, especially when Sibel shoots back,

"You don't understand shit." This line, which precedes the gory action, is also directed at the spectator, who may be attuned to interpreting Sibel's actions through schematic formulations of melodramatic victimhood. Violence is connected to the assumption of knowing, understanding, and judging. As Deleuze claims, cinematic acts that aim for audience affect reinforce "immanent evaluation, instead of judgment as transcendent value: 'I love or I hate' instead of 'I judge.'"[56] Affect deters the impersonal judgment and brings out the specificity of the individual action, passion, and life into the audience's realm of perception. The sheer raw physicality of the wrist-slitting and the self-victimization involved take the characters outside the realm of facile ethical judgment or clear moral legibility.

Extreme forms of self-victimization in the film cut down melodramatic moral legibility and clarity, as well as immediate social legibility. Jane Shattuc's commentary on self-victimization in Fassbinder's melodramas is telling: "the victim as his or her own victimizer contradicts both the active agency of the classical protagonist and the passive victim status of the melodramatic Mary Pickfords, Mildred Pierces or even the Sirkean Cary Scotts. Yet it also undercuts the potential critique of the social sources of victimization. There are no simple or direct social causes in Fassbinder's melodrama."[57] Rather than disregarding the potential familial forces of victimization, the self-victimizing character in *Head-On*, as in Fassbinder, filters the social in a more complex manner. The self-inflicted violence along with its raw affect introduces moral ambivalence into a narrative that is commonly interpreted through the frame of moral clarity.[58]

The self-destruction of characters becomes further discomforting through tactile details that highlight the visceral violence: blood gushing toward Cahit's face after Sibel's suicide attempt at the bar, Cahit dancing with his bloodied hands up in the air after breaking the glasses with his bare hands, an extreme close-up on the suturing of Sibel's slit wrists after her second on-screen suicide attempt. The self-inflicted violence is not irrational, for it does not exist in a vacuum of the inexplicable, yet it is excessive and unexpected. The moments of visceral immediacy in the film call for the erasure of preassigned meaning and signification about who the victim and perpetrator are. In Steven Shaviro's words, the character "lures [the spectator] into an excessive intimacy, one so extreme that it is also, immediately, a distance precluding identification."[59] Thus, screen violence disturbs the audience in its uncalled-for intimacy, as it does not leave room for compassion from a distance. Sheer raw violence and affect not only preclude identification, they also deter easy rationalizations or readings of the actions and identity of the character through predesignated markers.

Identitarian frames and borders are put up against the wall through the use of excessive affect in *Head-On*. Just as the main characters get closer to each other through multisensory contacts (Cahit smells Sibel's sheets, Sibel cleans the blood off Cahit's face, in an intimate moment they eat together), violence becomes a way for the film to touch its spectator.[60] Akın's style may be situated within a larger movement in cinema, a movement toward what Martine Beugnet calls the cinema of sensuality, which pours out of the screen and collapses the border between the film and its audience, making film a sensual experience. This cinema destabilizes the Cartesian division of the body and the mind, weaves together the sensual and the conceptual, breaks the hierarchy between the subjective and the objective, the raw sensation and so-called objective positive knowledge. This cinema includes more tactile details as a marked shift away from the centrality of the gaze. It calls for a different epistemology, a wider sense of reality, a bodily identification with cinema, "a more embodied and multisensory relationship to the image in films," an attempt to "use film to approach some borderline experiences of the human condition."[61] While Beugnet explores French cinema of the later 1990s and early 2000s within this framework, Akın's melodrama similarly disorients perception and also calls for a multisensory, border-crossing relationship between the spectator and the characters. Such affective disturbance brings the melodramatic world of fiction in close proximity, calling for a suspension of ethical judgment and distant empathy.

Sibel's second on-screen suicide attempt brings the character and her self-inflicted violence even closer to the spectator. Leading into scene, the camera cuts abruptly from Niko's murder to a close-up on Sibel's hand inserting the CD of a soundtrack from a Turkish melodrama.[62] The song "Cry My Love" ties together the disconcerting editing that moves between close-ups and long-distance shots in this central sequence titled "Family Honor" (DVD). A close-up shows Sibel looking into the mirror with her eyes red from crying; then a long shot shows her framed in a doorway with bloody hands, followed by a close-up on the bathroom sink that reveals bloodstains and a razor—evidence of a suicide attempt. Then an extreme close-up shows her skin being sutured. We then see a close-up of a newspaper headline that reads: "Jealousy Drama in St. Pauli" with a picture of Sibel and Cahit from their wedding and that of the victim, Niko. While Sibel's family grieves over the news in the next shot, her father burns Sibel's childhood pictures: in an extreme close-up we see the crumbling texture of the photographs.

The fast-paced close-ups followed by long shots move between personal space and public space without mediation. The newspaper headline frames the lack of mediation: the individual's story is bluntly placed within the public space. In this absence of mediation, the procession of close-ups is significant: the blood in the sink with the razor blade, Sibel's wrist being surgically sutured (with remarkable attention to details such as the mark of the old suicide attempt on her skin), the news of the "Jealousy Drama" and the burning of Sibel's photographs. The literal suturing of the two parts of the skin is juxtaposed with the suturing of Sibel's image in a sensational story of "jealousy drama." As her skin is parched and revealed, her story is displayed for the public eye and her photos are burned: "the skin conceals and reveals, protects and exposes not only our innards but also our emotional states and our personal histories."[63] The "objective" world of the news media becomes sutured with the subjective pain of the body through the editing; the self-objectification of the body through the suicide corresponds to the objectification of Sibel's story in the news. The suturing of Sibel's body is a metacommentary on the melodramatic suturing of images to create an illusion of minority visibility. A careful spectator would, however, notice that placed next to the news headline "Jealousy Drama" is another news item that contains sexual violence against women. The title reads, "The Rapist Is Finally Caught." With this news item, Sibel and Cahit's story is situated among other instances of gender-related violence in Germany. Once Sibel's family read the news, they burn her photographs, an act that can be interpreted as metaphorical domestic violence, but Akin reminds us that in no way is there isolated gender-related "minority" violence, and that violence against women has nothing ethnic about it.

Imitation and Performance

Throughout the film Sibel's self-destructive behavior accompanies her search for identity, marked by her repeated gaze into the mirror. With the dynamism of this search Sibel takes over the film narrative. As mentioned before, Sibel dominates the earlier scenes as the camera traces Cahit's movements until Sibel suddenly barges into the frame and takes the camera and Cahit's gaze or self with her. She takes initiative and she leads the plot. Her actions reflect a search rather than a direction, for they are frequently mimetic, echoing other characters' actions. Sibel follows multiple role models. She gets a tattoo similar to her boss Maren's and cuts her hair in the same style. In Istanbul she starts to live like her cousin, a hardworking single woman. Soon she imitates Cahit's route into perdition. Sibel experiments with various liberatory promises through imitation: sexualized femininity, economic independence through hard work, and androgynous punk rebellion. At the end of the film there is no clear resolution for her, since none of these identities serve her well.

Hereby, the film focuses on the conception of imitation and performance. Judith Butler, in her article "Imitation and Gender Insubordination," suggests that "imitation does not copy that which is prior, but produces and inverts the very terms of priority and derivativeness."[64] What is imitative is potentially explosive, exposing the performative nature of the original; it shows that what is considered to be original is really "an incessant and panicked imitation of its own idealization."[65] Sibel's various imitations, of certain models of agency within both liberal femininity and masculinity, reveal the performativity of all these normative identifications, the supposed imitation by the minority character who risks revealing the theatricality of the "original." As Fatima el-Tayib notes for Germany and the larger European context, "racialized Europeans use queer performative strategies in continuously rearranging the components of the supposedly stable identities assigned to them."[66] El-Tayeb suggests that young European minorities are actively "queering ethnicity" in their insistence to reveal the "unstable, strategic, shifting, and always performative" nature of identity. Sibel's imitations as much as the director's own imitation of media melodramas point to the nature of performance expected from the minority citizen.

The narrative structure of the film is, like the character herself, based on repetition and mimicry of previous structures and themes. Not only Sibel's actions but film images repeat themselves: the image and the sound of the alarm clock that awakens Cahit in the clinic is identical to the one that awakens Sibel in Istanbul; the soundtrack that repeats the same song ("I Feel You") calls for the more embedded sonic memory;[67] Sibel arrives to Istanbul and her vision from the car parallels the way Cahit experiences Istanbul in a cab when he arrives later on. In more subtle ways, after Cahit hits Niko with an ashtray, knocking him down, Sibel enters the bar and the couple gaze at each other; at the intersection of their gaze Cahit says, "Call a doctor!" This line recalls the clinic scene where Sibel and Cahit first met when the doctor called his name.

The film repeats its own sounds and images and imitates itself. This circularity hints at the inevitable fate of a minority couple: locked in the circle of melodrama. Even more, the circularity, imitation, and repetition gesture toward the director's play with the performativity expected from him, shooting the expected "authentic" melodrama: that which involves domestic violence, aggressive Turkish man and victimized Turkish woman. Mimesis starts with the question of marriage, an imitation of marriage, an arbitration. Like the character of his film, Sibel, who taps into the conventional visibility (marriage) in order to gain freedom, the director too capitulates on conventional imagery (moral legibility of melodrama) to gain freedom of expression as a minority filmmaker. The image aims to go beyond the literal and deterministic; hence it is a metacommentary on literality and fatality; the film reflects on its own realm of limited visibility. Repetition and imitation remind the spectator of expected routines of performativity through which minorities reveal the absence of the original and the authentic.

Conclusion

Transnational cinema by minority directors in Europe is considered to have taken a step in the direction of the postethnic by moving away from involvement with political issues concerning minorities such as racism and discrimination.[68] Depoliticization of the film becomes a synonym for transnational hybridity in the cinema of a minority director. *Head-On* does not make an overt political statement about racism and discrimination against minorities in Germany. Yet *Head-On* is tightly connected to its historical context and surrounding discourses such as the melodramatization or moral legibility of the Muslim Other that became further delineated after 9/11, a context that shaped the production and reception of this film. Fatih Akın explains in an interview, "Those characters aren't typical. They aren't representatives of the general Turkish minority in Germany. But the conflict is representative. This film came after 9/11. The world really changed after that. The Muslim world is considered in a much different way after 9/11."[69] While the film is not a direct reference to or an index of the post-9/11 context, it cannot be detached from it. The excess of fear and compassion have become conventional states of affect when it comes to minority visibility, especially since 9/11, and Akin's melodrama shows the constructed nature of this visibility. As Akın is critical of media melodramas, he uses the same modality to reveal the limited nature of minority visibility in its reflection of the diversity of minority experience.

In a context where *Head-On* was evaluated in the mainstream media as a window into Turkish-German society (as Ateş's interview in the prologue shows), Akın had to explain in his interviews that his characters are marginals, exceptions, that they are crazy and fictional.[70] Hence, definitions of Akın's oeuvre as European or transnational have been crucial in broadening the terms of analyses and opening up the ghettoization of his work as ethnic. However, the celebration of hybridity in Akın's films at times introduces a new form of ethnic culturalism. Focusing on its transnationalism could sideline both a historically situated reading of the films and the works' metanarrative commentary that counters the reductive analyses of their minority characters.

In terms of identity politics, this chapter presents a move from the ethnic-blind to the ethnic-conscious approach.[71] It presents an alternative to erasing the ethnic identity of the filmmaker and his characters by describing them as cosmopolitan "abject," "queer," or "Metropolitan urbanites" in Germany, or the definition of characters and the filmmaker as situated "between two worlds." Turkish-German or diaspora ethnicity is part of the film, yet it is never a given, for it is shaped from within and left unresolved. The film and its characters could very well be hybrid or multicultural but also ethnic, and calling them "ethnic" does not have to connote essentialism.[72] Ethnic identity in Akin's work is not distant from "German" in a hyphenated unbelonging. Ethnic in Akin's cinema is a category that needs to be analyzed in its terms and frames of visibility.

The chapter opens to debate these frames of visibility by focusing on the film's multisensory relationship with its audience. The contact and contradiction of senses is a critique of the melodramatization of ethnic Others in popular media and also wields the melodrama as a mode with a potential for revealing new possible relationships between the spectator and the characters in the film. *Head-On* confuses both the melodramatic moral and racial legibility of the characters, and the compassionate distance in the spectator's relationship with the characters. The film is not representative, but affective and symptomatic. Akın's melodrama does not resist the emotional power of melodrama but taps into its affective force, going beyond the clichés that mark the terms for minority visibility and at times repeating some clichés that give authenticity to the director.

The question of melodramatic imitation and performance is at the heart of Akın's work. The clichéd musical postcards from Istanbul that divide the film hint at the director's acute awareness of the spectator's desire for minority performativity in front of a public who gazes with the eyes of tourists searching for the authentic representation of the Oriental Other. The market demand for an authentic representation of "his" community from a minority director meets the desire to subvert the demand and also necessitates feeding the demand. A telling example in this regard is provided by the *New York Times* article on the film. The author gives the film certain authenticity by drawing parallels between the script and the characters' and the director's own life stories. Here Akin's own comments and confessions help the author of the article support his narrative:

> Ms. Kekilli, 25, who was spotted by a casting agent in a department store in Cologne, seemed well suited to play Sibel because she too had run away from her immigrant parents and because she was willing to appear naked on screen. After "Head-On" was released, however, German tabloids disclosed that she had previously acted in pornographic films, and a huge media storm erupted. . . . Mr. Akin said in a telephone interview from Hamburg, ". . . When it came out, she got into enormous trouble. Her parents read about it in the newspapers. Her sister said they were burning her photos. It was like a scene in the movie, witchcraft stuff." Even Mr. Akin's life is not too distant from the world he portrays in his movie. While he has made a career in German cinema . . . his Turkish roots still pull at him. "A couple of years ago," he recalled, "I married a girl of German-Mexican background and, for sure, my parents were like: 'Ah, don't you want to have a Muslim girl, a Turkish girl? It will be easier.'"[73]

In the interview Akın mentions his own experience of controversy with his family, underlining how the film has elements from his own life experience and is foretelling in other ways. He explains that the scene in which Sibel's parents burn her photographs in the film became real when Sibel Kekilli's parents learned about her pornographic career. The real-life melodrama is connected to the film melodrama. Akın's film, to a certain extent, benefited from the identification of the star with the character and from the scandal aroused by the star's hidden past, revealed after *Head-On*'s premiere as he confesses: "Head-On had like 800,000 [spectators in Germany], but the thing with Sibel Kekilli was porno scandal stuff; they were real notorious people, and it made people curious somehow. Not on purpose, but that helped."[74]

As the reception of the film reveals, Sibel is no easy antidote to the melodramatic stereotype of woman as victim. At the end of the film there awaits no emancipation for this Turkish-German protagonist, a conclusion that led certain critics to read the film as regressive, reproducing the stereotypes of victimized Turkish women.[75] The idea that there needs to be an emancipation for the minority woman at the end of the film, as discussed with regard to films that conclude with such promise (Tevfik Başer's films *Farewell to False Paradise* and *40 Square Meters of Germany* and Hark Bohm's *Yasemin*), can be all the more politically regressive. As explained throughout this chapter, Sibel's victimhood is not a typical melodramatic one. Her strong presence and purposeful actions in her search for a better life direct the camera and the narrative. In that sense, she is different from Kee's character in *Children of Men*, a strong-willed refugee who eventually has no control over her destiny and is left to be defended by humanitarian intentions of white characters. Sibel's acts of self-victimization are also different from that of minority character Majid's visceral suicide in front of the camera in Michael Haneke's *Hidden*. Haneke uses the sheer affect of the self-destruction to materialize Majid's haunting absence in the narrative, while Akın employs a similar raw violence to detach Sibel from a moralizing gesture and facile political conclusions about violence. However, this differential character development in the two films does not change the fact that the driving force behind the construction of agency is yet again acts of self-victimization. Just like the Albanian migrant character in Constantinos Giannaris's film *Hostage*, Elion, whose agency is established in a crime that eventually becomes his self-victimization, Sibel's identitarian search results again and again in her victimization of herself: from her first suicide attempt to get rid of her family's oppression to her verbal provocation that calls for an attack in the streets of Istanbul. Hence the problem is, as in other films discussed throughout the book, Sibel suffers the limited terms of agency attributed to so many refugee, migrant and minority characters, one gained through victimhood. The camera introduces Sibel first through her self-victimization, a shot of her slit wrist. The last image of her in the film is in her bedroom, suggesting that she is locked in the very family structure that she tried to avoid years ago by slitting her wrist. Akin too seems to suffer the dilemma that all other politically well-meaning directors whose works are explored in this book face: victimhood is set as the default option for the ethnic and racial Others in Europe in their search for a better life. While these directors point to the limits of minority visibility, to some extent they themselves are caught within the limits they present by reiterating (in so many complex ways) the same trope of inescapable victimhood for refugees, migrants, and minorities of Europe.

Epilogue

The Overarching Trope of Victimhood

Fear and pity are not political affects.

—JACQUES RANCIÈRE, "THE CAUSE OF THE OTHER."[1]

I would say that the booty in contemporary politics is still about whose suffering matters more, and, relatedly, what forms of repair the representation of such suffering would intend.

—LAUREN BERLANT, "AFFECT IN THE END OF TIMES: CONVERSATION WITH LAUREN BERLANT."[2]

When I started working on this epilogue in the spring of 2013 a terrorist bombing took place at the Boston Marathon. The bombing, which killed three people and injured more than 260, was committed by the Tsarnaev brothers—U.S. citizens originally from Chechnya. The younger of the two brothers was repeatedly described in the news as an atypical criminal because he was well integrated into the American society. The news on the French TV channel France 2 compared the Boston bombing with the killings of Mohamed Merah in March 2012. Merah, a French citizen of Algerian descent, shot four kids in a Jewish school in Montauban and three soldiers in Toulouse in three separate acts. According to France 2, what brought together the terror acts in France and in the United States was the previous invisibility of their perpetrators to intelligence agencies, as their connections to al-Qaeda or another fundamentalist organization were marginal and feeble. The news anchor demanded of a specialist of

Islam his opinion on how to ensure security at a time when even seemingly well-integrated minorities could turn into threats.

After the news I watched an episode of the French polar series *Femmes de loi*. The show features two intelligent and strong heroines, a lawyer and a detective who solve crimes in collaboration. In this particular episode the heroines were faced with the mysterious murder of a wealthy businessman. An illegal immigrant from Kenya—the housemaid, exploited by the businessman both sexually and economically—was involved in the mystery. The two feisty heroines first blamed the migrant maid for the murder. Soon they discovered that the cultprit was the infertile wife of the murdered man who felt threatened by the impregnated maid and killed her husband. The locked-room mystery ended with the heroines' promise to help out the migrant maid in her asylum case. They claimed that she had high chances of gaining asylum as she expected a "French" baby.

It is the problems that appear in such representations of refugees, migrants, and minorities of migrant origin in Europe that I have explored in this book. The integration of minorities seems to never be complete, as they can prove to be potential security menaces at all times, while illegal migrants who appear as victims of various forms of bodily exploitation can easily turn into threats as hyperreproductive bodies. These examples are indicative of the limited yet recurrent frames of representation through which refugees, migrants, and minorities of migrant background become publicly visible in Europe: in relation to violent events that hide social crises lurking in the background. They appear either as threats that call for security measures or as victims that call for aid, frequently shifting back and forth between the affective registers of fear and pity. As the above examples show, these tropes have currency here and now, in the visual media ranging from the news to a TV series. The affects of fear and pity, as the epigraph by Rancière points out, are not necessarily political, yet they are indeed part of the visibility and knowability of refugees, migrants, and minorities. Hence, I have argued in this study that these affects need to be explored in their social and political meanings as they appear in generic formulations that involve refugees, migrants, and minorities.

In a global context in which fear and pity became the mobilizing principles for the prominent politics of "war on terror" and "humanitarian action," studies on violence and victimhood have gained political, theoretical, and social significance. Along with the wars waged in humanitarian disguise and the emergence of high levels of structural violence—poverty and social inequality—under neoliberal global economics, we see an increase in the number of the debates on violence in political philosophy. Etienne Balibar[3] and Simon Critchley[4] question the place of violence in the realm of the political, while Judith Butler inquires into war, mourning, torture, and the representations of violence with the fundamental question: "what form political reflection and deliberation ought to take if we take injurability and aggression as two points of departure for political life?"[5] Slavoj Žižek discusses violence in relation to neoliberal economics as "systemic violence."[6] These larger conceptualizations of violence suggest a theoretical move away from the established liberal focus on physical violence and its bodily connotations, a bodily focus that looks for a subject and an object of violence, an identifiable agent responsible for the act of violence and a particular victim who suffers from it. In light of these larger theoretical discussions on the topic, this study has zoomed in on the following contradiction. While structural violence and precariousness are read, seen, and experienced by many on a daily basis, on the discursive level they are often attributed to a realm excluded from the everyday and confined to the realm of the Other.

In each of the European contexts that I have explored, different social issues are both addressed and cloaked through discussions on refugee-migrant- and minority-related violent events. In other words, refugees, migrants, and minorities of migrant origin have become central in filtering the structural violences perpetrated by the neoliberal economies and liberal democracies of Europe. While the categories of criminality and victimhood inform how refugees, migrants and minorities are imagined in European mass media, these imaginings reflect a particular European sense of self. The public discourse on these communities frequently establishes them as threats to and devoid of some central tenets of liberal humanist subjectivity: rationality, autonomy, tolerance, and secularism. Refugees, migrants, and minorities become the necessary Others for the liberal European state that distances them from the realm of politics and contains them in the realm of legality (with a right to control and punish) or compassion (with a vague ethical but no political obligation to act upon). Both the politics of fear that dictates security measures to protect the liberal subject and state, and the universal rights of humanitarianism, strip these populations of their status as social beings with political rights to "bare life"[7] who need to be contained or aided. Refugees, migrants, and minorities in Europe today are central to the notion of liberal subjectivity and its self-legitimization through a perpetual state of contradiction between the need for security and the call for humanitarianism.[8] As inclusion and exclusion are in the nature of a liberal polity (without the existence of outsiders there would not be free and equal citizens) universalism always conceals particularism:

historically it concealed racism in the colonies and imperial histories of violence; today it conceals racism against refugees, migrants, and minorities of migrant origin.[9] This particularism is reinforced through the discourses of right for security and humanitarian treatment, both claiming the universal right to be protected against violence.

I traced in this book how these seemingly contradictory discourses of security and humanitarianism are pursued through a historicity of emergency in contemporary Europe. Within this conception of history as a chain of crises refugees, migrants and minorities become the crux of disasters and dystopias that intertwine anxieties ranging from security concerns after September 11 and economic concerns due to high unemployment rates and declining welfare protections, to cultural concerns over the feasibility of a united European identity. I have shown how these anxieties find their outlet in the repeatedly mediatized scandals of "bogus" asylum seekers in Britain, "explosive" urban riots in France, "invasion" from the Balkans in Greece, and "honor killings" in Germany. I have investigated in detail the generic quality of such minority-related violent events: what determines a media event, what gets lost in the crevices of history when it comes to minorities in Europe and how generic conventions formulate ethnic and racial minority visibility in the media—fear of minority youth embedded in thrilling narratives of eruptive *banlieue* violence, and pity for Muslim women's victimhood in honor crime melodramas or in dystopias of humanitarian crisis involving refugees. Genre conventions that the auteur films appeal to are in interaction with the affects created in the mass media in relation to minority-related events of violence. The directors' critique of melodramas, tragedies, and dystopias of ethnic and racial Others in the mass media goes hand in hand with their wielding of the affective potential of these genre conventions. This tapping of the affective source of genres creates a space to bring together the cognitive and the emotional, the memory and the present, the "here" of immigration and the "there" of emigration. The films use genre conventions to connect the events' present to their historical fragments and geographical stretch that crosses European borders.

All the films explored in this work are tightly linked to their historical context and the surrounding discourses on the racial and ethnic Others in today's Europe. That being said, this book has moved away from a representative framework to a symptomatic one that explores genres as forms that unfold affective pathologies and crises in Europe's relationship with its growing multiethnicity and multiraciality. That is, the question that I have pursued is not whether or not these genre films represent migrant and minority lives and experiences truthfully or justly. The genre conventions in films reflect social anxieties often articulated in the apolitical yet symptomatic affects. Fear and compassion are symptoms of the problematic conception of violence and crisis in Europe.

Violence defines the borders of liberal subjectivity, but at the same time its representation often fascinates the liberal subject. The films under scrutiny simultaneously reconsider, cash in on, and undermine the idea of crisis and violence as the realm of the Other. They allude to the typical descriptions of violence associated with migrants and minorities (violence as eruptive, inherent, pathological, or traditional) only to challenge their assumptions of distance and obscurity and make violence homely and familiar, both temporally and spatially. Their critique goes together with their wielding of the commodity value of violence and the affects attached to crisis.

The most striking aspect of these films is that, while their politically well-meaning directors point to the limits of minority visibility through discourses of violence and eventfulness, they themselves reproduce, in many different ways but repeatedly, the trope of inescapable victimhood for refugees, migrants, and minorities of Europe. The progressive politics of each film hits a limit as it ends up recycling the generic frame of victimhood when it comes to justifying the actions and even the ways of existence of migrants and minorities in Europe. *Children of Men* follows a trend of refugee representation in films that are produced in Europe: devoid of their political and social characters, refugees embody victimhood in need of humanitarian aid in an apocalyptic world. It is indicative of how refugees as well as migrants are portrayed as the ultimate victims of globalization, whose bodies are often rendered bare symbols of the world's misery in many European film productions—including Damjan Kozole's *Spare Parts*, Alejandro González Iñárritu's *Biutiful*, Michael Winterbottom's *In This World*, Phillip Lioret's *Welcome*, the Dardenne brothers' *La promesse* (1996), Stephen Frears's *Dirty Pretty Things* (2002), Lukas Moodysson's *Lilya 4-Ever* (2002), and Ulrich Siedl's *Import/ Export* (2007). Under these conditions humanitarian conscience and sentiments (of the film characters and/or of the spectators) become the preliminary condition for political awareness, while the absence of reaction to the misery of the world becomes the target of critique, which inadvertently puts into the center white men's conscience and potential guilt.

Taking up from this point, my analysis of Haneke's *Hidden* proceeded to map out a much more skeptical approach to individual action and conscience in relation to the suffering Other. While this time the white male protagonist presents a conformist denial of guilt instead of a selfless humanitarian death as in *Children of Men*, the ethnic and racial Others in both films prove to be equally voiceless. The refugees and minorities similarly reveal through corporeal means, either the "truthfulness" of their physical fragility and plausibility of their demand for humanitarian aid or their innocence, the honesty of their psychological fragility, suffering, and trauma. In these two chapters, I indicated how both films show ethnic and racial Others as objects instead of subjects of their tragic fate, while biology and bare life rather than an active political involvement for their social, political, and historical rights defines their existence. The humanitarian intentions of white characters, or lack thereof, are at the center of these narratives. The corporeal acts of the Others have the sheer effect of proving their presence (as it needs proving) or revealing their haunting absence in the eyes of the white male protagonists.

Then I showed that the migrant is trapped in the dilemma of victimology even in a narrative that places him at the center of action as the noble protagonist of a Greek tragedy, as in Constantinos Giannaris's *Hostage*. While the invisibility of systematic and routinized situations of violence—economic (workplace exploitation), political (random ID checks and detentions by the police), and social (discriminatory treatment due to xenophobic prejudices)—are revealed against the mediatic visibility of migrant and minority acts of violence, once again sheer bodily suffering appears above the other forms of violence when it comes to justifying migrants' actions. Corporeal suffering and finally death render the migrant Other the ultimate victim of uncontrollable transnational forces, as in the string of nameless refugees crushed under multiple catastrophic events in *Children of Men* and the Algerian-French orphan of the 1961 massacre in *Hidden*. And finally, as I have traced in my analysis of Fatih Akin's *Head-On*, even when the representation of raw bodily violence is used to detach a minority character from facile political conclusions about victimhood perpetrated by domestic oppression, the driving force behind the construction of agency circles once again around victimization—that of the self.

The hyperfertile refugee, the potentially vengeance-seeking Algerian-French citizen, an Albanian criminal, a Turkish-German woman fighting for her freedom against domestic constraints—all end up victims, be it a self-chosen or an imposed identity. All these thought-provoking and politically progressive films set victimhood as the framework through which ethnic and racial Others in Europe are rendered visible as desiring subjects. They ascribe the declaration of pain as the sole option for these individuals in search of a better life. "Abetting the steady slide of political into therapeutic discourse"[10] bodies and "wounds" become the ultimate sites for the assertion of identity as well as that of rebellion. Contemporary representations of ethnic and racial Otherness in European films are symptomatic of a discursive shift toward a dialectic of humanitarianism in which racialized bodies function as affective objects (revealed to draw affects from the spectators) rather than political subjects.

While arguing against the conventional conceptualization of victimhood, I do not deny the instances of violence that refugees, migrants, and minorities suffer or the injustices they face. Instead, I aim to draw attention to the problems of a naturalized and essentialized category of "victim" (like that of the criminal or the terrorist), the politics of its wholesale attribution to a certain group of people, the resulting detachment from multiple forms of political and social identity, and a relegation to the realm of "bare" humanity. Despite their variety of generic forms and their good intentions, all the discussed films portray the refugee, migrant, and minority characters as victims—of history, of state violence, of globalization and if not any of these larger forces, victims of their own self-destructive violence due to psychological suffering, trauma, or lack of other options to alter their lives.

The frequent convergence of the ethnic and racial Other with the "victimized" Other has roots in today's ethical orientation, which, as Alain Badiou explains, prioritizes the protection of universal human rights in "Other" territories and "subordinates the identification of [universal human subject] to the universal recognition of the evil that is done to him. Ethics thus defines man *as a victim*."[11] The status of this man/victim, however, is negative and reduces the human subject to the simple reality of his living. In this way, Western humanitarian aid to the victims from the non-Western world assumes the "subhumanity" of these communities, and ethics becomes the new framework to delineate hierarchies between the Global South and North. Badiou asks, "Who cannot see that this ethics which rests on the misery of the world hides, behind its victim-Man, the good-Man, the white-man?"[12] Hence, the human in the Other emerges from his or her victimhood, while the good in the "white-man" emanates from humanitarian action. If we transfer this ethics to the level of representation, we observe that the migrant, the refugee, or the minority who is portrayed as a victim, or as the passive suffering body, serves the conscience as it safely advocates morality and compassion, posing no challenge to the established class and race hierarchies.

Rancière evokes the challenge for artists to take their underprivileged characters beyond the established class and race hierarchies of visibility, in which, for instance, the "freedom of fiction" is given for the citizens of the Global North while the documentary and "the reality of news" is assigned for that of the Global South:

> The main enemy of artistic creativity as well as of political creativity is consensus—that is, inscription within given roles, possibilities, and competences. Godard said ironically that the epic was for Israelis and the documentary for Palestinians. Which is to say that the distribution of genres—for example, the division between the freedom of fiction and the reality of the news—is always a distribution of possibilities and capacities: To say that, in the dominant regime of representation, documentary is for the Palestinians, that is to say that they can only offer the bodies of their victims to the gaze of news cameras or to the compassionate gaze at their suffering. That is, the world is divided between those who can and those who cannot afford the luxury of playing with words and images. Subversion begins when this division is contested, as when a Palestinian filmmaker like Elia Suleiman makes a comedy about the daily repression and humiliation that Israeli checkpoints represent and transforms a young Palestinian resistance fighter into a manga character.[13]

An oversight in this critique is that the epic also has conventions that frame Israelis in repeated narratives of historical belonging to the land, just as the realism of documentaries contain generic repetitions that are carefully constructed to make the Palestinian victim's suffering credible for the compassionate spectator. But no doubt the documentary continues to be the dominant form of visibility assigned to the underprivileged of the Global South instead of genres like the thriller and science fiction. The multiplicity of genres through which ethnic and racial Others are represented, however, does not guarantee that their characters will assume less conventional personalities. It is essential that the structural change (from realist to popular genres) be accompanied by a change in characterization (from the depiction of victimhood to that of resistance or another form of existence). The generic originality needs to go along with the change in content, from representation of suffering to that of desires that are not fixated on the wound and injury. I end this book with a hope for the visibility of ethnic and racial Others as fictional characters with more elusive desires as they enjoy the "luxury of playing with words and images," characters who enable their spectators to experience anew, reflect on, and hopefully alter for the better the current limited palette of affects associated with the multicultural landscape of Europe.

Notes

Introduction

1. Achille Mmembe, "The Republic and Its Beast: On the Riots in the French *Banlieues*," in *Frenchness and the African Diaspora: Identity and Uprising in Contemporary France*, ed. Charles Tshimanga, Didier Gondola, and Peter J. Bloom (Bloomington: Indiana University Press, 2009), 49.

2. Lauren Berlant, *The Anatomy of National Fantasy: Hawthorne, Utopia and Everyday Life* (Chicago: University of Chicago Press, 1991), 180.

3. Ginette Vincendeau, "*La Haine* and After: Arts, Politics, and the *Banlieue*," *The Criterion Collection Film Essays*, May 8, 2012, accessed March 20, 2013. http://www.criterion.com/current/posts/642-la-haine-and-after-arts-politics-and-the-banlieue.

4. For a longer discussion on the exchange see Colin Nattelbeck, "Kassovitz's "'*France d'en bas*' and Sarkozy's '*racaille*': Art and the Alienation of Politics in Contemporary France," in *French History and Civilization: Papers from the George Rude Seminar* 2 (2009): 70–81, accessed March 23, 2013. http://www.h-france.net/rude/rude%20volume%20ii/Nettelbeck%20Final%20Version%202.pdf.

5. Serge July and Marie Genin, "Un film & son époque: Il était une fois . . . la haine," *France 5*, February, 27, 2012, accessed March 7, 2012. http://www.youtube.com/watch?v=ApoBrixM8EM.

6. For a detailed description of affective economy, a circulation akin to that of commodities see Sara Ahmed, "Affective Economies," *Social Text* 22, no. 2 (Summer 2004): 117–39. Ahmed examines the figures of asylum seeker and terrorist as objects of racist hate and fear, emotions that become stronger in the absence of a particular "fixed referent." This economy of circulating emotions implicates any Other as the potentially menacing Other who may justify fear or hate, two emotions central to racial discrimination.

7. Throughout the book I use the term "migrant" rather than "immigrant," following Nicolas de Genova's problematization of the terms "immigration" and "immigrant." As de Genova suggests, these terms take at their center the experi-

ence of the receiver country rather than that of the individual who migrates and draw an "implicitly unilinear teleology . . . (posited always from the standpoint of the migrant-receiving nation-state, in terms of outsiders coming in, presumably to stay) (421)." In his work on Mexican migrants to the United States de Genova explains that the category of "immigrant" connotes "an essentialized, generic, and singular object, subordinated to that same teleology by which migrants inexorably become permanent settlers and the U.S. nation-state assumes the form of a 'promised land'—a self-anointed refuge of liberty and opportunity." Such framing of "immigrant" in search for an imagined "promised land" applies to Europe as much as to the United States, although the former, as opposed to the latter, has never promoted itself as an "immigrant nation." Nicolas de Genova, "Migrant 'Illegality' and Deportability in Everyday Life," *Annual Review of Anthropology* 31 (1998): 419–47.

8. For instance, Thilo Sarrazin, former politician and Deutsche Bank board member, published a controversial book, *Germany Abolishes Itself,* in 2010. The book claimed that Germany's high rate of immigration was leading to a civilizational decline. Sarrazin's racist argument claimed that the right sort of German women were not having enough babies, while Muslims with little education were reproducing excessively. The result, according to Sarrazin, is not only that Germany's so-called native population is shrinking, it is also becoming less intelligent. Thilo Sarrazin, *Deutschland schafft sich ab* (Berlin: Deutsche Verlags-Anstalt, 2010).

9. For injury as basis of political identity see Wendy Brown, *States of Injury: Power and Freedom in Late Modernity* (Princeton: Princeton University Press, 1995).

10. For debates on honor crimes and so-called paternalistic oppression of Muslim women in Germany see chapter 4. For refugees and asylum based on compassionate health care policies see Fassin and Ticktin, discussed in chapter 1: Didier Fassin, *Empire of Trauma: An Inquiry into the Condition of Victimhood* (Princeton: Princeton University Press, 2009), Miriam Ticktin, "Where Ethics and Politics Meet: The Violence of Humanitarianism in France," *American Ethnologist* 31, no. 1 (2006): 33–49.

11. Slavoj Žižek, *Violence: Six Sideways Reflections* (New York: Picador, 2008).

12. For culture as race see Etienne Balibar, "Is There a 'Neo-racism,'" in *Race, Nation, Class: Ambiguous Identities,* by Etienne Balibar and Immanuel Wallerstein (London: Verso, 1991), 17–29.

13. For a further discussion on the debates on women's rights and Islam in Germany see Beverly Weber, *Violence and Gender in the "New" Europe: Islam in German Culture* (New York: Palgrave Macmillan, 2013).

14. For an extended consideration of migration from the Balkans and the reflections of identitarian challenge in Greek literature and cinema see Vangelis Calotychos, *The Balkan Prospect: Identity, Culture, and Politics in Greece after 1989* (New York: Palgrave Macmillan, 2013).

15. Talal Asad, *Formations of the Secular: Christianity, Islam, Modernity* (Stanford: Stanford University Press, 2003), 180.

16. An illustration of this may be found in the way that the European Commission describes its role and responsibilities with regard to its citizens. In the mid-2000s, the European Commission launched a website in an effort to show that "in its everyday activities, the Union in fact addresses many of your con-

cerns as citizens, consumers or workers." Each year it listed ten areas in which the EU was most actively serving its citizens. In 2006, the number one issue was enabling "cheaper phone calls when travelling," while number ten was "tackling illegal immigration." (*Europe and You in 2006.* "A Snapshot of EU Achievements," accessed December 27, 2014, http://ec.europa.eu/archives/snapshot2006/index_en.htm) The selection of these particular topics highlights the EU's role as facilitating the movement of consumption, capital, and European citizens while tightly controlling the non-European's movement and labor. In the 2007 top ten citizen-friendly list, there is even more emphasis on borderless travel and consumption, with the appearance of issues such as "passport-free travel extended" and "more choice and cheaper fares on flights to USA" (*Europe and You in 2007*, "A Snapshot of EU Achievements," accessed December 27, 2014, http://ec.europa.eu/archives/snapshot2007/index_en.htm).

17. For more on Europe's schizophrenic regime of border control and mobility see Ginette Verstraete, *Tracking Europe: Mobility, Diaspora, and the Politics of Location* (Durham: Duke University Press, 2010).

18. Manuela Bojadzijev and Isabelle Saint-Saens, "Borders, Citizenship, War, Class: A Discussion with Etienne Balibar and Sandro Mezzadra," *New Formations* 58, no. 1 (2006): 22–23.

19. For an insightful study of these issues through analyses of road movies see Ewa Mazierska and Laura Rascaroli, *Crossing New Europe: Postmodern Travel and the European Road Movie* (London: Wallflower Press, 2006).

20. Yosefa Loshitsky's study of contemporary European cinema explores these issues, *Screening Strangers: Migration and Diaspora in Contemporary European Cinema* (Bloomington: Indiana University Press, 2010). Also, as its title suggests *Moving People, Moving Images: Cinema and Trafficking in the New Europe* focuses on close analyses of the filmic representations of trafficking connected to illegal migration in post-1989 Europe. William Brown, Dina Iordanova and Leshu Torchin, *Moving People, Moving Images: Cinema and Trafficking in the New Europe* (St. Andrews: St. Andrews Film Studies, 2010).

21. The edited volume by Daniela Berghahn and Claudia Sternberg focuses on these themes, see "Locating Migrant and Diasporic Cinema in Contemporary Europe," in *European Cinema in Motion: Migrant and Diasporic Film in Contemporary Europe*, ed. Daniela Berghahn and Claudia Sternberg (New York: Palgrave Macmillan, 2010).

22. Thomas Elsaesser, *European Cinema: Face-to-Face with Hollywood* (Amsterdam: Amsterdam University Press, 2005), 27–28.

23. Rosalind Galt's comprehensive book that maps the post-1990s European cinema also calls for a similar trajectory for analyzing European cinema: a cartography with historical dimensions, considering a spatiality that cannot be separated from historicity. She focuses on films that convey a sense of loss, nostalgia, or disenchantment and formulate "a new set of relations with the national and European past." Rosalind Galt, *The New European Cinema: Redrawing the Map* (New York: Columbia University Press, 2006), 3. Also, for a recent study on European cinema that defines the concept of borders in a more extensive manner and contains articles on films that "identify, challenge and imagine frontiers of another kind: social, ethnic, religious borderlines, which are equally important and historically constructed," see Raita Merivirta, Kimmo Ahonen, Heta Mulari,

Rami Mahka eds., *Frontiers of Screen History: Imagining European Borders in Cinema, 1945–2010* (Bristol: Intellect, 2013), 8.

24. Fatima El-Tayeb, *European Others: Queering Ethnicity in Postnational Europe* (Minneapolis: University of Minnesota Press, 2011), xii. For a specific example, see Algerian-French rapper's Médine's statement against Muslim and minority exclusion from French identity, Médine, "How Much More French Can I Be?" *Time,* November 6, 2005, accessed January 23, 2012. http://www.time.com/time/magazine/article/0,9171,1126720,00.html. Also, for a wonderful ironic take on the quotidian exclusion of minority Germans, especially through the assumption that one day they will return to their "native" countries, see a short video made by Kanak-Attak, minority activists against racism in Germany, "Philharmonie Köln—40 Jahre Einwanderung" *Kanak TV,* November 6, 2001, accessed May 15, 2011. http://www.kanak-tv.de/popup/philharmonie_video.html.

25. Etienne Balibar, *Politics and the Other Scene* (London: Verso, 2002), 92.

26. Etienne Balibar, *We, the People of Europe? Reflections on Transnational Citizenship* (Princeton: Princeton University Press, 2003), x.

27. "Anti-terror Searches Continuing," *BBC News,* April 10, 2009, accessed December 20, 2012. http://news.bbc.co.uk/2/hi/uk_news/7993748.stm.

28. This perceived threat and ever tightening rules applied on student visas are being brought to our attention every consequent year, with headlines such as "Tougher Rules to Stop Abuse of Student Visa System," *BBC News* February 7, 2010, accessed December 20, 2012, http://news.bbc.co.uk/2/hi/uk_news/8502640.stm, and "Tighter Rules for the UK Student Visas," *BBC News,* March 22, 2011, accessed December 20, 2012, http://www.bbc.com/news/education-12820645.

29. "Κώστας Καραμανλής: 'Κλείνετε το μάτι στους κουκουλοφόρους,'" *H Kathimerini,* April 9, 2009, accessed May 10, 2011. http://news.kathimerini.gr/4dcgi/_w_articles_ell_2_09/04/2009_310488. Regarding the Greek government officials' frequent statements that associate migration with criminality and the government's misuse of the statistical data, see chapter 3.

30. Andreas Kalyvas, "An Anomaly? Some Reflections on the Greek December 2008," *Constellations* 17, no. 2 (2010): 351–65.

31. Jessika Ter Wal, *Europe Day of Media Monitoring: Quantitative Analysis of Daily Press and TV Contents in the 15 EU Member States* (Utrecht: ERCOMER, University of Utrecht, 2004).

32. Prati Taneja, ed., "State of the World's Minorities and Indigenous Peoples: Events of 2009," *Minority Rights International Report,* July 1, 2010, accessed May 20, 2011. http://www.minorityrights.org/10068/state-of-the-worlds-minorities/state-of-the-worlds-minorities-and-indigenous-peoples-2010.html.

33. Katrin Elger, Ansbert Kneip, and Merlind Theile, "Einwanderung: Für immer fremd," *Der Spiegel,* January 26, 2009, accessed May 15, 2011. http://www.spiegel.de/spiegel/print/d-63806907.html. English translation is presented under the title of "Immigration: Survey Shows Alarming Lack of Integration in Germany," in *Der Spiegel International,* http://www.spiegel.de/international/germany/0,1518,603588,00.html.

34. The global financial crisis severely hit the poorest and most marginalized communities, illegal migrants among them, in Europe as elsewhere. For instance, in early 2009 when the crisis was in full swing the two sectors (manufacturing and

construction) that employ a substantial number of migrant workforce were hit severely. "The Impact of the Global Economic Crisis on Illegal Migration to the EU," *Frontex Report: European Agency for the Management of Operational Cooperation at the External Borders of the Member States of the European Union*, August 2009, accessed January 12, 2012. http://www.europarl.europa.eu/meetdocs/2009_2014/documents/libe/dv/frontex_/frontex_en.pdf.

35. In 2009 European parliamentary elections the radical-right parties increased their seats in a number of member countries including Austria, Denmark, Finland, Greece, Hungary, Italy, the Netherlands, Slovakia, Romania and the UK. In the Netherlands, the Freedom Party of Geert Wilders (known for his short film *Fitna* [2008], which juxtaposed verses from the Koran with images of violence) won around 17 percent of the vote and became the second strongest party. In Finland and Denmark right-wing populist parties raised their votes significantly. Italy's separationist and anti-migration Northern League won around 10 percent of the vote, while in the UK the far-right British National Party won four seats. More recently, in the 2014 European Parliament elections there has been a further rise in the representation of far-right parties (overall fifteen more seats). Most striking results came from France, as the National Front won 25 percent of the votes, increasing its seats in the parliament from three to twenty-four, and from Denmark where Danish People's Party won almost 27 percent of the votes, doubling its members in the European Parliament. Also, openly neo-Nazi parties such as NDP in Germany, Golden Dawn in Greece, and Jobbik in Hungary won seats in the European Parliament for the first time.

36. It needs to be noted that in Cologne that day, thousands of people turned out for an alternative rally against racism and neo-Nazism.

37. See Talal Asad, Judith Butler, Wendy Brown, and Saba Mahmood, *Is Critique Secular? Blasphemy, Injury, and Free Speech* (Berkeley: University of California Press, 2009) for an extended discussion on the cartoon debate. Asad and Mahmood provide elaborate discussions of the controversy as they draw the debate away from a liberal formulation of tolerance versus nontolerance. Asad questions the dichotomy assumed between criticism/free speech as secular and blasphemy/censorship as religious, while Mahmood focuses on the problems arising from conceptualizing Islamic piety through a perspective that ignores its particular hermeneutics and approach to iconography.

38. Kira Kosnick, "Cosmopolitan Capital or Multicultural Community? Reflections on the Production and Management of Different Mobilities in Germany's Capital City," in *Cosmopolitanism in Practice*, ed. Magdalena Nowicka and Maria Rowisko (Surrey: Ashgate, 2009), 169.

39. Slavoj Žižek, "Multiculturalism, or, The Cultural Logic of Multinational Capitalism," *New Left Review* 225 (September–October 1997), 44.

40. Žižek, *Violence*, 40–41. A perfect illustration of this phenomenon that Žižek talks about is the creation of the Ministry of Citizen Protection (2009–12) in Greece. The ministry was established to take over some of the responsibilities of the Ministry of Interior, responsibilities such as internal security, combating crime, disaster management, border security, and management of illegal migration. Even more to the point, in 2012, this institution was renamed the Ministry of Public Order and Citizen Protection. Many thanks to Alexis Rappas for bringing this to my attention.

41. Jacques Rancière, *The Nights of Labor: The Workers' Dream in Nineteenth-Century France* (Philadelphia: Temple University Press, 1989).

42. These questions on the efficiency of workers and the allocation of nighttime for rest continue to be debated. See "Do Early Pub Closings Make for Better Workers? That's What a UK Study Contends," *MSN Money*, April 5, 2013, accessed May 10, 2013. http://money.msn.com/now/post.aspx?post=ff6ac16a-cf3d-4ea9-9baa-0461ea456b5a.

43. Johannes Fabian, *Time and the Other: How Anthropology Makes Its Object* (New York: Columbia University Press, 1983), 144. Fabian's observation on the political use of temporality for establishing Western hierarchies of the Other is followed by his argument on coevalness as a solution to this West-rest hierarchy. For a critique of this solution see Berber Bevernage, "Against Coevalness: A Belated Critique of Johannes Fabian's Project of Radical Contemporaneity and a Plea for a New Politics of Time," May 2012, accessed March 12, 2013. http://www.inth.ugent.be/wp-content/uploads/2012/05/AgainstCoevalness.pdf. Also, it needs to be noted that Fabian's discourse is not unprecedented. Denial of coevalness of the Other was central to theories of economic modernization; hence dependency and world systems theorists such as Cardoso, Gunther, Wallerstein, and Samir Amin in the 1970s were critical of linear temporality as movement toward modernization in the Global South. Even as early as the mid-1920s, political theories of underdevelopment articulated by Antonio Gramsci and Jose Carlos Mariátegui posed questions about the different zones of temporality and modernity within the capitalist system created within regions of Italy and Peru respectively, and discussed the racist assumptions of barbarism and backwardness based on regional difference. Antonio Gramsci, "Some Aspects of the Southern Question," October 1926, accessed May 12, 2013. http://www.uky.edu/~tmute2/geography_methods/readingPDFs/gramsci-southern-question1926.pdf. Jose Carlos Mariátegui, *Seven Interpretive Essays on Peruvian Reality*, 1928, accessed May 23, 2013. http://www.marxists.org/archive/mariateg/works/1928/. For a recent analysis of temporal divergence (anachronism, regression, and backwardness) in the discourses of race and sexuality in the United States see Valerie Rohy, *Anachronism and Its Others: Sexuality, Race, Temporality* (Albany: SUNY Press, 2009).

44. Balibar and Wallerstein, *Race, Nation, Class*, 24–25.

45. Levent Soysal, "Diversity of Experience, Experience of Diversity: Turkish Migrant Youth Culture in Berlin," *Cultural Dynamics* 13, no. 1 (March 2001): 21–22. See also Rita Chin, *The Guest Worker Question in Postwar Germany* (Cambridge: Cambridge University Press, 2007) and Leslie Adelson, "Against Between: A Manifesto," in *Zafer Senocak: Contemporary German Writers*, ed. Tom Cheesman and Karin E. Yesilada (Cardiff: University of Wales Press, 2003), 130–43 on this so-called unbridgeable gap between Turkish and German temporalities.

46. Chin, *The Guest Worker Question*, 141.

47. Some notorious incidents are pogroms against an asylum seekers' hostel in Hoyerswerda and Rostock-Lichtenhagen (1992), and arson attacks against minority houses in Mölln (1992) and Solingen (1993), and an asylum seekers' hostel in Lübeck (1996).

48. For this "ethical turn" in history see Jacques Rancière, "The Ethical Turn of Aesthetics and Politics," in *Dissensus: On Politics and Aesthetics* (London: Continuum, 2010).

49. Francis Fukuyama, *The End of History and the Last Man* (New York: Free Press, 1992).

50. Fredric Jameson, "Postmodernism, or the Cultural Logic of Late Capitalism," *New Left Review* 146 (July–August 1984): 59–92. Also, Pierre Nora's consideration of "the realm of memory" puts emphasis on the spatial dimension of history. Nora observes an "acceleration of history" as well as "an increasing slippage of the present into a historical past that is gone for good, a general perception that anything and everything may disappear—these indicate a rupture of equilibrium." Pierre Nora, "Between Memory and History: *Les Lieux de Mémoire* [1984]," *Representations* 26 (Spring 1989): 7. For a discussion of 1990s philosophical emphasis on theories of spatiality and avoidance of historicity see Kristin Ross, "Historicizing Untimeliness," in *Jacques Rancière: History, Politics, Aesthetics*, ed. Gabriel Rockhill and Philip Wattson (Durham: Duke University Press, 2009), 15–29.

51. Harry Harootunian, "Remembering the Historical Present," *Critical Inquiry* 33 (Spring 2007): 471–94.

52. Mary Ann Doane, "Information, Crisis, Catastrophe," in *Historical Film: History and Memory in Media*, ed. Marcia Landy (New Brunswick: Rutgers University Press, 2001), 270.

53. Doane, "Information, Crisis, Catastrophe," 283. Chapter 1 focuses on such intermeshing of crisis and catastrophe in contemporary understanding of historical experience and how, in this context, refugees have become central to catastrophism and to the humanitarian politics of urgency that surrounds it.

54. Alain Badiou, *Being and Event*, trans. Oliver Feltham (London: Continuum, 2005); Alain Badiou, *The Rebirth of History*, trans. Gregory Elliott (London: Verso, 2012).

55. Badiou, *The Rebirth of History*, 25.

56. Badiou, *The Rebirth of History*, 19–20.

57. Badiou, *The Rebirth of History*, 23.

58. While I refer to Mahmood Mamdani's seminal work here, I do not at all propose a comparison between George W. Bush, whom Mamdani quotes as establishing a discourse that reinforces such a split between "good" and "bad" Others (Muslims in his case) and Badiou's perceptive comments about history and the revolutionary event. As Mahmood Mamdani suggests, distinguishing such a split, be it conscious or unconscious, could simply disguise a certain "failure to make a political analysis of our times." Mahmood Mamdani, *Good Muslims, Bad Muslims: America, the Cold War, and the Roots of Terror* (New York: Three Leaves Press, 2005), 16.

59. Furthermore, when the revolutionary event is considered the mover of history, this limits historicity to a certain impact and influence of actions whose validity as "historical" is determined by the intellectual himself. For a critique of the intellectual's role in determining historicity in Badiou's event theory, see Jacques Rancière, "A propos de *L'Etre et l'Evénement* d'Alain Badiou," *Le cahier du Collège international de philosophie* 8 (October 1989). horlieu-editions.com/textes-en-ligne/philosophie/ranciere-a-propos-d-etre-et-evenement-d-alain-badiou.pdf.

60. Arlette Farge, "Penser et définir l'événement en histoire," *Terrain: Revue*

d'ethnologie de l'Europe, no. 38 (March 2002), accessed May 12, 2013. http://terrain.revues.org/1929.

61. Gilles Deleuze, *Cinema 2: The Time-Image*, trans. Hugh Tomlinson and Robert Galeta (Minneapolis: University of Minnesota Press), 255. For Deleuze, the time-image in cinema addresses this silence and reveals the geological layers of divergent temporalities by opposing a linear focus on events or characters in the movement-image. Deleuze suggests that the sensory "disjunction" or "dissociation" of sound and image is productive for approaching the event and capturing its resistance against representation. Deleuze, *Cinema 2*, 256. I will talk more about the possibilities that this disjuncture allows in the fourth chapter, on Akın's *Head-On*.

62. I borrow this conceptualization (horizontalizing the event) from Kristin Ross, who suggests that Rimbaud's poetry has a horizontal approach to the Paris Commune as a historical event, in Kristin Ross, *The Emergence of Social Space: Rimbaud and the Paris Commune* (London: Verso, 2008). See also Michel Foucault, who suggests that the event shall be approached as "a process, a 'polygon' or rather a 'polyhedron' of intelligibility, the number of whose faces is not given in advance and can never properly be taken as finite." Michel Foucault, "Questions of Method," in *The Foucault Effect: Studies in Governmentality*, ed. Gordon Burchell and Peter Miller (Chicago: University Chicago Press, 1991), 77.

63. Here is Harootunian's particular intervention: he draws the Husserlian "lifeworld," which remains detached and abstracted from quotidian experience, into the everyday. Harootunian, "Remembering the Historical Present."

64. Rey Chow, *Primitive Passions* (New York: Columbia University Press, 1995).

65. Peter Bloom, "*Beur* Cinema and the Politics of Location: French Immigration Politics and the Naming of a Film Movement," in *Multiculturalism, Postcoloniality, and Transnational Media*, ed. Ella Shohat and Robert Stam (New Brunswick: Rutgers University Press, 2003), 60.

66. Tom Conley, "Cronos, Cosmos, and *Polis*: *La Haine*," in *Cartographic Cinema* (Minneapolis: University of Minnesota Press, 2007), 189.

67. For more on the media visibility of the Sürücü murder versus the lack of visibility in the Sherbini case see Beverly Weber, "A Regime of Gender Violence: Honor Killings, Familial Violence, and Muslim Women's Subjectivities," in *Violence and Gender*, 39–76.

68. For the connection between melodramatic and racial legibility of victims and villains see Linda Williams, *Playing the Race Card: Melodramas of Black and White from Uncle Tom to O.J. Simpson*, (Princeton: Princeton University Press, 2002). I will further discuss this issue in the fourth chapter, which analyzes Fatih Akın's melodrama *Head-On*.

69. Lauren Berlant, "The Compulsion to Repeat Femininity," in *The Female Complaint: The Unfinished Business of Sentimentality in American Culture* (Durham: Duke University Press, 2008), 259–60.

70. Berlant, *The Female Complaint*, 3–4.

71. I focus on Berlant's description mainly for the connection she draws between genre and affect. Of course, film scholars of genre theory have long dismissed the definition genres as formal categories, and similar to Berlant's description they focused on the spectator's particular relationship with genres. As

early as the 1980s Rick Altman explained how a semantic approach to genre is not sufficient to understand its contextual application—the social context that defines the emotional, habitual, and institutional framework of the audience's relationship with genre. Thereby, Altman provided a place for the spectators and for their reception to enter into formulation of genres. Rick Altman, "A Semantic/Syntactic Approach to Film Genre," *Cinema Journal* 23, no. 3 (Spring 1984): 6–18. Along the same lines Christine Gledhill conceives of genres as "dialogic"; what is productive about film genres is that their boundaries are always blurred, as they are redefined and redrawn in infinite dialogue with social life. Christine Gledhill, "Rethinking Genre," in *Reinventing Film Studies*, ed. Christine Gledhill and Linda Williams (London: Oxford University Press, 2000), 221–43. Gledhill brings Bakhtin's notion of heteroglossia and dialogism to genre theory, emphasizing genres' infinite dialogue with social life: "genres are fictional worlds, but they do not stay within fictional boundaries: their conventions cross into cultural and critical discourse, where we—as audiences, scholars, students, and critics—make and remake them" (241). Relatedly, Steve Neale describes genres as continuously reinvented processes: "dominated by repetition, but they are also marked fundamentally by difference, variation and change." "Questions of Genre," in *Film and Theory: An Anthology*, ed. Robert Stam and Toby Miller (New York: Blackwell, 2000), 165.

72. Elsaesser, *European Cinema*, and Paul Cooke, ed., *World Cinema's Dialogues with Hollywood* (New York: Palgrave Macmillan, 2007).

73. For an insightful article that explores the ways that auteurs rework popular genres see Jaimey Fischer, "German *Autoren* Dialogue with Hollywood? Refunctioning the Horror Genre in Christian Petzold's *Yella*," in *New Directions in German Cinema*, ed. Paul Cooke and Chris Homewood (London: I.B. Tauris, 2011), 182–200.

74. Scott Foundas, "INTERVIEW: Michael Haneke: The Bearded Prophet of "Code Inconnu" and "The Piano Teacher"," *Indiewire*, December 4, 2001, accessed September 21. http://www.indiewire.com/article/interview_michael_haneke_the_bearded_prophet_of_code_inconnu_and_the_piano_.

75. Reiner Werner Fassbinder, "Six Films by Douglas Sirk," *New Left Review* 91 (May–June 1975), 88–96.

76. To a large extent auteur films are not read through genre frames. At times, though, there can be a valorization of genre in minority filmmaking. The use of genre conventions by certain minority auteurs such as Fatih Akin can be interpreted as a welcome way to break away from the constrictions of expected authenticity from a minority director (the reception of his Turkish-German characters and themes through sociological frameworks), and to give his cinema a transnational legibility that surpasses the boundaries of German or Turkish nationalism and national cinemas. This will be explored in chapter 4.

77. Martin O'Shaughnessy, "Post-1995 French Cinema: Return of the Social, Return of the Political?" *Modern and Contemporary France* 11, no. 2 (2003): 189. Recently, however, there have been inspiring analyses of auteur cinema through the frames of genre conventions and affect. Especially, the Dardenne brothers' films are explored through the affective intensities they use. Lauren Berlant describes the Dardenne brothers' films as belonging to the new

genre of "situation tragedy" that conveys the affect of the precariousness of underclass lives in contemporary Europe. Berlant, *Cruel Optimism* (Durham: Duke University Press, 2011). Martin O'Shaughnessy analyzes the same films as a new form of political cinema that incorporates "melodramatic strategies in a broadly realist mode of film-making." Martin O'Shaughnessy, *The New Face of Political Cinema: Commitment in French Film since 1995* (London: Berghahn Books, 2007), 157. These works identify a trend in which political commitment in contemporary cinema distinguishes itself from an earlier mode of commitment, for instance that in Godard films of the 1960s and early 1970s. Through use of the affective appeal of genres the Dardenne brothers' cinema, reflecting "the violence and exclusions of the system as well as areas of the social that defy its grasp, clinging onto fragile possibilities and alliances, . . . disrupts neoliberalism's utopian and totalizing claims." O'Shaughnessy, *New Face of Political Cinema,* 201.

78. Rancière's references extend from Plato's cave allegory to Bertolt Brecht's epic theater, Antonin Artaud's theater of cruelty, and Guy Debord's *Society of Spectacle* (1967).

79. Jacques Rancière, *The Emancipated Spectator* (New York: Verso, 2009), 9.

80. Jacques Rancière, "Aesthetic Separation, Aesthetic Community: Scenes from the Aesthetic Regime of Art," *Art and Research: A Journal of Ideas, Contexts, and Methods* 2, no. 1 (Summer 2008), accessed July 26, 2012. http://www.artandresearch.org.uk/v2n1/ranciere.html.

81. For instance, Linda Williams's influential essay "Film Bodies" examines the affective relationship of "low culture" film genres with the spectators. Genres such as horror, porn, and "weepie" melodrama, "body genres" according to Williams, privilege the body and the sensational. The measure of their success has been the extent of audiences' bodily reaction, the extent to which the audience's body mimics the body on the screen: in porn the degree of erection, in horror the screams and fainting, in melodramas the amount of crying and number of handkerchiefs used has been the proof of a skillful "body genre" film. Linda Williams, "Film Bodies: Genre, Gender, and Excess," *Film Quarterly* 44, no. 4 (Summer 1991): 2–13.

82. Hamid Naficy, *An Accented Cinema: Exilic and Diasporic Filmmaking* (Princeton: Princeton University Press, 2001).

83. Laura Marks, *The Skin of the Film: Intercultural Cinema, Embodiment, and the Senses* (Durham: Duke University Press, 2000).

84. Similar to my position here, in her insightful critique of Naficy's work Asuman Suner mentions that the some of the stylistic and thematic aspects that Naficy attributes to "accented cinema" are found in numerous examples of world cinema and yet are categorized under national cinema. She suggests widening the category of "accented cinema" beyond that of exilic and diasporic directors in which the basis is "a narrowly defined notion of 'situatedness.'" She proposes instead to redefine accented cinema "as critical positionality vis-à-vis the questions of belonging and identity." Asuman Suner, "Outside in: 'accented cinema' at large," Inter-Asia Cultural Studies 7, no. 3 (2006), accessed 10 January, 2015. http://www.nbcfilm.com/uzak/press_screenasuman2.php.

Chapter 1

1. Michael Joshua Rowin, "*Children of Men,*" *Cineaste* 32, no. 2 (Spring 2007): 60–61.

2. Jon Stratton, "'Welcome to Paradise': Asylum Seekers, Neoliberalism, Nostalgia and *Lucky Miles,*" *Continuum: Journal of Media & Cultural Studies* 23, no. 5 (2009): 629–45.

3. W. J. T. Mitchell, *What Do Pictures Want? The Lives and Loves of Images* (Chicago: University of Chicago Press, 2005): 12.

4. In Dan Bulley, "'Foreign Terror'? Resisting/Responding to the London Bombings," in *Terrorism and the Politics of Response,* ed. Angharad Closs Stephens and Nick Vaughan-Williams (New York: Routledge, 2009), 83.

5. Javaid Rehman, "Islam, 'War on Terror' and the Future of Muslim Minorities in the United Kingdom: Dilemmas of Multiculturalism," *Human Rights Quarterly* 29, no. 4 (2007): 831–78.

6. Published on January 16, 2000, in Jessica Autumn Brown and Myra Marx Ferree, "Close Your Eyes and Think of England: Pronatalism in the British Print Media," *Gender & Society* 19, no. 1 (2005): 5–24.

7. European anxiety over reproduction is a recurrent fear that most forcefully appeared in the past during the interwar years. See Mark Mazower, "Healthy Bodies, Sick Bodies," in *Dark Continent: Europe's Twentieth Century* (New York: Vintage, 1998), 76–104. I am grateful to Alexis Rappas for bringing this to my attention.

8. Maggie Haberman, "Swedish Tennis Stud Recommends Borg-asms," *New York Post,* March 11, 2001, accessed January 4, 2013. http://www.nypost.com/p/news/item_ sGXUbuHN02bgsEZcXHa64K. The image of the ad may be found on the following website: http://www.olalax.com/bb_3.html (accessed September 2, 2012).

9. Kathryn Joyce, "Missing the 'Right' Babies," *The Nation,* February, 14, 2009, accessed June 6, 2011. http://www.thenation.com/article/missing-right-babies.

10. Oriana Fallaci, *La Forza Della Ragione,* in Luiza Bialasiewicz, "'The Death of the West': Samuel Huntington, Oriana Fallaci and a New 'Moral' Geopolitics of Births and Bodies," *Geopolitics* 11, no. 4 (July 2006), 705.

11. Brown and Ferree, "Close Your Eyes."

12. *The Mail on Sunday,* "Open Door for Bogus Refugees," March 15, 1998, accessed January 4, 2015. http://www.highbeam.com/doc/1G1-109823367.html.

13. *Daily Mail,* "Britain Is Top Asylum Haven," February 2, 2002, accessed January 4, 2015. http://www.dailymail.co.uk/news/article-98148/Britain-asylum-haven.html.

14. *Daily Express,* "Asylum: Time to Pull Down the Shutters," August 30, 2001, accessed January 4, 2015. http://www.ukpressonline.co.uk/ukpressonline/database/search/preview.jsp?fileName=DExp_2001_08_30_001&sr=1. For a historical analysis of such alarming headlines in the UK see Anna Karpf article in The Guardian, "We've Been Here Before," June 8, 2002, accessed January 4, 2015. http://www.theguardian.com/uk/2002/jun/08/immigration.immigrationandpublicservices.

15. British National Front Poster (2003) quoted in Sara Ahmed, *The Cultural Politics of Emotion* (Edinburgh: Edinburgh University Press, 2004), 1.

16. Catherine Wihtol de Wenden, "La crise de l'asile," *Hommes et migrations* 1238: 6–12 and Peter Stalker, *The No-Nonsense Guide to International Migration* (Oxford: New Internationalist Publications, 2008).

17. Brad Brevet, "Exclusive: Alfonso Cuarón on *Children of Men*," *Rope of Silicon*, December 22, 2006, accessed December 27, 2012. http://www.ropeofsilicon.com/exclusive_alfonso_cuaron_on_children_of_men/.

18. Alfonso Cuarón, "DVD Bonus Features: Futuristic Design," *Children of Men*, directed by Alfonso Cuarón (Universal City: Universal Pictures, 2007).

19. *Blade Runner*, for instance, has been analyzed as a film that reflects the anxieties about the US inner cities imagined as dark, chaotic and lawless in the 1980s. Fredric Jameson suggests that good science fiction enables the spectator to grasp the present as history since we are dissociated from the present and the everyday life rendered "inaccessible directly, is numb, habituated, empty of affect." Science fiction calls upon the present rather than the future and the challenging task for the director or the author is to find an effective strategy to make the spectators/readers experience the present anew. Jameson explains, "Elaborate strategies of indirection are therefore necessary if we are somehow to break through our monadic insulation and to 'experience,' for some first and real time, this 'present' which is after all all we have." Jameson, "Progress Versus Utopia," 287.

20. Darko Suvin, *Metamorphosis of Science Fiction: On the Poetics and History of a Literary Genre* (New Haven: Yale University Press, 1979).

21. Susan Sontag famously claimed that there has always been a tight connection between science fiction and representation of disasters: "Science fiction films are not about science. They are about disaster, which is one of the oldest subjects of art." Susan Sontag, "The Imagination of Disaster," in *Liquid Metal: The Science Fiction Film Reader*, ed. Sean Redmond (London: Wallflower Press, 2004), 41. What has changed, however, since Sontag's article was first published in the mid-1960s is the very conception of disaster and that of its immediate effect on the human body, as I will discuss further in this chapter.

22. Vivian Sobchack, *Screening the Space: The American Science Fiction* (New Brunswick: Rutgers University Press, 1987).

23. Slavoj Žižek, *Welcome to the Desert of the Real! Five Essays on September 11 and Related Dates* (London: Verso, 2002), 16.

24. Similarly, in the horror films after September 11 the elements of terror are less frequently monsters, aliens or cyborgs. In films such as *Hostel* (2005), *Saw* (2004) and *The Devil's Rejects* (2005), horror emerges from humanity and the threat to humans is nothing else than other humans. Aaron Kerner, "Faculty Profile: Aaron Kerner," *SFSU Cinema Department Video*, 4:49, posted July 2012, accessed January 10, 2013. http://www.youtube.com/watch?v=lhXFFOFEBWg&list=PLC3367192BD41107C&index=10.

25. Henri Lefebvre, "The Everyday and Everydayness," *Yale French Studies*, no. 73 (1987), 10–11.

26. Harootunian, "Remembering the Historical Present," 472.

27. Kristin Ross uses this phrase to describe "endisms" declared in the post-Cold War era, in "Historicizing Untimeliness," 28.

28. Didier Fassin and Mariella Pandolfi, "Introduction: Military and Humanitarian Government in the Age of Intervention," in *Contemporary States of Emergency: The Politics of Military and Humanitarian Interventions*, ed. Didier Fassin and Mariella Pandolfi (New York: Zone Books, 2010), 9.

29. Slavoj Žižek, "DVD Bonus Features: *Children of Men* Comments by Slavoj Žižek," in *Children of Men*, DVD.

30. For an analysis of *Children of Men* through the light of Rancière's theory of the "ethical turn," see Ozan Kamiloglu, "The Ethical Turn and Cinema: The Politics and Aesthetics of Jacques Rancière," MA thesis, Bilkent University, 2011, 4, accessed December 20, 2012. http://www.thesis.bilkent.edu.tr/0004048.pdf.

31. Rancière, "Ethical Turn," 192.

32. The global connectedness of the historical events presented in the film's background is explored in Kirk Boyle in "*Children of Men* and *I Am Legend*: The Disaster-Capitalism Complex Hits Hollywood," *Jump Cut: A Review of Contemporary Media* 51 (Spring 2009), accessed September 9, 2012, http://www.ejumpcut.org/archive/jc51.2009/ChildrenMenLegend/text.html; and also in Alfonso Cuarón, "DVD Bonus Features: The Possibility of Hope," in *Children of Men*, DVD.

33. Rowin, "*Children of Men*," 61.

34. John Berger, *The Success and Failure of Picasso* (New York: Pantheon Books, 1965), 169, and A. K. Thompson, "Matter's Most Modern Configurations: Rivera, Picasso, and Benjamin's Dialectic," Scapegoat 2 (Winter 2011), 2–6, accessed December 26, 2012. http://www.scapegoatjournal.org/docs/02/02_Thompson_MattersMostModern.pdf.

35. Nonfiction writer Russell Martin suggests the affective power and universality of *Guernica* by narrating how his encounter with the painting in Madrid both coincides and corresponds with the experience of September 11: "None of us was aware as we stood across from the brutal, horrific, yet somehow mesmerizing images of Picasso's war, that in those same moments the twenty-first century had been forced forever onto a new tack, that once more—as had happened in little Gernika—humans had transformed themselves into demons, and other humans suddenly search for reasons why." Russell Martin, *Picasso's War* (New York: Plume, 2003), 7.

36. It is no coincidence that one of the references in the film is Diego Velázquez's *Las Meninas*, a painting famous for its *mise en abyme* effect.

37. Kim Voynar, "Interview: *Children of Men* Director Alfonso Cuarón," *Cinematical*, December 25, 2006, accessed December 29, 2012. http://blog.moviefone.com/2006/12/25/interview-children-ofmen-director-alfonso-cuaron/.

38. The film shows art that witnesses human suffering but it criticizes valuing of art over human suffering. Theo's cousin, Nigel, the minister of art whom Theo visits to secure transit papers for Kee, brags about saving *Guernica* from disaster-struck Madrid at a posh dinner table. While Theo stresses the deaths of people in Madrid, Nigel insists on mourning the art destroyed or expressing with pride how he managed to save precious artworks. The project Nigel is involved with is called the Ark of the Arts, as he plays the modern Noah salvaging art instead of species from the destroyed parts of the world. Nigel's first words to Theo under the crushing presence of Michelangelo's *The Statue of David* are: "We couldn't save *La Pietà* . . . smashed up before we got there." Theo responds, "My mother had one in the bathroom; it was a lamp." The exchange evokes the questionable

function of the arts in a world that carries no future for humanity. Yet the film itself carries an intense desire for preservation and display of artworks. In terms of citing disasters Cuarón's references are global; in terms of representing art, however, his iconography remains particularly European and especially British. In the Ark of the Arts the spectator may observe that what are preserved are works at the core of European heritage (Michelangelo's *David* and *Guernica*) and British popular culture (Banksy's *Kissing Policemen*). This obsession with preservation of various symbols of European heritage in the Ark of the Arts is evident even in the soundtrack, which pays homage to British alternative rock of the 1970s, including highlights from King Crimson's "The Court of the Crimson King" and Deep Purple's "Hush" to the Rolling Stones' "Ruby Tuesday."

39. Anirban Kapil Baishya, "Trauma, Post-apocalyptic Science Fiction and the Post-human," *Wide Screen* 3, no. 1 (June 2011): 19.

40. Rancière, "Ethical Turn," 194–95.

41. Fredric Jameson describes the continent's present state thus: "Europe's image ambiguity—a kind of elegant museum or tourist playground which is also an evolutionary and economic dead end." Fredric Jameson, "Fear and Loathing in Globalization," *New Left Review* 23 (September–October 2003): 107. Nigel's Ark of the Arts and the preservation and representation of particularly British art in the film is telling in that it parallels the intense commodification of cultural heritage in today's Britain and Europe. Especially in the UK, economic benefits from cultural heritage are billions of pounds per year. See European Group on Museum Statistics, http://www.egmus.eu/nc/en/statistics/complete_data/. As opposed to Italy or France, most of the UK's cultural heritage revenues come from exhibitions of modern art, as the Tate Modern remains the most visited modern museum of art in the world. In *Children of Men*, the scene with Nigel's Ark of the Arts is shot in the Tate Modern, displaying the Battersea power station in the background. (Pink Floyd's 1977 *Animals* album cover shows the Battersea power station—which the film also makes a reference to by showing the inflated pig attached to Battersea's roof as in the album cover—in support of a campaign to preserve the building as a national heritage site after the power plant was closed down). This reference to the Tate is even more visible for an audience familiar with the museum site established inside the Bankside power station—both buildings being symbols of the emerging heritage industry that draws tourists to the postindustrial landscape of London.

42. For more on Europe's schizophrenic regime of border control and mobility see Verstraete, *Tracking Europe*.

43. The question of stunted mobility applies at times to other characters in the film as well. Theo keeps on losing his shoes throughout the film. In one of the most exciting action scenes in which the leader of the Fishes, Julian (Julianne Moore), is killed, the car is in reverse gear moving backward. As Theo and Kee try to escape from the Fishes the car fails to start, so they have to push it until it does.

44. The mobile long take has been used in genre cinema, with examples ranging from Hitchcock's *Rope* (1948) and Orson Welles's *Touch of Evil* (1958) to more recent films such as *Old Boy* by Park Chan-wook (2003) and *Strange Days* by Kathryn Bigelow (1995), to create tension, increase the anxiety, and sometimes to give a broader sense of the surrounding context.

45. Joshua Clover, "All That Is Solid Melts into War," *Film Quarterly* 61, no. 1 (Autumn 2007), accessed November 11, 2012. http://www.filmquarterly.org/2007/12/all-that-is-solid-melts-into-war/.

46. André Bazin, "The Evolution of the Language of Cinema," in *What Is Cinema?* trans. Hugh Gray (Berkeley: University of California Press, 2004).

47. Richard von Busack, "Making the Future: Richard von Busack Talks to Alfonso Cuarón about Filming *Children of Men*," *Metroactive*, October 1, 2007, accessed December 9, 2012. http://www.metroactive.com/metro/01.10.07/alfonso-cuaron-0702.html. The director effaces this binary logic—that editing seeks for effect and the long take does not—in this very comment when he admits his goal is to "create" "truthfulness," yet another effect. In any case, despite the claim of "registering," documentation, and reference to reality, the long take is not quite an invisible form that reflects the material it shoots in its ambiguity. Rather, the long take calls attention to its technical dimension and becomes in itself the spectacle of a director's expertise. See Geoff King, "Following in the Footsteps: Gus Van Sant's *Gerry* and *Elephant* in the American Independent Field of Cultural Production," *New Review of Film and Television Studies* 4, no. 2 (August 2006): 78. A dialogue on *Children of Men* between two Australian critics is indicative of the technique's effect on the connoisseurs; while one critic implies how she is skeptical about whether or not the film "soars" despite all the "interesting detail" and wealth of "substance," the other critic quickly reminds her, "It's a bit downbeat isn't it? I guess that's partly why . . . I was just dazzled by the way it's shot. . . . Just one of these long takes in some action scenes are really amazingly well done." "At the Movies with Margaret and David: Children of Men," ABC Australia, last modified October 11, 2006, accessed March 29, 2013. http://www.abc.net.au/atthemovies/txt/s1756228.htm. James Udden suggests that the long take in *Children of Men*, as with some other directors (such as Gus van Sant), functions as a declaration of independence from Hollywood conventions, as mobility and seeming lack of montage in the action scenes become spectacles in themselves, "endlessly talked about by reviewers, scholars and film aficionados alike. And that appears to have been precisely the reason why they are employed in the film during those particular sequences which proved to be the most challenging." James Udden, "Child of the Long Take: Alfonso Cuarón's Film Aesthetics in the Shadow of Globalization," *Style* 43, no. 1 (Spring 2009): 32.

48. Ironically, James Udden brings to our attention that a more technical film magazine (*Cinefex*) article explains that these scenes in *Children of Men* are not long takes but multiple shots put together digitally in postproduction. On the DVD extras, however, Cuarón appears proud of having tackled the challenges of the long takes used in action scenes.

49. *Children of Men* reveals science fiction and disaster genre's changing involvement with the human body in the 2000s. In the 1980s and 1990s, the body became the focus of anxieties; the elimination of the boundaries of human and machine and the question of the posthuman were at the center of debates in postapocalyptic action films such as *The Terminator* (1984) and *The Matrix* (1999). Jenny Wolmark, "Staying with the Body: Narratives of Post-human in Contemporary Science Fiction," in *Edging into the Future: Science Fiction and Contemporary Cultural Transformation*, ed. Veronica Hollinger and Joan Gordon (Philadelphia: University of Pennsylvania Press, 2002), 75–90. Anxieties about the body have

changed route, from anxiety about the interface between body and technology that dominated the dystopias of the 1990s to anxiety about the limited capacity of the human body, its vulnerability to biological horrors. For instance, in *I Am Legend* (2007), *28 Days Later* (2002), and *World War Z* (2013) the apocalypse hits the major capitals in the form of a virus that takes over the body and turns people into raging hordes. So, rather than further erosion, the dystopias of the 2000s reflect a surfacing of the body's boundaries.

50. For Berenike Jung, the most imminent danger that causes all the ensuing violence in the film is the invisible biological danger of infertility. For more on this point, see Berenike Jung, *Narrating Violence in Post-9/11 Action Cinema: Terrorist Narratives, Cinematic Narration, and Referentiality* (Wiesbaden: Springer, 2010).

51. This is Zahid Chaudhary's careful observation. His article on the film interprets this misspelling as an allegory of inassimilable alterity, an approach that I will soon elaborate. Zahid Chaudhary, "Humanity Adrift: Race, Materiality, and Allegory in Alfonso Cuarón's *Children of Men*," *Camera Obscura* 24, no. 3-72 (2009): 73–109.

52. Jacques Rancière, "The Intolerable Image," in *The Emancipated Spectator*, 96.

53. The vocabulary Jasper uses to describe how the future British government treats the refugees is possibly yet another historical reference to the way in which Hutus referred to Tutsis during the Rwandan genocide.

54. In an insightful analysis of *Children of Men* as adaptation, Patricia Nelson praises the film for having a clearer political agenda than the novel and a utopian promise: "While James' novel suggests the futility and cyclicality of human existence, engaging themes of Christianity, reproductive rights, political corruption and totalitarian regimes, and the apparent futility of political activism, Cuarón shifts the focus to immigration and environmentalism and inscribes in his film a hope for the future, activated by the promise of children, that remains notably absent in the novel version." Patricia Nelson, "The Politics of Film Adaptation: A Case Study of Alfonso Cuarón's *Children of Men*," MA thesis, University of Texas at Austin, 2010, 4, accessed December 12, 2012. https://repositories.lib.utexas.edu/bitstream/handle/2152/ETD-UT-2010-05- 1162/NELSON-THESIS.pdf.

55. Nelson, "Politics of Film Adaptation."

56. P. D. James, *Children of Men* (New York: Vintage, 2006), 58.

57. James, *Children of Men,* 111.

58. Alfonso Cuarón, Timothy J. Sexton, David Arata, Mark Fergus, and Hawk Ostby, "*Children of Men* Final Shooting Script," 70, accessed December 15, 2012. http://www.pages.drexel.edu/~ina22/splaylib/Screenplay-Children_of_Men.htm.

59. Craig Calhoun, "The Idea of Emergency: Humanitarian Action and Global (Dis)Order," in Fassin and Pandolfi, *Contemporary States of Emergency*, 49.

60. Cuarón's casting of Michael Caine for the role is in itself ironic, of course, considering Caine's openly right-wing politics with his support for Margaret Thatcher in the 1980s and recent public endorsement of the Conservative Party. I am grateful to Ozlem Koksal for pointing this out to me.

61. Calhoun, "The Idea of Emergency," 33.

62. Calhoun, "The Idea of Emergency," 34.

63. Giorgio Agamben, *Homo Sacer: Sovereign Power and Bare Life*, trans. Daniel Heller-Roazen (Stanford: Stanford University Press, 1998), 133–34.

64. For a critique of rights of man conceived as rights of citizens in Arendt and Agamben, see Jacques Rancière, "Who Is the Subject of the Rights of Men?," *South Atlantic Quarterly* 103, nos. 2–3 (Spring–Summer 2004): 297–310.

65. On the religious symbolism in *Children of Men* see Jung, *Narrating Violence*, 88.

66. Chaudhary, "Humanity Adrift," 100.

67. While allegory produces multiple meanings, what saves it, for the critic, from "a nihilistic surplus of meaning here *is* the figure of alterity." Chaudhary, "Humanity Adrift," 86.

68. Chaudhary, "Humanity Adrift," 100.

69. Fassin, *Empire of Trauma*, 270. Fassin mentions the exhibition "The Ills of Exile" in 2000 where the black-and-white photographs of wounded Algerians are presented along with a collection of personal narratives of torture, however, in the anthropologist's narrative the tortured refugees voices are rather absent, a striking similarity to the disinfected medical reports prepared along with conventions to secure asylum. Instead of the refugees, Fassin cites Jean Améry's narrative of Nazi torture in *At the Mind's Limits* and suggests that "Tamil or Mauritanian, Kurdish or Angolan asylum seekers are not likely to speak of torture with Améry's eloquence. They do not have the words, and even if they had, there is neither time or place for them to make their statement" (Fassin, *Empire of Trauma*, 271). Hence, even though Fassin critiques medical certificates for leaving the refugees voiceless, his own work seems to be trapped in the same dilemma.

70. Ticktin, "Where Ethics and Politics Meet." What Ticktin names the "illness clause" is a provision introduced in the French Immigration Act in 1998 recognizing the possibility that undocumented immigrants who faced severe health problems and who have no access to effective treatment at home might obtain a residence permit "for humanitarian reasons." In the case of the UK the treatment based on medical humanitarianism is slightly different than France; while the UK limits the free treatment of chronic diseases such as AIDS and TB within its borders, it still offers substantial development aid to treat these diseases abroad. See Richard Coker and Alan Ingram, "Passports and Pestilence: Migration, Security and Contemporary Border Control of Infectious Diseases," in *Medicine at the Border: Disease, Globalization and Security, 1850 to the Present*, ed. Alison Bashford (New York: Palgrave Macmillan, 2006).

71. Ticktin, "Where Ethics and Politics Meet," 39.

72. Ticktin, "Where Ethics and Politics Meet," 45.

73. Didier Fassin, "Of Words and Wounds: The Thin Evidence of Asylum Seekers," Brown University, Pembroke Seminar Research Lecture, March 2, 2010.

74. Lauren Berlant, "America, 'Fat,' the Fetus," in *The Queen of America Goes to Washington City: Essays on Sex and Citizenship* (Durham: Duke University Press, 1997), 84.

75. Berlant, "America, 'Fat,' the Fetus," 87.

76. Žižek, "DVD Bonus Features: *Children of Men* Comments by Slavoj Žižek."

77. This critique is made literal in a dinner table scene displaying Picasso's *Guernica* in the background as Theo and his cousin, the minister of art, talk about the destruction of Madrid.

78. Kirk Boyle maintains that in *Children of Men* "anamorphic advertisements of invented products ironize the consumerism of late capitalism." Boyle, "*Children of Men*."

79. This phrase is taken from an infamous speech by Michel Rocard (a former French prime minister who was a primary figure in passing laws that tightened the security measures against illegal migration). In response to the growing asylum applications that France was receiving, he claimed, "France cannot accommodate all the misery of the world." Thomas Deltombe, "'Accueillir toute la misère du monde': Michel Rocard, martyr ou mystificateur?" *Le Monde diplomatique,* September 30, 2009, accessed December 2, 2012. http://www.monde-diplomatique.fr/carnet/2009-09-30-Rocard.

80. Catherine Coroller, "Le film 'Welcome' fait polémique," *Libération,* March, 10, 2009, accessed November 23, 2012. http://www.liberation.fr/societe/0101553219-le-film-welcome-fait-polemique.

81. The controversial ministry that was created under the Sarkozy presidency (May 2007) and quickly earned itself an infamous name by initiating laws such as the expulsion of the Roma (2010) and the ban on the burka (2010).

82. It needs to be mentioned, though, that *sans papiers* protests for rights and papers are not uncommon in Europe. On March 18, 1996, three hundred *sans papiers* occupied the Church of St Ambroise in Paris and went on a hunger strike. Their spokesperson, Ababacar Diop, explained, "Whenever we go out to work, we are hunted down like animals and denied our dignity; we are stopped by police, often simply for the colour of our face, although we have committed no crime." In Madjiguène Cissé, "The *Sans-Papiers*: A Woman Draws the First Lessons," in *We Are Everywhere: The Irresistible Rise of Global Anti-capitalism* (London: Verso, 2003), 38. The police soon attacked with tear gas and evicted the *sans papiers* from the church. In January 2011, undocumented migrants occupied the University of Athens Law School and went on a hunger strike that lasted about a week until they decided to peacefully end their protest. In 2009 protests in many European cities (Paris, Brussels, and Zurich) were organized in conjunction with antiracist organizations. Therefore, my point here is not to underplay or ignore the activism for and of the *sans papiers* but to note that such activism is not the kind of reaction that the film incited.

83. Laura María Agustín, *Sex at the Margins: Migration, Labour Markets and the Rescue Industry* (London: Zed Books, 2007), 8.

Chapter 2

1. For a discussion on the 2005 riots and the value attributed to property over the lost lives of minority *banlieue* youth see Badiou, "Immediate Riot," 16–27.

2. Charles Tshimanga, Didier Gondola, and Peter J. Bloom, "Introduction: Examining Frenchness and the African Diaspora," in Tshimanga, Gondola, and Bloom, *Frenchness and the African Diaspora,* 5.

3. Etienne Balibar, "Uprising in the *Banlieues,*" *Constellations* 14, no. 1 (2007): 67.

4. Jean-Luc Einaudi, *La Bataille de Paris* (Paris: Seuil, 1991).

5. For a longer discussion on the memory politics around the 1961 massacre of Algerians in Paris and their relation to Haneke's film see my article, Ipek A. Celik, "'I Wanted You to Be Present': Guilt and the History of Violence in Michael Haneke's *Caché*," *Cinema Journal* 50, no. 1 (2010): 59–80.

6. Serge Toubiana, "Interview with Michael Haneke," in *Caché*, directed by Michael Haneke (Culver City: Sony Pictures Home Entertainment, 2006), DVD.

7. For a discussion on the ongoing moral panic in the media regarding violence in the *banlieues* see Laurent Mucchielli, "L'éphémère question des viols collectifs en France (2000–2002): Etude d'une panique morale," *Logos 26* 14, no. 1 (2007): 9–29.

8. Nicolas Sarkozy, "Déclaration de M. Nicolas Sarkozy, ministre de l'intérieur et de l'aménagement du territoire, président de l'UMP et candidat à l'élection présidentielle, sur son suhait de voir se réunifier l'espace méditerranéen pour le remettre au cœur de la civilisation occidentale et de la mondialisation, Toulon le 7 février 2007," Vie publique: Collection des discours publics, accessed February 25, 2010. http://discours.vie-publique.fr/notices/073000533.html. Unless otherwise stated, translations from French are mine.

9. Foundas, "INTERVIEW."

10. Rosalind Galt, "The Functionary of Mankind: Haneke and Europe," in *On Michael Haneke*, ed. Brian Price and John David Rhodes (Detroit: Wayne State University Press, 2010), 221.

11. Catherine Wheatley, *Michael Haneke's Cinema: The Ethic of the Image* (New York: Berghahn Books, 2009), 80. In addition to Wheatley's comment, it needs to be noted that among other genres the thriller has a particularly complicated and intricate history in European cinema that goes much beyond Haneke's comment of "parody." Especially in France via *la nouvelle vague* and its attention to and appreciation of Alfred Hitchcock's oeuvre, the French thriller is considered "the principal means by which the French cinema's relationship to Hollywood has been articulated," Jill Forbes, *The Cinema in France after the New Wave* (London: BFI, 1992), 48. Furthermore, the exchange between different regional and national cinemas on the thriller front has never been a one-way interaction; Hollywood conventions of genre have affected European and international filmmaking, but the opposite has also been valid: For instance, both Quentin Tarantino and John Woo stress the influence of Jean-Pierre Melville's thrillers on their filmmaking. Peter Lennon, "Poet of the Underworld," *The Guardian*, June 27, 2003, accessed May 20, 2010. http://www.guardian.co.uk/film/2003/jun/27/artsfeatures2.

12. In Haneke's earlier films one frequently finds traces of genre conventions. *Seventh Continent* (1989), for instance, is a family drama abundant with domestic scenes so as to emphasize how domesticity alienates and traps the characters until their deaths. At the very beginning of *Time of the Wolf* (2003), the sudden murder of the father breaks the typical trope of communal bonding in disaster films, and further highlights the utter fragmentation and anarchy in this postapocalyptic film. *Funny Games* (1997) is the most explicit genre-bender. It is a family-under-attack thriller that overrides the spectator's expectation of the victims' retribution by breaking the frame to have the villains rewind a scene in which the victim shoots one of them. Even in *Code Unknown* (2000), a film

without explicit generic markers, there is a film within the film—in which Juliette Binoche appears as the terrorized protagonist imprisoned by a serial killer—a sequence that prepares the audience for Binoche's role as a potential victim in *Hidden.*

13. For genre conventions common to thrillers see Charles Derry, *The Suspense Thriller: Films in the Shadow of Alfred Hitchcock* (Jefferson: McFarland, 1988).

14. Raymond Chandler explains that the concerns of novelists and filmmakers converge in thrillers that expose social conditions rather than propose arbitrary resolutions: "The ideal mystery was one you would read if the end was missing. We who tried to write it had the same point of view as the filmmakers." Raymond Chandler, *Trouble Is My Business* (New York: Vintage, 1950), ix.

15. Charles Derry admits that it is extremely difficult to define genre conventions that shape audience expectations in a thriller as it is the genre that is most conditioned by bending established rules and unsettling conventions. For instance, the attack on Roger O. Thornhill (Cary Grant) in *North by Northwest* (1959) in broad daylight and open field rather than a dark alley challenges our spatial coordinates of fear and exploits an uncharted territory of thrill: agoraphobia. Similarly, the rather early death of Marion Crane (Janet Leigh), the heroine of *Psycho* with whom the audience has identified, quickly changes the track of the film. The thriller is the genre of "ingenuity in playing with the audience's expectations." David Bordwell and Kristin Thompson, *Film Art: An Introduction* (New York: McGraw Hill, 2010), 332. Suspense and surprise are inherent to thriller, and misleading the audience is a frequent experiment. Such preoccupation with the unexpected and the novel make it even more difficult to define the thriller beyond its intimate attachment to Hitchcock's filmmaking as well as the structural devices that sustain the suspense and thrill. Hence, one of the rare books on the genre, Derry's *The Suspense Thriller* adopts this approach focusing on the Hitchcockian structural devices.

16. Quoted in Guy Austin, *Contemporary French Cinema* (Manchester: Manchester University Press, 1996), 100. As Austin notes, Hitchcock's use of gaze inspired numerous European thrillers: from Michael Powell's *Peeping Tom* (1960), in which the camera searches for the authentic expression of fear and literally becomes the tool for murder, to Chabrol's *Le Cri du hibou* (1987) and Patrice Leconte's *Monsieur Hire* (1989), which challenge the voyeur-criminal dynamic by making them victims of the person they watch or the bourgeois society's judgment of their "perversion."

17. Studies on the Hitchcockian gaze have a significant impact on feminist film studies through Laura Mulvey's famous article "Visual Pleasure and Narrative Cinema." Mulvey's analysis of the Hitchcockian gaze contributed to what Clifford Manlove calls the increasing significance of "gaze theory" with implications especially in postcolonial studies from Edward Said's *Orientalism* to Rey Chow's critique of Said in *Primitive Passions.* [Laura Mulvey, "Visual Pleasure and Narrative Cinema," *Screen* 16, no. 3 (Autumn 1975): 6–18; Clifford Manlove, "Visual 'Drive' and the Cinematic Narrative," *Cinema Journal* 46, no. 3 (2007): 83–108; Edward Said, *Orientalism* (New York: Vintage, 1978); Chow, *Primitive Passions.*

18. For a Lacanian analysis of the function of videotapes in *Hidden* as Georges' obsession to control the conditions of his visibility see James Penney, "'You Never Look at Me From Where I See You': Postcolonial Guilt in *Caché*," *New Formations*

70 (Winter 2011): 77–93. Also, Hugh Manon's insightful analysis of the gaze in *Hidden* concludes that while the video's gaze represents Georges' desire to come into contact with Majid, this encounter is bound to be disappointing since "for any desiring subject certain recognitions are constitutively impossible, beyond any hope of realization except in the form of an ego-shattering, perhaps revolutionary breakdown" in Hugh Manon, "'Comment ça, rien?' Screening the Gaze in *Caché*," in Price and Rhodes, *On Michael Haneke*, 122.

19. Ranjana Khanna, "From Rue Morgue to Rue des Iris," *Screen* 48, no. 2 (Summer 2007): 243.

20. Ara Osterweil, "*Caché*," *Film Quarterly* 59, no. 4 (Summer 2006): 35–39.

21. Thomas Levin, "Five Tapes, Four Halls, Two Dreams: Vicissitudes of Surveillant Narration in Michael Haneke's *Caché*" in *A Companion to Michael Haneke*, ed. Roy Grundmann (Oxford: Blackwell, 2010), 84.

22. Chow, *Primitive Passions*, 12.

23. Deleuze, *Cinema 2*, 82.

24. Deleuze, *Cinema 2*, 81.

25. Patricia Pisters, "New Subjectivity in Cinema: The Vertigo of Strange Days" in *Subjectivity*, ed. Willem van Reijen and Willem G. Weststeijn (Amsterdam: Rodopi, 2000), 305.

26. Rancière, *The Emancipated Spectator*.

27. Thomas Elsaesser, "Performative Self-Contradictions: Michael Haneke's Mind Games," in *A Companion to Michael Haneke*, ed. Roy Grundmann (Oxford: Blackwell, 2010), 64–65.

28. Toubiana, "Interview with Michael Haneke."

29. Kristin Ross, *Fast Cars, Clean Bodies: Decolonization and the Reordering of French Culture* (Cambridge, MA: MIT Press, 1995), 196.

30. Thomas Levin claims that ingraining real or fictional surveillance videos within a film's narrative is a way to compensate for unreliable film images with a supposedly objective and live referentiality, an attempt to get ever closer to reality: "If the unproblematic referentiality of cinematic photograms is under siege, it makes great sense to start appropriating a type of imaging characterized by definition . . . in terms of its seemingly unproblematic, reliable referentiality." Thomas Y. Levin, "Rhetoric of Temporal Index: Surveillant Narration and the Cinema of 'Real Time" in *Ctrl [space]: Rhetorics of Surveillance from Bentham to Big Brother*, ed. Thomas Y. Levin, Ursula Frohne, and Peter Weibel (Karlsruhe: ZKM Center for Art and Media; and Cambridge, MA: MIT Press, 2002), 585.

31. Dominik Kamalzadeh, "Cowardly and Comfortable: Interview with Michael Haneke" *Sign and Sight*, January 30, 2006, accessed August, 29, 2011. http://www.signandsight.com/features/577.html.

32. Antoine de Baecque, "Interview avec Michael Haneke: L'intelligence ne protège pas de la lâcheté," *Libération*, October 5, 2005, accessed October 10, 2011. http://next.liberation.fr/cinema/0101543833-l-intelligence-ne-protege-pas-de-la-lachete.

33. Brigitte Peucker, *The Material Image: Art and the Real in Film* (Stanford: Stanford University Press, 2007), 132.

34. Examples are Gaspar Noe's *Irreversible* (2002) with its unbearably long rape scene, Claire Denis's *Trouble Every Day* (2001) in which cannibalism is portrayed and a long list of films including Phillippe Grandrieux's *La Vie Nouvelle*

(2002), Catherine Breillat's *Anatomie de l'Enfer* (2004) and Virginie Despentes' *Baise-Moi* (2000) that depict other experiences of extreme bodily violence. This trend is not limited to French cinema, as the 2009 Cannes film festival attests: almost all screened and awarded international films were drenched in violence, most notably Lars von Trier's *Anti-Christ* (2009) and Brilliante Mendoza's *Slaughter* (2009), which won the best director award. The later is a Filipino film on police corruption that shows the abduction, beating, brutal rape, and dismembering of a prostitute for nearly forty-five minutes.

35. Williams, "Film Bodies."

36. Martine Beugnet, *Cinema and Sensation: French Film and the Art of Transgression* (Carbondale: Southern Illinois University Press, 2007).

37. Hampus Hagman, "'Every Cannes Needs Its Scandal': Between Art and Exploitation in Contemporary French Film," *Film International* 5, no. 29 (2007): 37.

38. Elsaesser, "Performative Self-Contradictions," 56.

39. "It seems to me that the ear is fundamentally more sensitive than the eye. To put it another way, the ear provides a more direct path to the imagination and to the heart of human beings. . . . Our sensibility in the visual domain is further diminished by the flood of pictures on television, so that it is now very difficult to create pictures that leave a strong impression, let alone evoke reaction." Michael Haneke, "71 Fragments of a Chronology of Chance: Notes to the Film," in *After Postmodernism: Austrian Literature and Film in Transition*, ed. Willy Riemer (Riverside: Ariadne, 2000), 174.

40. Jonathan Beller, "Capital/Cinema," in *Deleuze and Guattari: New Mappings in Politics, Philosophy and Culture*, ed. Eleanor Kaufman and Kevin Jon Heller (Minneapolis: University of Minnesota Press, 1998), 92.

41. See Steven Shaviro's insightful piece on *Hidden* and the question of white guilt as a self-fulfillment devoid of any political use. "*Caché*," Steven Shaviro's personal blog (The Pinocchio Theory), last modified February 14, 2006, accessed September 24, 2011. http://www.shaviro.com/Blog/?p=476.

42. Maurice Halbwachs, *The Causes of Suicide* (London: Routledge and Kegan Paul, 1978), 300.

43. Halbwachs, *The Causes of Suicide*, 300.

44. Deleuze in Jean Ma, "Discordant Desires, Violent Refrains: La Pianiste," *Grey Room* 28 (Summer 2007): 17.

45. Ma, "Discordant Desires, Violent Refrains," 18.

46. Jean-Paul Sartre, *Being and Nothingness*, trans. Hazel E. Barnes (New York: Washington Square Press, 1956), 492.

47. Sartre, *Being and Nothingness*, 518.

48. Sartre, *Being and Nothingness*, 529.

49. Sartre, *Being and Nothingness*, 531. Original emphasis.

50. Paul Gilroy, "Shooting Crabs in a Barrel," *Screen* 48, no. 2 (Summer 2007): 234.

51. For the video in French see "Les lascars: Cigarette," accessed August 21, 2011. http://www.youtube.com/watch?v=_pmdbXGT1jg.

52. See Balibar's discussion on the hierarchical regime of security and threat in Europe, podcast of seminar titled "Racism, Migration and Citizenship in Europe" (University of London, Goldsmiths College), August 5, 2007, accessed Oc-

tober 10, 2011. http://www.darkmatter101.org/site/2007/08/05/racisms-migration-citizenship-in-europe/.

53. Anne Donadey, "'Une certaine idée de la France': The Algeria Syndrome and Struggles over 'French' Identity," in *Identity Papers: Contested Nationhood in Twentieth-Century France*, ed. Steven Ungar and Tom Conley (Minneapolis: University of Minnesota Press, 1996), 221.

54. See Schneider for an insightful discussion on the tight historical connection between police violence and riots in the *banlieues*. Cathy Lisa Schneider, "Police Power and Race Riots in Paris," *Politics and Society* 36, no. 1 (March 2008): 133–59.

55. Clifford Rosenberg, *Policing Paris: The Origins of Modern Immigration Control between Wars* (Ithaca, NY: Cornell University Press, 2006).

56. For Les indigènes de la république's call to action in translation, "A Call to Action: 'We Are the Natives of the Republic!,' January 18, 2005," trans. Florence Bernault, in Tshimanga, Gondola, and Bloom, *Frenchness and the African Diaspora*, 277–81. For more information on the reactions against Les indigènes de la république see Florence Bernault, "Colonial Syndrome: French Modern and the Deceptions of History," in *Frenchness and the African Diaspora*, 120–45.

57. Les indigènes de la république, "A Call to Action," 277.

58. Paul Gormley, *The New-Brutality Film: Race and Affect in Contemporary Hollywood Cinema* (Bristol: Intellect, 2005), 30–31.

59. In the film, Georges accuses Majid of terrorizing his family.

60. Brown, *States of Injury*, 76.

61. While forming the Mandelkern commission that investigated the October 1961 events, the interior minister of the Socialist Party, Jean-Pierre Chevènement, declared that he was "fully ready to try to get the facts about (the repression of the October 17th, 1961 protests) in accordance with the duty of memory." The resulting report was not satisfactory, as some archives remained closed, and perpetrators were not brought to justice. Charles Forsdick, "'Direction les oubliettes de l'histoire': Witnessing the Past in the Contemporary French Polar," *French Cultural Studies* 12, no. 3 (2001): 345.

Chapter 3

1. Ali Behdad, *A Forgetful Nation: On Immigration and Cultural Identity in the United States* (Durham: Duke University Press, 2005), 144.

2. Penelope Papailias, "'Money of *Kurbet* Is Money of Blood': The Making of a 'Hero' of Migration at the Greek-Albanian Border," *Journal of Ethnic and Migration Studies* 29, no. 6 (2003): 1059–78.

3. "World/Europe: Two Killed in Bus Ambush," *BBC News*, May 29, 1999, accessed June 12, 2011. http://news.bbc.co.uk/2/hi/europe/355846.stm.

4. Georges Karyotis and Stratos Patrikios, "Religion, Securitization and Anti-Immigration Attitudes: The Case of Greece," Journal of Peace Research 47, no. 1 (2010), 47. Also as mentioned in the introduction, Prime Minister Kostas Karamanlis attributed the responsibility for inciting the December 2008 riots in Athens to illegal migrants as well as the extreme Left. "Κώστας Καραμανλής: «Κλείνετε το μάτι στους κουκουλοφόρους», *H Kathimerini*, April 9, 2009, accessed May 10, 2011. http://news.kathimerini.gr/4dcgi/_w_ articles_

politics_2_09/04/2009_310488. During the riots the mainstream Greek media depicted all migrant participation negatively, as looters, outlaws, and criminals, scapegoats for the worst kinds of violence. Kalyvas, "An Anomaly?"

5. Albanians constitute the highest number of migrants in Greece. For a history of conflicts between Greece and Albania and the bases of Albanian discrimination in Greece see Rodanthi Tzanelli, "'Not My Flag!' Citizenship and Nationhood in the Margins of Europe (Greece, October 2000/2003)," *Ethnic and Racial Studies* 29, no. 1 (2006): 27–49.

6. Giorgos Hatzios and Kostas Kantouris, "Πέρασε στην Αλβανία ο κακοποιός με τους ομήρους," *Ta Nea*, May 29, 1999, accessed April 19, 2011. http://www.tanea.gr/news/greece/article/4072240/?iid=2. Unless otherwise stated, translations from Greek are mine.

7. "Hijacker Seizes Bus for 350-mile Joyride," *The Herald: Scotland on Sunday*, May 29, 1999, accessed June 15, 2011, http://www.heraldscotland.com/sport/spl/aberdeen/hijacker-seizes-bus-for-350-mile-joyride-1.289161, and "Simitis says Greece has lowest crime rate in EU," Athens News Agency, June, 1, 1999, accessed June 19, 2011, http://www.hri.org/news/greek/apeen/1999/99-06-01.apeen.html.

8. In his critique of the hierarchical regimes of representation, Jacques Rancière states that for certain populations of the world fiction is considered as "luxury": "in the dominant regime of representation, documentary is for the Palestinians, that is to say that they can only offer the bodies of their victims to the gaze of news cameras or to the compassionate gaze at their suffering. That is, the world is divided between those who can and those who cannot afford the luxury of playing with words and images." For further discussion on this see the introduction and the conclusion. Jacques Rancière, Fulvia Carnevale, and John Kelsey, "Art of the Possible: Fulvia Carnevale and John Kelsey in Conversation with Jacques Rancière," *Artforum*, March 2007, accessed April 12, 2013. http://www.egs.edu/faculty/jacques-ranciere/articles/art-of-the-possible/.

9. "Θα παιχθεί αύριο;" *Eleftherotipia*, March 3, 2005, accessed June 20, 2011. http://archive.enet.gr/online/online_ text/c=113,dt=03.03.2005,id=36885080.

10. Statistics in "Κινηματογράφος / Κωνσταντίνος Γιάνναρης: Παραμένει αμετανόητος," *H Kathimerini*, December 31, 2005, accessed May 1, 2011. http://www.kathimerini.gr/237987/article/politismos/arxeio-politismoy/kinhmatografos–kwnstantinos-giannarhs. The tone of irony with which the *H Kathimerini* article refers to Greek spectators' reaction to the film and the director's choice of an Albanian protagonist is unmistakable: "Constantinos Giannaris is unrepentant. In his most recent film project ('Welcome Aboard' is its title) he 'explores the confines of our tolerance.' But hasn't he already tried that? When *Hostage* came out—in the spring of 2005—with 11,000 tickets, was it not a 'test drive' of Greek society, whether it 'withstands' an Albanian bus-pirate as the central hero of the film?" A further proof for the general discontent that the director's ruminations on migration through the eyes and acts of migrant heroes create, it took two years for the aforementioned film (under the title of *Men at Sea*) to be released in Greece after its premier in Berlin film festival in 2011.

11. *Hostage* official website, last accessed May 2009. http://www.hostage.gr/forum.php. The website is currently down.

12. Katerina Zacharia, "'Reel' Hellenisms: Perceptions of Greece in Greek Cinema," in *Hellenisms: Culture, Identity, and Ethnicity from Antiquity to Modernity*, ed. Katerina Zacharia (Aldershot: Ashgate, 2008), 325.

13. Wendy Everett, "Re-framing the Fingerprints: A Short Survey of European Film," in *European Identity in Cinema*, ed. Wendy Everett (Bristol: Intellect, 2005), 26.

14. Maria Katsounaki, "Ξένος, ανάμεσα σε τιμή και θάνατο," *H Kathimerini*, February 13, 2005, accessed June 15, 2011. http://www.kathimerini.gr/209084/article/politismos/arxeio-politismoy/3enos-anamesa-se-timh-kai-8anato.

15. During the shooting of *Suspended Step of the Stork* a far-right extremist Orthodox priest, Augustinos Kandiotis, organized demonstrations against Angelopoulos and his crew and excommunicated them for making a film that depicts Greek-Albanian border in an "unpatriotic" manner, claiming: "[People] have died to safeguard this border." In Wendy Everett, "'Between Here and There, Between Then and Now': The Theme of Border Crossing in the Films of Theo Angelopoulos," in *Border Crossings*, ed. Peter Wagstaff (Oxford: Peter Lang, 2004), 67.

16. Papailias, "Money of *Kurbet*," suggests that sociological research in Greece confronts figures of criminality with stories of honest Albanian workers in works such as Eleni Syrigou-Rigou, ed., *Conversations with Lida: An Albanian Woman Migrant Speaks about Her Life* (Athens: Ekdoseis Anoihta Sinora, 2000). In Germany, *Literatur der Betroffenheit* (literature of the affected) features the figure of noble and honest Turkish worker, while liberal German press focuses on figures of "successful integration" such as Cem Özdemir, the co-chairman of the German Green Party.

17. Jean-Marie Le Pen quoted in Rogers Brubaker, *Citizenship and Nationhood in France and Germany* (Cambridge, MA: Harvard University Press, 1992), 144.

18. Kay Warren, "Violence in Anthropology," *International Encyclopedia of Social and Behavioral Sciences* (London: Elsevier, 2002), 16205.

19. Stuart Hall, "The Spectacle of the 'Other,'" in *Representation: Cultural Representations and Signifying Practices*, ed. Stuart Hall (London: Sage, 1997), 274.

20. Hall, "The Spectacle of the 'Other,'" 274.

21. Gkazment Kaplani, "Θέλω να σκάψω την ανασφάλειά μας," *Ta Nea*, December 4, 2004, 12.

22. Keith Beattie, *Documentary Screens: Non-fiction Film and Television* (New York: Palgrave Macmillan, 2004), 19.

23. Elaine Scarry, *The Body in Pain: The Making and Unmaking of the World* (New York: Oxford University Press, 1985), 9.

24. Tzanelli, "'Not My Flag!'" 40.

25. Raymond Williams, *Modern Tragedy* (Stanford: Stanford University Press, 1966), 55–56.

26. Williams, *Modern Tragedy*, 49.

27. Williams, *Modern Tragedy*, 53.

28. Many thanks to Eleftheria Astrinaki for bringing this arc in the film to my attention.

29. Giannaris's depiction of this contractual relationship between Greek and Albanian police is not grounded on documented proof, yet the film's evoking of

the possibility itself opens a discussion of the regional power politics and neoliberal economics in the post–Cold War context, discussed further below.

30. Aihwa Ong, "The Gender and Labor Politics of Post-modernity," *Annual Review of Anthropology* 20 (1991): 279–309.

31. Abdelmalek Sayad, *The Suffering of the Immigrant,* trans. David Macey (Malden: Polity Press, 2004), 1–3.

32. Trajko Slaveski and Pece Nedanovski, "Foreign Direct Investment in the Balkans: The Case of Albania, FYROM, and Bulgaria," *Eastern European Economics* 40, no. 4 (2002): 83–99.

33. Michel Chossudovsky, "The Criminalization of Albania," in *Masters of the Universe? NATO's Balkan Crusade,* ed. Tariq Ali (New York: Verso, 2000), 302.

34. Out of the total amount of $458 million Italy's investment was about $200 million with six hundred companies, and Greece followed Italy with about $100 million with three hundred companies. Slaveski and Nedanovski, "Foreign Direct Investment," 90–91.

35. Chossudovsky, "The Criminalization of Albania."

36. Maria Vidali, "Living in a Policy Vacuum: The Plight of Albanian Immigrants in Greece," *Central Europe Review* 1, no. 21 (1999): 104.

37. Dina Iordanova, "Displaced? Shifting Politics of Place and Itinerary in International Cinema," *Senses of Cinema* 14 (2001). http://sensesofcinema.com/2001/feature-articles/displaced/.

38. Mazierska and Rascaroli, *Crossing New Europe.*

39. Jack Sargeant and Stephanie Watson, *Lost Highways: An Illustrated History of Road Movies* (London: Creation, 1999), 13–14.

40. Loshitsky, *Screening Strangers.*

41. In *40 Square Meters of Germany,* the source of suffocation emerges from the supposedly paternalistic family structure of the minorities and only secondarily from the diasporic condition. This gendered element will be discussed further in the next chapter.

42. Hamid Naficy, "Chronotopes of Life in Exile: Claustrophobie, Contemporaneity," in *An Accented Cinema,* 188–222.

43. Dina Iordanova, *Cinema of Flames: Balkan Film, Culture and the Media* (London: British Film Institute, 2001), 66.

44. Silvana Silvestri, "A Skein of Reversals: The Films of Gianni Amelio," *New Left Review* 10 (2001): 128.

45. Interview in Angela Baldassarre, *The Great Dictators: Interviews with Filmmakers of Italian Descent* (Toronto: Guernica, 1999). The way Amelio discusses his visit to Albania is quite different from how Giannaris discusses his experience in Albania: "In my visit to Albania I felt that as a Greek they approached me with a lot of distrust. When they alluded to bad experiences in Greece they were often talking about rape. As if negative experience gained the standard meaning of sexual harassment." *Ta Nea,* December 4, 2004. Both directors seem to reflect their respective experiences on the screen.

46. It is not a coincidence that cinemascope is the typical format of the American Western genre where "the frontier represented as lack of civilization and law, as well as domesticity," Mazierska and Rascaroli, *Crossing New Europe,* 152.

47. Mazierska and Rascaroli, *Crossing New Europe,* 152.

48. Katherine Fleming, "Orientalism, the Balkans, and Balkan Historiography," *American Historical Review* 105, no. 4 (2000): 1226.

49. Maria Todorova, *Imagining the Balkans* (New York: Oxford University Press, 1997), 36.

50. Rodica Diaconescu-Blumenfeld, "The Desire of the Other: Balkan Dystopia in Western European Cinema," in *Moving Pictures, Migrating Identities*, ed. Eva Rueschmann (Jackson: University Press of Mississippi, 2003), 100.

51. Diaconescu-Blumenfeld, "The Desire of the Other," 95.

52. Ien Ang, "Hegemony-in-Trouble: Nostalgia and the Ideology of the Impossible in European Cinema," in *Screening Europe: Image and Identity in Contemporary European Cinema*, ed. Duncan Petrie (London: BFI Publishing, 1992), 28.

53. Diaconescu-Blumenfeld, "The Desire of the Other," 95.

54. Chow, *Primitive Passions.*

55. Chow, *Primitive Passions*, 27–28.

56. Rancière, Carnevale, and Kelsey, "Art of the Possible."

57. Marco Abel, *Violent Affect: Literature, Cinema and Critique after Representation* (Lincoln: University of Nebraska Press, 2009), xiii.

58. Bhikhu Parekh, "The Liberal Discourse on Violence," in *Selves, People, and Persons: What Does It Mean to Be a Self?*, ed. Leroy S. Rouner (Notre Dame: University of Notre Dame Press, 1992), 125.

59. For an extended discussion on the history of the liberal position on violence and on the human right to be protected from physical violence see the Calas affair. In 1762 France was shaken by the debates on the death of French Protestant Jean Calas during judicial torture. Voltaire took up the cause and published a pamphlet "Treatise on Tolerance on the Occasion of the Death of Jean Calas." Voltaire's position was not so much defending religious tolerance as a human right, but standing against the use of judicial torture in protection of bodily integrity. See details in Lynn Hunt, *Inventing Human Rights: A History* (New York: W.W. Norton, 2007). I am grateful to Kenneth Haynes for bringing this historical background of the physical conceptualization of violence to my attention.

60. Žižek, *Violence.*

Chapter 4

1. Susanne Beyer and Henryk M. Broder, "Sie verglühen vor Leidenschaft: Gespräch mit Seyran Ates," *Der Spiegel*, October 12, 2009, accessed April 20, 2012. http://www.spiegel.de/spiegel/print/d-67282871.html. Unless otherwise stated, translations from German are mine.

2. Linda Williams's argument on the connection between melodramatic and racial legibility of victims and villains will be discussed further in the following pages of this chapter. Williams, *Playing the Race Card.*

3. Jane Shattuc, "Having a Good Cry over *The Color Purple*," in *Melodrama: Stage, Picture, Screen*, ed. Jacky Bratton, Jim Cook, and Christine Gledhill (Bloomington: Indiana University Press, 1994), 147–56.

4. Ayhan Sürücü in the documentary film *Verlorene Ehre: Der Irrweg der Familie Sürücü* (Lost Honor: The Folly of the Sürücü Family) by Matthias Deiß and Jo Goll, quoted in Barbara Hans's review of the documentary, "Murder in Ber-

lin: The Lost Honor of the Sürücü Family," *Der Spiegel Online International*, July 27, 2011, accessed May 2, 2012. http://www.spiegel.de/international/germany/murder-in-berlin-the-lost-honor-of-the-sueruecue-family-a-777109.html.

5. Society of Cinema and Media Studies, 2012 Annual Meeting program, 131.

6. Katherine Ewing quoted in "Violence against Women: A New Direction?" Inside Islam: Dialogues and Debates, last modified May 1, 2010, accessed May 5, 2011. http://insideislam.wisc.edu/europe.html.

7. Weber, "Regime of Gender Violence," 66.

8. For an extended discussion on the comparison of the media visibility of Sürücü murder versus the lack of visibility of Sherbini case see Weber, "Regime of Gender Violence."

9. Christine Huth-Hildebrandt, "Das Bild von der Migrantin—eine Folie zur Polarisierung der Debatte um Migration?" in *Gender und soziale Praxis*, ed. Margit Gottert and Karin Walser (Königstein: Taunus, 2001), 144–69.

10. Sara Lennox, "Divided Feminism: Women, Racism and German National Identity," *German Studies Review* 18 (1995): 481–502.

11. In Beverly M. Weber, "Headscarves and Mini-Skirts," PhD diss., University of Massachusetts, Amherst, 2006. Also, Kai Hafez's research on the representation of Islam in German media reveals that terrorism and domestic violence in Muslim countries constitute nearly 80 percent of the German news on Islam. Hence, he suggests that German media's agenda creates an "enlightened Islamophobia." Kia Hafez, "Images of Middle East and Islam in German Media: A Reappraisal," in *Mutual Misunderstandings? Muslims and Islam in the European Media / Europe in the Media of Muslim Majority Countries*, ed. Kerem Öktem and Reem Abou-El-Fadl (Oxford: European Studies Center, 2009), 29–52.

12. For a larger discussion on the topic see Deniz Göktürk's insightful article, "Turkish Women on German Streets: Closure and Exposure in Transnational Cinema," in *Space in European Cinema*, ed. Myrto Konstantarakos (Exeter: Intellect, 2000), 64–76.

13. Leslie Adelson uses "paradigm of victimology" as a term to describe the representation of *Gastarbeiter* or the migrant worker, generating liberal and leftist sympathies due to his working-class condition and supposed muteness / lack of language skills. Leslie Adelson, *The Turkish Turn in Contemporary German Literature: Toward a New Critical Grammar of Migration* (New York: Palgrave Macmillan, 2005).

14. See Beverly Weber on these autobiographies: "Freedom from Violence, Freedom to Make the World: Muslim Women's Memoirs, Gendered Violence, and Voices for Change in Germany," *Women in German Yearbook* 25 (2009): 199–222.

15. Tom Cheesman, *Novels of Turkish German Settlement: Cosmopolite Fictions* (Rochester: Camden House, 2007), 114.

16. Katherine Ewing, *Stolen Honor: Stigmatizing Muslim Men in Berlin* (Stanford: Stanford University Press, 2008).

17. "From Bare to Bear for Ex-Porn Queen," *Deutsche Welle*, February 18, 2004, accessed May 8, 2012. http://www.dw.de/from-bare-to-bear-for-ex-porn-queen/a-1118125.

18. Drawing parallels between the life of movie star and that of the charac-

ter she reenacts is not uncommon in melodrama. See Lucy Fischer's essay on Lana Turner, "Three-Way Mirror: Imitation of Life," in *Imitation of Life*, ed. Lucy Fischer (New Brunswick: Rutgers University Press, 1991).

19. Rüdiger Suchsland, "Interview with Fatih Akin: 'Ich bin wirklich davon ausgegangen,'" *artechock*, March 11, 2004, accessed March 12, 2012. http://www.artechock.de/film/text/interview/a/Akin_2004.htm.

20. Karin Lorssen, "Where Have All the Guest Workers Gone? Transcultural Role-Play and Performative Identities in Fatih Akın's *Gegen die Wand* (2004)," in *Finding the Foreign*, ed. Robert Schechtman and Suin Roberts (Newcastle: Cambridge Scholars Publishing, 2007), 13–32.

21. Thomas Elsaesser, "Double Occupancy and Small Adjustments: Space, Place and Identity in European Cinema" in *European Cinema*, 108-131 ; and for a deeper analysis of the film Elsaesser, "Politics, Multiculturalism and the Ethical Turn: The Cinema of Fatih Akın," in *Just Images: Ethics and the Cinematic*, ed. B. Hagen, S. Meiri, R. Yosef, and A. Zanger (Newcastle: Cambridge Scholars, 2011), 1–19.

22. Necia Chronister, "Topographies of Sexuality: Space, Movement, and Gender in German Literature and Film since 1989," PhD diss. Washington University in St. Louis, 2011.

23. Daniela Berghahn, "No Place Like Home? Or Impossible Homecomings in the Films of Fatih Akın," *New Cinemas* 4, no. 3 (2006): 141–57.

24. Explored by Daniela Berghahn, "'Seeing Everything with Different Eyes': The Diasporic Optic of Fatih Akın's *Head-On*," in Cooke and Homewood, *New Directions in German Cinema*, 239–56; Asuman Suner, "Dark Passion: Fatih Akın's *Head On*," *Sight and Sound* 15, no. 3 (March 2005): 18–21; and Mine Eren, "Cosmopolitan Filmmaking: Fatih Akın's *In July* and *Head-On*," in *Turkish German Cinema in the New Millennium: Site, Sounds, and Screens*, ed. Sabine Hake and Barbara Mennel (Oxford: Berghahn, 2012), 175–86.

25. Feridun Zaimoğlu, "Sex, Drogen und die Schocks der Moderne," in *Gegen die Wand: Das Buch zum Film* (Cologne: Kiepenheuer Witsch, 2004), 209–14.

26. Berghahn, "Seeing Everything with Different Eyes," 239.

27. Berna Gueneli, "Challenging European Borders: Fatih Akın's *Auteurist* Visions of Europe," PhD diss., University of Texas at Austin, 2011.

28. Deniz Göktürk, "Turkish Delight—German Flight: Migrant Identities in Transnational Cinema," Transnational Communities—Working Paper Series, and Economic and Social Council Research Program, University of Oxford, January 1999, 6, accessed May 5, 2012. http://www.transcomm.ox.ac.uk/working%20papers/mediated.pdf.

29. Berghahn and Sternberg, "Locating Migrant and Diasporic Cinema," 15.

30. Rey Chow, *The Protestant Ethnic and the Spirit of Capitalism* (New York: Columbia University Press, 2002), 130.

31. Higbee and Lim, in their inquiry into the prospects and pitfalls of transnational cinema, talk about a similar loophole. For Higbee and Lim one of the weaknesses of the label "transnational cinema" is in the way "it risks celebrating the supranational flow or transnational exchange of peoples, images and cultures at the expense of specific cultural, historical or ideological context in which these exchanges take place." Will Higbee and Song Hwee Lim, "Concepts

of Transnational Cinema: Towards a Critical Transnationalism in Film Studies," *Transnational Cinemas* 1, no. 1 (2010): 11.

32. Mahmut Mutman, "Up Against the Wall of the Signifier: *Gegen die Wand*," in *Shifting Landscapes: Film and Media in the European Context*, ed. Miyase Christensen and Nezih Erdoğan (Newcastle: Cambridge Scholars Publishing, 2008), 318.

33. For an insightful review of the generic conventions of the melodramatic mode that traces their emergence in European theater of the eighteenth and nineteenth centuries and crystallization in Douglas Sirk's films, see John Mercer and Martin Shingler, *Melodrama: Genre, Style, Sensibility* (London: Wallflower, 2004). It goes without saying that the definition of melodrama changes through time and place, yet Hollywood of the 1940s and 1950s provides a palate of conventions that gives melodramas a global legibility that many directors, including Akın in *Head-On*, draw from.

34. Deniz Göktürk, "Sound Bridges: Transnational Mobility as Ironic Melodrama," in Berghahn and Sternberg, *European Cinema in Motion*, 217. A similar argument was made with regard to *Kebab Connection*, the use of comedy within the film as enabling transnational legibility: "Indeed, the mixture of genres the film references such as kung-fu, gangster, comedy and melodrama might actually be said to add to its transnational identity, matching the film's overall theme of multiculturalism." Victoria Fincham, "Violence, Sexuality and the Family: Identity 'Within and Beyond Turkish-German Parameters' in Fatih Akın's *Gegen die Wand*, Kutluğ Ataman's *Lola+Bilidikid* and Anno Saul's *Kebab Connection*," *German as Foreign Language Journal* 1 (2008): 66, accessed May 10, 2012. http://www.gfl-journal.de/1-2008/fincham.pdf.

35. Thomas Elsaesser, "Tales of Sound and Fury," in *Film Theory and Criticism*, ed. G. Mast, M. Cohen, and L. Braudy (New York: Oxford University Press, 1992), 244–58.

36. Peter Brooks, *The Melodramatic Imagination: Balzac, Henry James, Melodrama, and the Mode of Excess* (New Haven: Yale University Press, 1995).

37. Christine Gledhill, "The Melodramatic Field: An Investigation," in *Home Is Where the Heart Is: Studies in Melodrama and the Woman's Film* (London: BFI Publishing, 1987), 33.

38. Williams, *Playing the Race Card*, 344.

39. We can add to this list the 2012 Trayvon Martin murder by George Zimmerman. The depiction of this murder reveals the Manichaean nature of the representation of African-American men in the US media. While Zimmerman considered Martin a threat and justified his shooting through self-defense and stand-your-ground law, the news on the event emphasized the innocent youth of the victim by repeated declaration of the fact that he was shot while walking back from the supermarket with a packet of candies in his pocket.

40. Williams, *Playing the Race Card*, xiv.

41. Although a highly emotional mode, melodrama is rarely valued for its affective potential. The Marxist tradition of melodrama studies that emerged in the 1970s with the analyses of Douglas Sirk's films has valued melodrama's affective excess only in its potential for stimulating an ideological critique. The contrast between the content and the form that colors the mise-en-scène be-

comes the alienating factor that resists the complacent scenarios of the Hollywood studio system. Jane Shattuc argues for the need to explore the power of affect in melodramas instead of seeing the affective excess as a path to an enlightened ideological contradiction. Shattuc points out the elitist implications of this theoretical framework that separates the intellectuals who can discern the alienation and popular viewers who are drawn into the film world. The reading of melodramatic excess as ideological contradiction enforces the dichotomy of the rational intellectual spectator versus the emotional masses. Shattuc, "Having a Good Cry."

42. Marks, *Skin of the Film*, 190.

43. That having been said, such criticism shall by no means be disregarded. Senta Siewert's article on sound in *Head-On* insightfully applies Thomas Elsaesser's concept of "double occupancy" on Akın's hybrid music-scape. Siewert argues that mixing of different genres of music in *Head-On* creates a hybrid space of "double occupancy," a "sound bridge [that] transcends cultural borders and reveals a state of double occupancy" (200). Senta Siewert, "Soundtracks of Double Occupancy: Sampling Sounds and Cultures in Fatih Akın's *Head On*," in *Mind the Screen: Media Concepts according to Thomas Elsaesser*, ed. Jaap Kooijman, Patricia Pisters, and Wanda Strauven (Chicago: University of Chicago Press, 2008), 198–208.

44. Michel Chion, "The Audiovisual Contract: Projections of Sound on Image," in *Audio-Vision: Sound on Screen* (New York: Columbia University Press, 1994), 1–24.

45. Taking the wall as a literal reference is especially difficult when one considers the dual vocabulary for "wall" in German. While *die Wand* implies a wall that separates private from public space, *die Mauer* means a stand-alone fortification wall, and it is the latter that is used to name the Berlin Wall: *die Berliner Mauer*. I thank Luis Calva Salgado for reminding me of this crucial difference.

46. Karen Beckman, *Crash: Cinema and the Politics of Speed and Stasis* (Durham: Duke University Press, 2010), 8.

47. In this category Naficy includes Turkish films in Germany such as the aforementioned Tevfik Başer film *40 Square Meters of Germany*, the narrative of Turkish minority women's containment within a patriarchal household in Germany. In Naficy's description, "For many exiles, the separation from homeland, the loss of status, language, culture, and family, and the fear of the hostile host society may constitute sufficiently 'excessive adverse life events; to lead us to expect to see in their lives and their films agoraphobic and claustrophobic spatiality." Naficy, *An Accented Cinema*, 189.

48. Rey Chow, "Postcolonial Visibilities: Questions Inspired by Deleuze's Method," in *Entanglements, or Transmedial Thinking about Capture* (Durham: Duke University Press, 2012), 151–68. Chow uses "visibility" in the Foucauldian sense, being entrapped into a certain bound of institutional visibility. Although it is beyond the scope of this chapter, it would be interesting to do a Foucauldian reading of *Head-On* considering that the psychiatric clinic, the nuclear family, and the prison are at the center of the film, shaping the crucial events that mark changes in the characters' lives. For more on visibility, power, ethnicity, and Foucault see Chow, "Postcolonial Visibilities."

49. Chow, "Postcolonial Visibilities," 154.

50. Rey Chow, *Sentimental Fabulations, Contemporary Chinese Films: Attachment in the Age of Global Visibility* (New York: Columbia University Press, 2007), 11.

51. Michel Chion, *The Voice in Cinema* (New York: Columbia University Press, 1999).

52. In the original script this dialogue is longer and punctuated with a clear political message. In the script, the two men's conversation involves conspiracy theories about 9/11: that Bush is a friend of bin Laden and he arranged the terrorist attack and that Bush and his family are part of the Skulls and Bones, a secret society that also funded Hitler. This excessively long and politically forced part of the dialogue is truncated in the actual film, which allows the political critique to emerge in a subtler manner. *Gegen die Wand.*

53. Michel Chion, "Lines and Points: Horizontal and Vertical Perspectives on Audiovisual Relations," in *Audio-Vision: Sound on Screen* (New York: Columbia University Press, 1994), 38.

54. Lauren Berlant, "Introduction: Compassion (and Withholding)," in *Compassion: The Culture and Politics of an Emotion* (New York: Routledge, 2004), 4.

55. The chapter on Michael Haneke's *Hidden* extensively discussed the minority character's (Majid's) visceral suicide in front of the camera and the film's protagonist. The raw affect enhances the thrill, but Majid's passive-aggressive death has no meaning beyond the imposition of guilt on the protagonist and the spectator; it is a "special effect" that ends up making the Other even more inaccessible than he already was. In *Hidden,* the excessive self-inflicted violence has a different effect on the narrative and character development. In *Head-On,* the suicidal violence does not eliminate the minority character; it marks her ongoing search for an identity beyond the clichéd frames offered to her. Whether victimhood as driving force for the identitarian search is a successful strategy or not is debatable in itself and will be discussed in the conclusion of this chapter.

56. Deleuze, *Cinema 2,* 141.

57. Jane Shattuc, *Television, Tabloids, and Tears: Fassbinder and Popular Culture* (Minneapolis: University of Minnesota Press, 1995), 119. In Fassbinder's *Bitter Tears of Petra von Kant* the social critique is omnipresent (in the relationship of higher- and lower-class characters, that of Petra von Kant with her maid Marlene and with her lover Karin), yet Petra's self-victimization removes the clear-cut villain-bourgeoisie/victim–lower class dichotomy.

58. The fluidity of gender or androgyny that is later introduced to the narrative when Sibel goes to Istanbul also interferes with the moral legibility of gendered victim and victimizer dynamic.

59. Steven Shaviro, *The Cinematic Body* (Minneapolis: University of Minnesota Press, 1993), 52–53.

60. See Martin Seel on the aesthetics of violence and its haptic relationship with spectators of art and film, and readers of literature. Martin Seel, "Variations on Art and Violence," in *Aesthetics of Appearing* (Stanford: Stanford University Press, 2005), 186–206.

61. Beugnet, *Cinema and Sensation,* 74.

62. Senta Siewert observes that Akın frequently enhances the emotional power of *Head-On* by using diegetic soundtrack. Siewert, "Soundtracks of Double Occupancy."

63. Jennifer Barker, *The Tactile Eye: Touch and the Cinematic Experience* (Berkeley: University of California Press, 2009), 56.

64. Judith Butler, "Imitation and Gender Insubordination," in *The Lesbian and Gay Studies Reader*, ed. Henry Abelove (New York: Routledge, 1993), 313.

65. Butler, "Imitation and Gender Insubordination," 314.

66. El-Tayeb, *European Others*, 170.

67. Articulated in Siewert, "Soundtracks of Double Occupancy."

68. Rob Burns, "Turkish-German Cinema: From Cultural Resistance to Transnational Cinema?" in *German Cinema since Unification*, ed. David Clarke (London: Continuum, 2006), 127–41.

69. Wendy Mitchell, "Going to Extremes: Fatih Akın on His Turkish-German Love Story *Head-On*," *Indiewire*, January 19, 2005, accessed May 20, 2012. http://www.indiewire.com/article/going_to_extremes_fatih_akin_on_his_turkish-german_love_story_head-on.

70. Eleanora Volodina, "Interview with Fatih Akın," *Deutsche Welle Culture*, February 14, 2004, accessed May 11, 2012. http://www.dw.de/interview-with-fatih-akin/a-1114779.

71. See, for color consciousness, K. Anthony Appiah and Amy Gutmann, *Color Conscious: The Political Morality of Race* (Princeton: Princeton University Press, 1998).

72. Here it would be important to note the transnational form of "ethnic" in Akin's description of his cinema. When asked, Akın rejects any connection of his cinema with Fassbinder's, pointing out that Fassbinder's background in theater and the latter's working methods make them different. Instead, he associates his filmmaking with that of Spike Lee and Martin Scorsese, explaining that these directors were able to move outside the Italian-American and African-American ethnic niche in their filmmaking. Amin Farzanefar, "Film ist Punk: Interview mit dem Regisseur Fatih Akın," *IFA Kultur Austausch Online*, March 2004, accessed September 10, 2012, http://cms.ifa.de/index.php?id=akin&type=98&L=; Suchsland, "Interview mit Fatih Akın"; Lars-Olav Beier and Matthias Matussek, "From Istanbul to New York: Spiegel Interview with Director Fatih Akın," *Spiegel Online International*, September 28, 2007, accessed March 20, 2012, http://www.spiegel.de/international/zeitgeist/ spiegel-interview-with-director-fatih-Akın-from-istanbul-to-new-york-a-508521.html.

73. Alan Riding, "On Screen, Tackling Europe's New Reality," *New York Times*, January 18, 2005, accessed June 5, 2014. http://www.nytimes.com/2005/01/18/movies/18head.html?_r=0.

74. Sam Adams, "Interview: Director Fatih Akin," *AV Club*, August 20, 2010, accessed June 7, 2014. http://www.avclub.com/article/director-fatih-akin-44341.

75. Screenwriter Hatice Ayten suggests that the depiction of Sibel's life in Istanbul runs the risk of undermining the initial deconstruction of female clichés in the streets of Hamburg. Hatice Ayten, "Was Sie schon immer über die Türken wissen wollten," *epd medien*, April 24, 2004, 3–6. Mine Eren also tackles the question of how to interpret "Akın's image of the so-called 'oppressed Muslim woman'" and asks, "is there perhaps a specific meaning behind Akın's presentation of violence, female subjectivity, and subjectivity, other than the intention to shock viewers?" Mine Eren, "Breaking the Stigma? The Anti-heroine

in Fatih Akın's Head-On," in *Muslim Women, Transnational Feminism and the Ethics of Pedagogy: Contested Imaginaries in Post-9/11 Cultural Practice,* ed. Lisa Taylor and Jasmin Zine (New York: Routledge, 2014), 83. I am very thankful to Mine Eren for sharing with me the manuscript of her article before it was published.

Epilogue

1. Jacques Rancière, "The Cause of the Other," *Parallax* 4 (1998): 28.

2. Lauren Berlant, "Affect in the End of Times: Conversation with Lauren Berlant," *Qui Parle: Critical Humanities and Social Sciences* 20, no. 2 (2012): 82.

3. Etienne Balibar, "Some Questions on Politics and Violence," *Assemblage* 20 (April 1993): 12–13, Balibar, "Violence and Civility: On the Limits of Political Anthropology," *differences* 20, nos. 2–3 (2009): 9–35.

4. Simon Critchley, *Infinitely Demanding: Ethics of Commitment, Politics of Resistance* (London: Verso, 2007).

5. Judith Butler, *Precarious Life: The Powers of Mourning and Violence* (London: Verso, 2006), xii.

6. Zizek, *Violence.*

7. Agamben, *Homo Sacer.*

8. Talal Asad, in his work on the Western fascination with suicide bombers, suggests that the contradiction between humanitarianism and "ruthlessness" in defense of security is a crucial constituent in the functioning of liberal thought and subject today: "on the one hand, there is the imperative to use any means necessary to defend the nation-state that constitutes one's worldly identity and defends one's health and security and, on the other hand, the obligation to revere all human life, to offer life in place of death to universal humanity; the first presupposes a capacity for ruthlessness, the second for kindness. The contradiction itself constitutes a particular kind of human subject whose functioning depends on the fact that the contradiction has to be continually worked through without ever being resolved." Talal Asad, *On Suicide Bombing* (New York: Columbia University Press, 2007), 88.

9. Phillip Cole, *Philosophies of Exclusion: Liberal Political Theory and Immigration* (Edinburgh: Edinburgh University Press, 2000).

10. Brown, *States of Injury,* 75.

11. Alain Badiou, *Ethics: An Essay on the Understanding of Evil,* trans. Peter Hallward (New York: Verso, 2001), 10.

12. Badiou, *Ethics,* 13.

13. Rancière, Carnevale, and Kelsey, "Art of the Possible."

Bibliography

ABC Australia. "At the Movies with Margaret and David: Children of Men." Last modified October 11, 2006, accessed March 29, 2013. http://www.abc.net.au/atthemovies/txt/s1756228.htm.

Abel, Marco. *Violent Affect: Literature, Cinema and Critique after Representation*. Lincoln: University of Nebraska Press, 2009.

Adams, Sam. "Interview: Fatih Akin." *AV Club*, August 20, 2010. Accessed June 7, 2014. http://www.avclub.com/article/director-fatih-akin-44341.

Adelson, Leslie. "Against Between: A Manifesto." In *Zafer Senocak: Contemporary German Writers*, edited by Tom Cheesman and Karin E. Yesilada, 130–43. Cardiff: University of Wales Press, 2003.

Adelson, Leslie. *The Turkish Turn in Contemporary German Literature: Toward a New Critical Grammar of Migration*. New York: Palgrave Macmillan, 2005.

Agamben, Giorgio. *Homo Sacer: Sovereign Power and Bare Life*. Translated by Daniel Heller-Roazen. Stanford: Stanford University Press, 1998.

Agustín, Laura María. *Sex at the Margins: Migration, Labour Markets and the Rescue Industry*. London: Zed Books, 2007.

Akin, Fatih. *Gegen die Wand: Das Buch zum Film*. Cologne: Kiepenheuer Witsch, 2004.

Ahmed, Sara. "Affective Economies." *Social Text* 22, no. 2 (Summer 2004): 117–39.

Ahmed, Sara. *The Cultural Politics of Emotion*. Edinburgh: Edinburgh University Press, 2004.

Altman, Rick. "A Semantic/Syntactic Approach to Film Genre." *Cinema Journal* 23, no. 3 (Spring 1984): 6–18.

Ang, Ien. "Hegemony-in-Trouble: Nostalgia and the Ideology of the Impossible in European Cinema." In *Screening Europe: Image and Identity in Contemporary European Cinema*, edited by Duncan Petrie, 21–31. London: BFI Publishing, 1992.

Appiah, K. Anthony, and Amy Gutmann. *Color Conscious: The Political Morality of Race*. Princeton: Princeton University Press, 1998.

Asad, Talal. *Formations of the Secular: Christianity, Islam, Modernity.* Stanford: Stanford University Press, 2003.

Asad, Talal. *On Suicide Bombing.* New York: Columbia University Press, 2007.

Asad, Talal, Judith Butler, Wendy Brown, and Saba Mahmood. *Is Critique Secular? Blasphemy, Injury, and Free Speech.* Berkeley: University of California Press, 2009.

Athens News Agency. "Simitis Says Greece Has Lowest Crime Rate in EU." June 1, 1999, accessed June 19, 2011. http://www.hri.org/news/greek/apeen/1999/99-06-01.apeen.html.

Austin, Guy. *Contemporary French Cinema.* Manchester: Manchester University Press, 1996.

Ayten, Hatice. "Was Sie schon immer über die Türken wissen wollten." *epd medien,* April 24, 2004, 3–6.

Badiou, Alain. *Being and Event.* Translated by Oliver Feltham. London: Continuum, 2005.

Badiou, Alain. *Ethics: An Essay on the Understanding of Evil.* Translated by Peter Hallward. New York: Verso, 2001.

Badiou, Alain. "Immediate Riot." In *The Rebirth of History,* translated by Gregory Elliott, 16–26. London: Verso, 2012.

Baishya, Anirban Kapil. "Trauma, Post-apocalyptic Science Fiction and the Posthuman." *Wide Screen* 3, no. 1 (June 2011): 1–25.

Baldassarre, Angela. *The Great Dictators: Interviews with Filmmakers of Italian Descent.* Toronto: Guernica, 1999.

Balibar, Etienne. *Politics and the Other Scene.* London: Verso, 2002.

Balibar, Etienne. "Racism, Migration and Citizenship in Europe" Seminar, University of London, Goldsmiths College, August 5, 2007, accessed October 10, 2011. http://www.darkmatter101.org/site/2007/08/05/racisms-migration-citizenship-in-europe/.

Balibar, Etienne. "Some Questions on Politics and Violence." *Assemblage* 20 (April 1993): 12–13.

Balibar, Etienne. "Uprising in the *Banlieues.*" *Constellations* 14, no. 1 (2007): 47–71.

Balibar, Etienne. "Violence and Civility: On the Limits of Political Anthropology." *Differences* 20, nos. 2–3 (2009): 9–35.

Balibar, Etienne. *We, the People of Europe? Reflections on Transnational Citizenship.* Princeton: Princeton University Press, 2003.

Balibar, Etienne, and Immanuel Wallerstein. *Race, Nation, Class: Ambiguous Identities.* London: Verso, 1991.

Barker, Jennifer. *The Tactile Eye: Touch and the Cinematic Experience.* Berkeley: University of California Press, 2009.

Bazin, André. "The Evolution of the Language of Cinema." In *What is Cinema?* translated by Hugh Gray, 23–40. Berkeley: University of California Press, 2004.

BBC News. "Anti-terror Searches Continuing." April 10, 2009, accessed December 20, 2012. http://news.bbc.co.uk/2/hi/uk_news/7993748.stm.

BBC News. "Tighter Rules for the UK Student Visas." March 22, 2011, accessed December 20, 2012. http://www.bbc.co.uk/news/education-12820645.

BBC News. "Tougher Rules to Stop Abuse of Student Visa System." February

7, 2010, accessed December 20, 2012. http://news.bbc.co.uk/2/hi/uk_news/8502640.stm.

BBC News. "Two Killed in Bus Ambush." May 29, 1999, accessed June 12, 2011. http://news.bbc.co.uk/2/hi/europe/355846.stm.

Beattie, Keith. *Documentary Screens: Non-fiction Film and Television.* New York: Palgrave Macmillan, 2004.

Beckman, Karen. *Crash: Cinema and the Politics of Speed and Stasis.* Durham: Duke University Press, 2010.

Behdad, Ali. *A Forgetful Nation: On Immigration and Cultural Identity in the United States.* Durham: Duke University Press, 2005.

Beier, Lars-Olav, and Matthias Matussek. "From Istanbul to New York: Spiegel Interview with Director Fatih Akin." *Spiegel Online International,* September 28, 2007, accessed March 20, 2012. http://www.spiegel.de/international/zeitgeist/spiegel-interview-with-director-fatih-akin-from-istanbul-to-new-york-a-508521.html.

Beller, Jonathan. "Capital/Cinema." In *Deleuze and Guattari: New Mappings in Politics, Philosophy and Culture,* edited by Eleanor Kaufman and Kevin Jon Heller, 77–95. Minneapolis: University of Minnesota Press, 1998.

Berger, John. *The Success and Failure of Picasso.* New York: Pantheon Books, 1965.

Berghahn, Daniela. "No Place Like Home? Or Impossible Homecomings in the Films of Fatih Akin." *New Cinemas* 4, no. 3 (2006): 141–57.

Berghahn, Daniela. "'Seeing Everything with Different Eyes': The Diasporic Optic of Fatih Akin's *Head-On.*" In *New Directions in German Cinema,* edited by Paul Cooke and Chris Homewood, 239–56. London: I.B. Tauris, 2011.

Berghahn, Daniela, and Claudia Sternberg. "Locating Migrant and Diasporic Cinema in Contemporary Europe." In *European Cinema in Motion: Migrant and Diasporic Film in Contemporary Europe,* edited by Daniela Berghahn and Claudia Sternberg, 12–49. New York: Palgrave Macmillan, 2010.

Berlant, Lauren. "Affect in the End of Times: Conversation with Lauren Berlant." *Qui Parle: Critical Humanities and Social Sciences* 20, no. 2 (2012): 71–89.

Berlant, Lauren. "America, 'Fat,' the Fetus." In *The Queen of America Goes to Washington City: Essays on Sex and Citizenship,* 83–144. Durham: Duke University Press, 1997.

Berlant, Lauren. *The Anatomy of National Fantasy: Hawthorne, Utopia and Everyday Life.* Chicago: University of Chicago Press, 1991.

Berlant, Lauren. "The Compulsion to Repeat Femininity." In *The Female Complaint: The Unfinished Business of Sentimentality in American Culture,* 233–64. Durham: Duke University Press, 2008.

Berlant, Lauren. *Cruel Optimism.* Durham: Duke University Press, 2011.

Berlant, Lauren. "Introduction: Compassion (and Withholding)." In *Compassion: The Culture and Politics of an Emotion,* edited by Lauren Berlant, 1–14. New York: Routledge, 2004.

Berlant, Lauren. "Intuitionists: History and the Affective Event." *American Literary History* 20, no. 4 (Winter 2008): 845–60.

Berlant, Lauren, and Dana Luciano. "Conversation: Lauren Berlant with Dana Luciano." *Social Text: Periscope,* January 13, 2013, accessed April 26, 2013. http://socialtextjournal.org/periscope_article/conversation-lauren-berlant-with-dana-luciano/.

Bernault, Florence. "Colonial Syndrome: French Modern and the Deceptions of History." In *Frenchness and the African Diaspora: Identity and Uprising in Contemporary France*, edited by Charles Tshimanga, Didier Gondola, and Peter J. Bloom, 120–45. Bloomington: Indiana University Press, 2009.

Beugnet, Martine. *Cinema and Sensation: French Film and The Art of Transgression.* Carbondale: Southern Illinois University Press, 2007.

Bevernage, Berber. "Against Coevalness: A Belated Critique of Johannes Fabian's Project of Radical Contemporaneity and a Plea for a New Politics of Time." May 2012, accessed March 12, 2013. http://www.inth.ugent.be/wp-content/uploads/2012/05/Against Coevalness.pdf.

Beyer, Susanne, and Henryk M. Broder. "Sie verglühen vor Leidenschaft: Gespräch mit Seyran Ateş." *Der Spiegel*, October 12, 2009, accessed April 20, 2012. http://www.spiegel.de/spiegel/print/d-67282871.html.

Bloom, Peter. "*Beur* Cinema and the Politics of Location: French Immigration Politics and the Naming of a Film Movement." In *Multiculturalism, Postcoloniality, and Transnational Media*, edited by Ella Shohat and Robert Stam, 44–62. New Brunswick: Rutgers University Press, 2003.

Bojadzijev, Manuela, and Isabelle Saint-Saens. "Borders, Citizenship, War, Class: A Discussion with Etienne Balibar and Sandro Mezzadra." *New Formations* 58, no. 1 (2006): 10–30.

Bordwell, David, and Kristin Thompson. *Film Art: An Introduction.* New York: McGraw Hill, 2010.

Boyle, Kirk. "*Children of Men* and *I Am Legend*: The Disaster-Capitalism Complex Hits Hollywood." *Jump Cut: A Review of Contemporary Media* 51 (Spring 2009). Accessed September 9, 2012. http://www.ejumpcut.org/archive/jc51.2009/ChildrenMenLegend/text.html.

Bradshaw, Peter. "Children of Men." *The Guardian*, September 22, 2006, accessed December 16, 2012. http://www.guardian.co.uk/film/2006/sep/22/juliannemoore.thriller.

Brevet, Brad. "Exclusive: Alfonso Cuarón on *Children of Men*." *Rope of Silicon*, December 22, 2006, accessed December 27, 2012. http://www.ropeofsilicon.com/exclusive_alfonso_cuaron_on_children_of_men/.

Brooks, Peter. *The Melodramatic Imagination: Balzac, Henry James, Melodrama, and the Mode of Excess.* New Haven: Yale University Press, 1995.

Brown, Jessica Autumn, and Myra Marx Ferree. "Close Your Eyes and Think of England: Pronatalism in the British Print Media." *Gender and Society* 19, no. 1 (2005): 5–24.

Brown, Wendy. *States of Injury: Power and Freedom in Late Modernity.* Princeton: Princeton University Press, 1995.

Brown, William, Dina Iordanova and Leshu Torchin. *Moving People, Moving Images: Cinema and Trafficking in the New Europe.* St. Andrews: St. Andrews Film Studies, 2010.

Brubaker, Rogers. *Citizenship and Nationhood in France and Germany.* Cambridge, MA: Harvard University Press, 1992.

Bulley, Dan. "'Foreign Terror'? Resisting/Responding to the London Bombings." In *Terrorism and the Politics of Response*, edited by Angharad Closs Stephens and Nick Vaughan-Williams, 81–95. New York: Routledge, 2009.

Burns, Rob. "Turkish-German Cinema: From Cultural Resistance to Transna-

tional Cinema?" In *German Cinema since Unification*, edited by David Clarke, 127–41. London: Continuum, 2006.
Butler, Judith. "Imitation and Gender Insubordination." In *The Lesbian and Gay Studies Reader*, edited by Henry Abelove, 307–20. New York: Routledge, 1993.
Butler, Judith. *Precarious Life: The Powers of Mourning and Violence*. London: Verso, 2006.
Calhoun, Craig. "The Idea of Emergency: Humanitarian Action and Global (Dis)Order." In *Contemporary States of Emergency: The Politics of Military and Humanitarian Interventions*, edited by Didier Fassin and Mariella Pandolfi, 29–58. New York: Zone Books, 2010).
Calotychos, Vangelis. *The Balkan Prospect: Identity, Culture, and Politics in Greece after 1989*. New York: Palgrave Macmillan, 2013.
Celik, Ipek A. "'I Wanted You to Be Present': Guilt and the History of Violence in Michael Haneke's *Caché*." *Cinema Journal* 50, no. 1 (2010): 59–80.
Chandler, Raymond. *Trouble Is My Business*. New York: Vintage, 1950.
Chaudhary, Zahid. "Humanity Adrift: Race, Materiality, and Allegory in Alfonso Cuarón's *Children of Men*." *Camera Obscura* 24, no. 3-72 (2009): 73–109.
Cheesman, Tom. *Novels of Turkish German Settlement: Cosmopolite Fictions*. Rochester: Camden House, 2007.
Chin, Rita. *The Guest Worker Question in Postwar Germany*. Cambridge: Cambridge University Press, 2007.
Chion, Michel. *Audio-Vision: Sound on Screen*. New York: Columbia University Press, 1994.
Cho, Michelle. "Generic Realities: The Transnational Spaces of South Korean Cinema." PhD diss., University of California, Irvine, 2011.
Chossudovsky, Michel. "The Criminalization of Albania." In *Masters of the Universe? NATO's Balkan Crusade*, edited by Tariq Ali, 285–316. New York: Verso, 2000.
Chow, Rey. "Postcolonial Visibilities: Questions Inspired by Deleuze's Method." In *Entanglements, or Transmedial Thinking about Capture*, 151–68. Durham: Duke University Press, 2012.
Chow, Rey. *Primitive Passions: Visuality, Sexuality, Ethnography, and Contemporary Chinese Cinema*. New York: Columbia University Press, 1995.
Chow, Rey. *The Protestant Ethnic and the Spirit of Capitalism*. New York: Columbia University Press, 2002.
Chow, Rey. *Sentimental Fabulations, Contemporary Chinese Films: Attachment in the Age of Global Visibility*. New York: Columbia University Press, 2007.
Chronister, Necia. "Topographies of Sexuality: Space, Movement, and Gender in German Literature and Film since 1989." PhD diss., Washington University in St. Louis, 2011.
Cissé, Madjiguène. "The *Sans-Papiers*: A Woman Draws the First Lessons." In *We Are Everywhere: The Irresistible Rise of Global Anti-capitalism*, 38–45. London: Verso, 2003.
Clover, Joshua. "All That Is Solid Melts into War." *Film Quarterly* 61, no. 1 (Autumn 2007), accessed November 11, 2012. http://www.filmquarterly.org/2007/12/all-that-is-solid-melts-into-war/.
Coker, Richard, and Alan Ingram. "Passports and Pestilence: Migration, Security and Contemporary Border Control of Infectious Diseases." In *Medicine at the*

Border: Disease, Globalization and Security, 1850 to the Present, edited by Alison Bashford, 159–76. New York: Palgrave Macmillan, 2006.
Cole, Phillip. *Philosophies of Exclusion: Liberal Political Theory and Immigration.* Edinburgh: Edinburgh University Press, 2000.
Conley, Tom. "Cronos, Cosmos, and *Polis*: *La Haine*." *Cartographic Cinema.* Minneapolis: University of Minnesota Press, 2007: 173–90.
Cooke, Paul, ed. *World Cinema's Dialogues with Hollywood.* New York: Palgrave Macmillan, 2007.
Coroller, Catherine. "Le film 'Welcome' fait polémique." *Libération,* March, 10, 2009, accessed November 23, 2012. http://www.liberation.fr/societe/0101553219-le-film-welcome-fait-polemique.
Critchley, Simon. *Infinitely Demanding: Ethics of Commitment, Politics of Resistance.* London: Verso, 2007.
Cuarón, Alfonso. "DVD Bonus Features: Futuristic Design." In *Children of Men.* DVD. Directed by Alfonso Cuarón. Universal City: Universal Pictures, 2007.
Cuarón, Alfonso. "DVD Bonus Features: The Possibility of Hope." In *Children of Men.* DVD. Directed by Alfonso Cuarón. Universal City: Universal Pictures, 2007.
Cuarón, Alfonso, Timothy J. Sexton, David Arata, Mark Fergus, and Hawk Ostby. *Children of Men* final shooting script. Accessed December 15, 2012. http://www.pages.drexel.edu/~ina22/splaylib/Screenplay-Children_of_Men.htm.
Daily Express, "Asylum: Time to Pull Down the Shutters," August 30, 2001. Accessed January 4, 2015. http://www.ukpressonline.co.uk/ukpressonline/database/search/preview.jsp?fileName=DExp_2001_08_30_001&sr=1.
Daily Mail. "Britain Is Top Asylum Haven," February 2, 2002. Accessed January 4, 2015 http://www.dailymail.co.uk/news/article-98148/Britain-asylum-haven.html.
de Baecque, Antoine. "Interview avec Michael Haneke: L'intelligence ne protège pas de la lâcheté." *Libération,* October 5, 2005, accessed October 10, 2011. http://next.liberation.fr/cinema/0101543833-l-intelligence-ne-protege-pas-de-la-lachete.
de Genova, Nicolas. "Migrant 'Illegality' and Deportability in Everyday Life." *Annual Review of Anthropology* 31 (1998): 419–47.
Deleuze, Gilles. *Cinema 2: The Time-Image.* Translated by Hugh Tomlinson and Robert Galeta. Minneapolis: University of Minnesota Press.
Deltombe, Thomas. "'Accueillir toute la misère du monde': Michel Rocard, martyr ou mystificateur?" *Le Monde diplomatique,* September 30, 2009, accessed December 2, 2012. http://www.monde-diplomatique.fr/carnet/2009-09-30-Rocard.
Derry, Charles. *The Suspense Thriller: Films in the Shadow of Alfred Hitchcock.* Jefferson: McFarland, 1988.
Deutsche Welle. "From Bare to Bear for Ex-Porn Queen." February 18, 2004, accessed May 8, 2012. http://www.dw.de/from-bare-to-bear-for-ex-porn-queen/a-1118125.
Diaconescu-Blumenfeld, Rodica. "The Desire of the Other: Balkan Dystopia in Western European Cinema." In *Moving Pictures, Migrating Identities,* edited by Eva Rueschmann, 90–104. Jackson: University Press of Mississippi, 2003.

Doane, Mary Ann. *The Emergence of Cinematic Time: Modernity, Contingency, the Archive.* Cambridge, MA: Harvard University Press, 2002.

Doane, Mary Ann. "Information, Crisis, Catastrophe." In *Historical Film: History and Memory in Media,* edited by Marcia Landy, 269–85. New Brunswick: Rutgers University Press, 2001.

Donadey, Anne. "'Une certaine idée de la France': The Algeria Syndrome and Struggles over 'French' Identity." In *Identity Papers: Contested Nationhood in Twentieth- Century France,* edited by Steven Ungar and Tom Conley, 215–33. Minneapolis: University of Minnesota Press, 1996.

Einaudi, Jean-Luc. *La Bataille de Paris.* Paris: Seuil, 1991.

Eleftherotipia. "Θα παιχθεί αύριο." March 3, 2005, accessed June 20, 2011. http://archive.enet.gr/online/online_ text/c=113,dt=03.03.2005,id=36885080.

Elger, Katrin, Ansbert Kneip, and Merlind Theile. "Einwanderung: Für immer fremd." *Der Spiegel,* January 26, 2009, accessed May 15, 2011. http://www.spiegel.de/spiegel/print/d-63806907.html.

Elsaesser, Thomas. *European Cinema: Face to Face with Hollywood.* Amsterdam: Amsterdam University Press, 2005.

Elsaesser, Thomas. "Performative Self-Contradictions: Michael Haneke's Mind Games." In *A Companion to Michael Haneke,* edited by Roy Grundmann, 53–74. Oxford: Blackwell, 2010.

Elsaesser, Thomas. "Politics, Multiculturalism and the Ethical Turn: The Cinema of Fatih Akin." In *Just Images: Ethics and the Cinematic,* edited by B. Hagen, S. Meiri, R. Yosef, and A. Zanger, 1–19. Newcastle: Cambridge Scholars, 2011.

Elsaesser, Thomas. "Tales of Sound and Fury." In *Film Theory And Criticism,* edited by G. Mast, M. Cohen, and L. Braudy, 244–58. New York: Oxford University Press, 1992.

Eren, Mine. "Breaking the Stigma? The Anti-heroine in Fatih Akin's *Head-On.*" In *Muslim Women, Transnational Feminism and the Ethics of Pedagogy: Contested Imaginaries in Post-9/11 Cultural Practice,* edited by Lisa Taylor and Jasmin Zine (New York: Routledge, 2014), 82–109. New York: Routledge, 2014

Eren, Mine. "Cosmopolitan Filmmaking: Fatih Akın's *In July* and *Head-On.*" In *Turkish German Cinema in the New Millennium: Site, Sounds, and Screens,* edited by Sabine Hake and Barbara Mennel, 175–86. Oxford: Berghahn, 2012.

Europe and You in 2006. "A Snapshot of EU Achievements." Accessed December 27, 2014. http://ec.europa.eu/archives/snapshot2006/index_en.htm.

Europe and You in 2007. "A Snapshot of EU Achievements." Accessed December 27, 2014. http://ec.europa.eu/archives/snapshot2007/index_en.htm.

Everett, Wendy. "'Between Here and There, Between Then and Now': The Theme of Border Crossing in the Films of Theo Angelopoulos." In *Border Crossings,* edited by Peter Wagstaff, 55–80. Oxford: Peter Lang, 2004.

Everett, Wendy. "Re-framing the Fingerprints: A Short Survey of European Film." In *European Identity in Cinema,* edited by Wendy Everett, 19–33. Bristol: Intellect, 2005.

Ewing, Katherine. *Stolen Honor: Stigmatizing Muslim Men in Berlin.* Stanford: Stanford University Press, 2008.

Fabian, Johannes. *Time and the Other: How Anthropology Makes Its Object.* New York: Columbia University Press, 1983.

Farge, Arlette. "Penser et définir l'événement en histoire." *Terrain: Revue d'ethnologie de l'Europe* 38 (March 2002). Accessed May 12, 2013. http://terrain.revues.org/1929.

Farzanefar, Amin. "Film ist Punk: Interview mit dem Regisseur Fatih Akin." *IFA Kultur Austausch Online*, March 2004, accessed September 10, 2012. http://cms.ifa.de/index.php?id=akin&type=98&L=.

Fassbinder, Reiner Werner. "Six Films by Douglas Sirk." *New Left Review* 91 (May–June 1975): 88–96.

Fassin, Didier. "Of Words and Wounds. The Thin Evidence of Asylum Seekers." Brown University, Pembroke Seminar Research Lecture, March 2, 2010.

Fassin, Didier, and Mariella Pandolfi. "Introduction: Military and Humanitarian Government in the Age of Intervention." In *Contemporary States of Emergency: The Politics of Military and Humanitarian Interventions*, edited by Didier Fassin and Mariella Pandolfi, 9–25. New York: Zone Books, 2010.

Fassin, Didier, and Richard Rechtmann. *Empire of Trauma: An Inquiry into the Condition of Victimhood.* Princeton: Princeton University Press, 2009.

Fincham, Victoria. "Violence, Sexuality and the Family: Identity 'Within and Beyond Turkish-German Parameters' in Fatih Akin's *Gegen die Wand*, Kutluğ Ataman's *Lola+Bilidikid* and Anno Saul's *Kebab Connection*." *German as Foreign Language Journal* 1 (2008): 66. Accessed May 10, 2012. http://www.gfl-journal.de/1-2008/fincham.pdf.

Fischer, Jaimey. "German *autoren* Dialogue with Hollywood? Refunctioning the Horror Genre in Christian Petzold's *Yella*." In *New Directions in German Cinema*, edited by Paul Cooke and Chris Homewood, 182–200. London: I.B. Tauris, 2011.

Fischer, Lucy. "Three-Way Mirror: Imitation of Life." In *Imitation of Life*, edited by Lucy Fischer, 3–37. New Brunswick: Rutgers University Press, 1991.

Fleming, Katherine. "Orientalism, the Balkans, and Balkan Historiography." *American Historical Review* 105, no. 4 (2000): 1218–33.

Forsdick, Charles. "'Direction les oubliettes de l'histoire': Witnessing the Past in the Contemporary French Polar." *French Cultural Studies* 12, no. 3 (2001): 333–50.

Foucault, Michel. "Questions of Method." In *The Foucault Effect: Studies in Governmentality*, edited by Gordon Burchell and Peter Miller, 73–86. Chicago: University Chicago Press, 1991.

Foundas, Scott. "Decade: Michael Haneke Talks *Code Inconnu* and *The Piano Teacher*." *Indiewire*, December 4, 2001, accessed September 21. http://www.indiewire.com/article/interview_michael_haneke_the_bearded_prophet_of_code_inconnu_and_the_piano_.

Frontex Report: European Agency for the Management of Operational Cooperation at the External Borders of the Member States of the European Union. "The Impact of the Global Economic Crisis on Illegal Migration to the EU." August 2009, accessed January 12, 2012. http://www.europarl.europa.eu/meetdocs/2009_2014/documents/libe/dv/frontex_/frontex_en.pdf.

Fukuyama, Francis. *The End of History and the Last Man.* New York: Free Press, 1992.

Galt, Rosalind. "The Functionary of Mankind: Haneke and Europe." In *On Mi-*

chael Haneke, edited by Brian Price and John David Rhodes, 221–44. Detroit: Wayne State University Press, 2010.

Galt, Rosalind. *The New European Cinema: Redrawing the Map*. New York: Columbia University Press, 2006.

Gilroy, Paul. "Shooting Crabs in a Barrel." *Screen* 48, no. 2 (Summer 2007): 233–35.

Gledhill, Christine. "The Melodramatic Field: An Investigation." In *Home Is Where the Heart Is: Studies in Melodrama and the Woman's Film*, 5–39. London: BFI Publishing, 1987.

Gledhill, Christine. "Rethinking Genre." In *Reinventing Film Studies*, edited by Christine Gledhill and Linda Williams, 221–43. London: Oxford University Press, 2000.

Gramsci, Antonio. "Some Aspects of the Southern Question." October 1926, accessed May 12, 2013. http://www.uky.edu/~tmute2/geography_methods/readingPDFs/gramsci-southern-question1926.pdf.

Göktürk, Deniz. "Sound Bridges: Transnational Mobility as Ironic Melodrama." In *European Cinema in Motion: Migrant and Diasporic Film in Contemporary Europe*, edited by Daniela Berghahn and Claudia Sternberg, 215–34. New York: Palgrave Macmillan, 2010.

Göktürk, Deniz. "Turkish Delight—German Flight: Migrant Identities in Transnational Cinema." Transnational Communities—Working Paper Series, and Economic and Social Council Research Program, University of Oxford. January 1999, 6, accessed May 5, 2012. http://www.transcomm.ox.ac.uk/working%20papers/mediated.pdf.

Göktürk, Deniz. "Turkish Women on German Streets: Closure and Exposure in Transnational Cinema." In *Space in European Cinema*, edited by Myrto Konstantarakos, 64–76. Exeter: Intellect, 2000.

Gormley, Paul. *The New-Brutality Film: Race and Affect in Contemporary Hollywood Cinema*. Bristol: Intellect, 2005.

Gueneli, Berna. "Challenging European Borders: Fatih Akin's *Auteurist* Visions of Europe." PhD diss., University of Texas at Austin, 2011.

Haberman, Maggie. "Swedish Tennis Stud Recommends Borg-asms." *New York Post*, March 11, 2001, accessed January 4, 2013. http://www.nypost.com/p/news/item_ sGXUbuHN02bgsEZcXHa64K.

Hafez, Kia. "Images of Middle East and Islam in German Media: A Reappraisal." In *Mutual Misunderstandings? Muslims and Islam in the European Media / Europe in the Media of Muslim Majority Countries*, edited by Kerem Öktem and Reem Abou-El-Fadl, 29–52. Oxford: European Studies Center, 2009.

Hagman, Hampus. "'Every Cannes Needs Its Scandal': Between Art and Exploitation in Contemporary French Film." *Film International* 5, no. 29 (2007): 32–41.

Halbwachs, Maurice. *The Causes of Suicide*. London: Routledge and Kegan Paul, 1978.

Hall, Stuart. "The Spectacle of the 'Other.'" In *Representation: Cultural Representations and Signifying Practices*, edited by Stuart Hall, 223–90. London: Sage, 1997.

Haneke, Michael. "71 Fragments of a Chronology of Chance: Notes to the Film."

In *After Postmodernism: Austrian Literature and Film in Transition*, edited by Willy Riemer, 171–75. Riverside: Ariadne, 2000.

Hans, Barbara. “Murder in Berlin: The Lost Honor of the Sürücü Family.” *Der Spiegel Online International*, July 27, 2011, accessed May 2, 2012. http://www.spiegel.de/international/germany/murder-in-berlin-the-lost-honor-of-the-sueruecue-family-a-777109.html.

Harootunian, Harry. “Remembering the Historical Present.” *Critical Inquiry* 33 (Spring 2007): 471–94.

Hatzios, Giorgos, and Kostas Kantouris. “Πέρασε στην Αλβανία ο κακοποιός με τους ομήρους.” *Ta Nea*, May 29, 1999, accessed April 19, 2011. http://www.tanea.gr/news/greece/article/4072240/?iid=2.

The Herald: Scotland on Sunday. “Hijacker Seizes Bus for 350-Mile Joyride.” May 29, 1999, accessed June 15, 2011. http://www.heraldscotland.com/sport/spl/aberdeen/hijacker-seizes-bus-for-350-mile-joyride-1.289161.

Higbee, Will, and Song Hwee Lim. “Concepts of Transnational Cinema: Towards a Critical Transnationalism in Film Studies.” *Transnational Cinemas* 1, no. 1 (2010): 7–21.

Hunt, Lynn. *Inventing Human Rights: A History*. New York: W.W. Norton, 2007.

Huth-Hildebrandt, Christine. “Das Bild von der Migrantin—eine Folie zur Polarisierung der Debatte um Migration?” In *Gender und soziale Praxis*, edited by Margit Gottert and Karin Walser, 144–69. Königstein: Taunus, 2001.

Les indigènes de la république. “A Call to Action: ‘We Are the Natives of the Republic!.’ January 18, 2005.” Translated by Florence Bernault. In *Frenchness and the African Diaspora: Identity and Uprising in Contemporary France*, edited by Charles Tshimanga, Didier Gondola, and Peter J. Bloom, 277–81. Bloomington: Indiana University Press, 2009.

Iordanova, Dina. *Cinema of Flames: Balkan Film, Culture and the Media*. London: British Film Institute, 2001.

Iordanova, Dina. “Displaced? Shifting Politics of Place and Itinerary in International Cinema.” *Senses of Cinema* 14 (2001). http://sensesofcinema.com/2001/feature-articles/displaced/.

James, P. D. *Children of Men*. New York: Vintage, 2006.

Jameson, Fredric. “Fear and Loathing in Globalization.” *New Left Review* 23 (September–October 2003): 105–14.

Jameson, Fredric. “Postmodernism, or the Cultural Logic of Late Capitalism.” *New Left Review* 146 (July–August 1984): 59–92.

Jameson, Fredric. “Progress versus Utopia, Or, Can We Imagine the Future?” In *Archaeologies of the Future: The Desire Called Utopia and Other Science Fictions*, 281–95. New York: Verso, 2005.

Joyce, Kathryn. “Missing the ‘Right’ Babies.” *The Nation*, February 14, 2009, accessed June 6, 2011. http://www.thenation.com/article/missing-right-babies.

July, Serge, and Marie Genin. “Un film & son époque: Il était une fois . . . la haine.” *France* 5, February, 27, 2012, accessed March 7, 2012. http://www.youtube.com/watch?v=ApoBrixM8EM.

Jung, Berenike. *Narrating Violence in Post-9/11 Action Cinema: Terrorist Narratives, Cinematic Narration, and Referentiality*. Wiesbaden: Springer, 2010.

Kalyvas, Andreas. “An Anomaly? Some Reflections on the Greek December 2008.” *Constellations* 17, no. 2 (2010): 351–65.

Kamalzadeh, Dominik. "Cowardly and Comfortable: Interview with Michael Haneke." *Sign and Sight*, January 30, 2006, accessed August, 29, 2011. http://www.signandsight.com/features/577.html.

Kamiloglu, Ozan. "The Ethical Turn and Cinema: The Politics and Aesthetics of Jacques Rancière." MA Thesis, Bilkent University, 2011. http://www.thesis.bilkent.edu.tr/ 0004048.pdf.

Kanak-Attak. "Philharmonie Köln-40 Jahre Einwanderung." *Kanak TV*, November 6, 2001, accessed May 15, 2011. http://www.kanak-tv.de/popup/philharmonie_video.html.

Kaplani, Gkazment. "Θέλω να σκάψω την ανασφάλειά μας." *Ta Nea*, December 4, 2004, 12.

Karpf, Anna. "We've Been Here Before." The Guardian, June 8, 2002, accessed January 4, 2015. http://www.theguardian.com/uk/2002/jun/08/immigration.immigrationandpublicservices.

Karyotis, Georges and Stratos Patrikios, "Religion, Securitization and Anti-Immigration Attitudes: The Case of Greece," Journal of Peace Research 47, no. 1 (2010): 43-57

H Kathimerini. "Κινηματογράφος/Κωνσταντίνος Γιάνναρης: Παραμένει αμετανόητος." December 31, 2005, accessed May 1, 2011. http://www.kathimerini.gr/237987/article/politismos/arxeio-politismoy/kinhmatografos–kwnstantinos-giannarhs.

H Kathimerini. "Κώστας Καραμανλής: 'Κλείνετε το μάτι στους κουκουλοφόρους.'" April 9, 2009, accessed May 10, 2011. http://news.kathimerini.gr/4dcgi/_w_articles_ell_2_09/04/2009 _310488.

Katsounaki, Maria. "Ξένος, ανάμεσα σε τιμή και θάνατο." *H Kathimerini*, February 13, 2005, accessed June 15, 2011. http://www.kathimerini.gr/209084/article/politismos/arxeio-politismoy/3enos-anamesa-se-timh-kai-8anato.

Kėrner, Aaron. "Faculty Profile: Aaron Kellner." SFSU Cinema Department video. 4:49. Posted July 2012, accessed January 10, 2013. http://www.youtube.com/watch?v= lhXFFOFEBWg&list=PLC3367192BD41107C&index=10.

Khanna, Ranjana. "From Rue Morgue to Rue des Iris." *Screen* 48, no. 2 (Summer 2007): 237–44.

Kim, Soyoung. "Genre as Contact Zone: Hong Kong Action and Korean Hwalkuk." In *Hong Kong Connections: Transnational Imagination in Action Cinema*, edited by Meaghan Morris, Siu- Leung Li, and Stephen Chan Ching-kiu, 97–110. Durham: Duke University Press, 2006.

King, Geoff. "Following in the Footsteps: Gus Van Sant's *Gerry* and *Elephant* in the American Independent Field of Cultural Production." *New Review of Film and Television Studies* 4, no. 2 (August 2006): 75–92.

Kosnick, Kira. "Cosmopolitan Capital or Multicultural Community? Reflections on the Production and Management of Different Mobilities in Germany's Capital City." In *Cosmopolitanism in Practice*, edited by Magdalena Nowicka and Maria Rowisko, 161–80. Surrey: Ashgate, 2009.

Les lascars: Cigarette. Accessed August 21, 2011. http://www.youtube.com/watch?v=_pmdbXGT1jg.

Lefebvre, Henri. "The Everyday and Everydayness." *Yale French Studies* 73 (1987): 7–11.

Lennon, Peter. "Poet of the Underworld." *The Guardian*, June 27, 2003, accessed May 20, 2010. http://www.guardian.co.uk/film/2003/jun/27/artsfeatures2.

Lennox, Sara. "Divided Feminism: Women, Racism and German National Identity." *German Studies Review* 18 (1995): 481–502.

Levin, Thomas. "Five Tapes, Four Halls, Two Dreams: Vicissitudes of Surveillant Narration in Michael Haneke's *Caché*." In *A Companion to Michael Haneke*, edited by Roy Grundmann, 75–90. Oxford: Blackwell, 2010.

Levin, Thomas. "Rhetoric of Temporal Index: Surveillant Narration and the Cinema of 'Real Time." In *Ctrl [space]: Rhetorics of Surveillance from Bentham to Big Brother*, edited by Thomas Y. Levin, Ursula Frohne, and Peter Weibel, 578–93. Karlsruhe: ZKM Center for Art and Media; Cambridge, MA: MIT Press, 2002.

Lorssen, Karin. "Where Have All the Guest Workers Gone? Transcultural Role-Play and Performative Identities in Fatih Akin's *Gegen die Wand* (2004)." In *Finding the Foreign*, edited by Robert Schechtman and Suin Roberts, 13–32. Newcastle: Cambridge Scholars Publishing, 2007.

Loshitsky, Yosefa. *Screening Strangers: Migration and Diaspora in Contemporary European Cinema.* Bloomington: Indiana University Press, 2010.

Ma, Jean. "Discordant Desires, Violent Refrains: La Pianiste." *Grey Room* 28 (Summer 2007): 6–29.

The Mail on Sunday. "Open Door for Bogus Refugees." March 15, 1998. http://www.highbeam.com/doc/1G1-109823367.html.

Mamdani, Mahmood. *Good Muslims, Bad Muslims: America, The Cold War, and the Roots of Terror.* New York: Three Leaves Press, 2005.

Manlove, Clifford. "Visual 'Drive' and the Cinematic Narrative." *Cinema Journal* 46, no. 3 (2007): 83–108.

Manon, Hugh. "'Comment ça, rien?' Screening the Gaze in *Caché*." In *On Michael Haneke*, edited by Brian Price and John David Rhodes, 105–26. Detroit: Wayne State University Press, 2010.

Mariátegui, Jose Carlos. *Seven Interpretive Essays on Peruvian Reality.* 1928, accessed May 23, 2013. http://www.marxists.org/archive/mariateg/works/1928/.

Marks, Laura. *The Skin of the Film: Intercultural Cinema, Embodiment, and the Senses.* Durham: Duke University Press, 2000.

Martin, Russell. *Picasso's War.* New York: Plume, 2003.

Mazierska, Ewa, and Laura Rascaroli. *Crossing New Europe: Postmodern Travel and the European Road Movie.* London: Wallflower Press, 2006.

Mazower, Mark. "Healthy Bodies, Sick Bodies." In *Dark Continent: Europe's Twentieth Century*, 76–104. New York: Vintage, 1998.

Médine. "How Much More French Can I Be?" *Time*, November 6, 2005, accessed January 23, 2012. http://www.time.com/time/magazine/article/0,9171,1126720,00.html.

Mercer, John, and Martin Shingler. *Melodrama: Genre, Style, Sensibility.* London: Wallflower, 2004.

Merivirta, Raita, Kimmo Ahonen, Heta Mulari, and Rami Mahka eds. Frontiers of Screen History: Imagining European Borders in Cinema, 1945–2010. Bristol: Intellect, 2013.

Mezzadra, Sandro, and Brett Neilson. "Né qui, né altrove—Migration, Detention, Desertion: A Dialogue." *Borderlands: Online Journal* 2, no. 1 (2003). http://www.borderlands.net.au/vol2no1_2003/mezzadra_neilson.html.

Mitchell, W. J. T. *What Do Pictures Want? The Lives and Loves of Images.* Chicago: University of Chicago Press, 2005.

Mitchell, Wendy. "Going to Extremes: Fatih Akin on His Turkish-German Love Story *Head-On.*" *Indiewire,* January 19, 2005, accessed May 20, 2012. http://www.indiewire.com/article/going_to_extremes_fatih_akin_on_his_turkish-german_love_story_head-on.

Mmembe, Achille. "The Republic and Its Beast: On the Riots in the French *Banlieues.*" In *Frenchness and the African Diaspora: Identity and Uprising in Contemporary France,* edited by Charles Tshimanga, Didier Gondola, and Peter J. Bloom, 47–55. Bloomington: Indiana University Press, 2009.

Moylan, Thomas. *Scraps of the Untainted Sky: Science Fiction, Utopia, Dystopia.* Boulder: Westview Press, 2000.

MSN Money. "Do Early Pub Closings Make for Better Workers? That's What a UK Study Contends." April 5, 2013, accessed May 10, 2013. http://money.msn.com/now/post.aspx?post=ff6ac16a-cf3d-4ea9-9baa-0461ea456b5a.

Mucchielli, Laurent. "L'éphémère question des viols collectifs en France (2000–2002): Etude d'une panique morale." *Logos 26* 14, no. 1 (2007): 9–29.

Mulvey, Laura. "Visual Pleasure and Narrative Cinema." *Screen* 16, no. 3 (Autumn 1975): 6–18.

Mutman, Mahmut. "Up Against the Wall of the Signifier: *Gegen die Wand.*" In *Shifting Landscapes: Film and Media in the European Context,* edited by Miyase Christensen and Nezih Erdoğan, 317–35. Newcastle: Cambridge Scholars Publishing, 2008.

Naficy, Hamid. *An Accented Cinema: Exilic and Diasporic Filmmaking.* Princeton: Princeton University Press, 2001.

Naqvi, Fatima. *The Literary and Cultural Rhetoric of Victimhood: Western Europe, 1970–2005.* New York: Palgrave Macmillan, 2007.

Nattelbeck, Colin. "Kassovitz's '*France d'en bas*' and Sarkozy's '*racaille*': Art and the Alienation of Politics in Contemporary France." *French History and Civilization: Papers from the George Rude Seminar* 2 (2009): 70–81. Accessed March 23, 2013. http://www.h-france.net/rude/rude%20volume%20ii/Nettelbeck%20Final%20Version%202.pdf.

Neale, Steve. "Questions of Genre." In *Film and Theory: An Anthology,* edited by Robert Stam and Toby Miller, 157–78. New York: Blackwell, 2000.

Nelson, Patricia. "The Politics of Film Adaptation: A Case Study of Alfonso Cuarón's *Children of Men.*" MA thesis, University of Texas at Austin, 2010. Accessed December 12, 2012. https://repositories.lib.utexas.edu/bitstream/handle/2152/ ETD-UT-2010-05- 1162/NELSON-THESIS.pdf.

Noiriel, Gerard. *The French Melting Pot: Immigration, Citizenship, and National Identity.* Translated by Geoffroy De Laforcade. Minneapolis: University of Minnesota Press, 1996.

Nora, Pierre. "Between Memory and History: *Les Lieux de Mémoire* [1984]." *Representations* 26 (Spring 1989): 7–25.

O'Leary, Alan, and Catherine O'Rawe. "Against Realism: On a 'Certain Tendency' in Italian Film Criticism." *Journal of Modern Italian Studies* 16, no. 1 (2011): 107–28.

Ong, Aihwa. "The Gender and Labor Politics of Post-modernity. " *Annual Review of Anthropology* 20 (1991): 279–309.

O'Rawe, Catherine. "'I padri e i maestri': Genre, Auteurs, and Absences." *Italian Studies* 63, no. 2 (Autumn 2008): 173–94.

O'Shaughnessy, Martin. *The New Face of Political Cinema: Commitment in French Film since 1995*. London: Berghahn Books, 2007.

O'Shaughnessy, Martin. "Post-1995 French Cinema: Return of the Social, Return of the Political?" *Modern and Contemporary France* 11, no. 2 (2003): 189–203.

Osterweil, Ara. "*Caché*." *Film Quarterly* 59, no. 4 (Summer 2006): 35–39.

Papailias, Penelope. "'Money of *Kurbet* Is Money of Blood': The Making of a 'Hero' of Migration at the Greek-Albanian Border." *Journal of Ethnic and Migration Studies* 29, no. 6 (2003): 1059–78.

Parekh, Bhikhu. "The Liberal Discourse on Violence." In *Selves, People, and Persons: What Does It Mean to Be a Self?*, edited by Leroy S. Rouner, 187–204. Notre Dame: University of Notre Dame Press, 1992.

Pellegrini, Ann, and Jasbir Puar. "Affect." *Social Text* 27, no. 3 (Fall 2009): 35–38.

Penney, James. "'You Never Look at Me From Where I See You': Postcolonial Guilt in *Caché*." *New Formations* 70 (Winter 2011): 77–93.

Peucker, Brigitte. *The Material Image: Art and the Real in Film*. Stanford: Stanford University Press, 2007.

Pisters, Patricia. "New Subjectivity in Cinema: The Vertigo of Strange Days." In *Subjectivity*, edited by Willem van Reijen and Willem G. Weststeijn, 283–314. Amsterdam: Rodopi, 2000.

Rancière, Jacques. "Aesthetic Separation, Aesthetic Community: Scenes from the Aesthetic Regime of Art." *Art and Research: A Journal of Ideas, Contexts, and Methods* 2, no. 1 (Summer 2008). Accessed July 26, 2012. http://www.artandresearch.org.uk/v2n1/ranciere.html.

Rancière, Jacques. "A propos de *L'Etre et l'Evénement* d'Alain Badiou." *Le cahier du Collège international de philosophie* 8 (October 1989). horlieu-editions.com/textes-en-ligne/philosophie/ranciere-a-propos-d-etre-et-evenement-d-alain-badiou.pdf.

Rancière, Jacques. "The Cause of the Other." *Parallax* 4 (1998): 25–33.

Rancière, Jacques. *The Nights of Labor: The Workers' Dream in Nineteenth-Century France*. Philadelphia: Temple University Press, 1989.

Rancière, Jacques. *The Emancipated Spectator*. New York: Verso, 2009.

Rancière, Jacques. "The Ethical Turn of Aesthetics and Politics." In *Dissensus: On Politics and Aesthetics* (London: Continuum, 2010), 184–204.

Rancière, Jacques. "Who Is the Subject of the Rights of Men?" *South Atlantic Quarterly* 103, nos. 2–3 (Spring–Summer 2004): 297–310.

Rancière, Jacques, Fulvia Carnevale, and John Kelsey. "Art of the Possible: Fulvia Carnevale and John Kelsey in Conversation with Jacques Rancière." *Artforum*, March 2007, accessed April 12, 2013. http://www.egs.edu/faculty/jacques-ranciere/articles/art-of-the-possible/.

Rehman, Javaid. "Islam, 'War on Terror' and the Future of Muslim Minorities in the United Kingdom: Dilemmas of Multiculturalism." *Human Rights Quarterly* 29, no. 4 (2007): 831–78.

Riding, Alan. "On Screen, Tackling Europe's New Reality." *New York Times*, January 18, 2005. Accessed June 5, 2014. http://www.nytimes.com/2005/01/18/movies/18head.html?_r=0.

Rohy, Valerie. *Anachronism and Its Others: Sexuality, Race, Temporality.* Albany: SUNY Press, 2009.

Rosenberg, Clifford. *Policing Paris: The Origins of Modern Immigration Control between Wars.* Ithaca, NY: Cornell University Press, 2006.

Ross, Kristin. *The Emergence of Social Space: Rimbaud and the Paris Commune.* London: Verso, 2008.

Ross, Kristin. *Fast Cars, Clean Bodies: Decolonization and the Reordering of French Culture.* Cambridge, MA: MIT Press, 1995).

Ross, Kristin. "Historicizing Untimeliness." In *Jacques Rancière: History, Politics, Aesthetics,* edited by Gabriel Rockhill and Philip Watts, 15–29. Durham: Duke University Press, 2009.

Rowin, Michael Joshua. "*Children of Men.*" *Cineaste* 32, no. 2 (Spring 2007): 60–61.

Said, Edward. *Orientalism.* New York: Vintage, 1978.

Sargeant, Jack, and Stephanie Watson. *Lost Highways: An Illustrated History of Road Movies.* London: Creation, 1999.

Sarkozy, Nicolas. "Déclaration de M. Nicolas Sarkozy, ministre de l'intérieur et de l'aménagement du territoire, président de l'UMP et candidat à l'élection présidentielle, sur son suhait de voir se réunifier l'espace méditerranéen pour le remettre au cœur de la civilisation occidentale et de la mondialisation, Toulon le 7 février 2007." *Vie publique: Collection des discours publics.* Accessed February 25, 2010. http://discours.vie-publique.fr/notices/073000533.html.

Sarrazin, Thilo. *Deutschland schafft sich ab.* Berlin: Deutsche Verlags-Anstalt, 2010.

Sartre, Jean-Paul. *Being and Nothingness.* Translated by Hazel E. Barnes. New York: Washington Square Press, 1956.

Sayad, Abdelmalek. *The Suffering of the Immigrant.* Translated by David Macey. Malden: Polity Press, 2004.

Scarry, Elaine. *The Body in Pain: The Making and Unmaking of the World.* New York: Oxford University Press, 1985.

Schneider, Cathy Lisa. "Police Power and Race Riots in Paris." *Politics and Society* 36, no. 1 (March 2008): 133–59.

Seel, Martin. "Variations on Art and Violence." In *Aesthetics of Appearing,* 186–206. Stanford: Stanford University Press, 2005.

Shattuc, Jane. "Having a Good Cry over *The Color Purple.*" In *Melodrama: Stage, Picture, Screen,* edited by Jacky Bratton, Jim Cook, and Christine Gledhill, 147–56. Bloomington: Indiana University Press, 1994.

Shattuc, Jane. *Television, Tabloids, and Tears: Fassbinder and Popular Culture.* Minneapolis: University of Minnesota Press, 1995.

Shaviro, Steven. "*Caché.*" Personal blog (The Pinocchio Theory). Last modified February 14, 2006, accessed September 24, 2011. http://www.shaviro.com/Blog/?p=476.

Shaviro, Steven. *The Cinematic Body.* Minneapolis: University of Minnesota Press, 1993.

Siewert, Senta. "Soundtracks of Double Occupancy: Sampling Sounds and Cultures in Fatih Akin's *Head On.*" In *Mind the Screen: Media Concepts according to Thomas Elsaesser,* edited by Jaap Kooijman, Patricia Pisters, and Wanda Strauven, 198–208. Chicago: University of Chicago Press, 2008.

Silvestri, Silvana. "A Skein of Reversals: The Films of Gianni Amelio." *New Left Review* 10 (July–August 2001): 119–32.

Slaveski, Trajko, and Pece Nedanovski. "Foreign Direct Investment in the Balkans: The Case of Albania, FYROM, and Bulgaria." *Eastern European Economics* 40, no. 4 (2002): 83–99.

Sobchack, Vivian. *Screening the Space: The American Science Fiction.* New Brunswick: Rutgers University Press, 1987.

Sontag, Susan. "The Imagination of Disaster." In *Liquid Metal: The Science Fiction Film Reader*, edited by Sean Redmond, 41–47. London: Wallflower Press, 2004.

Soysal, Levent. "Diversity of Experience, Experience of Diversity: Turkish Migrant Youth Culture in Berlin." *Cultural Dynamics* 13, no. 1 (March 2001): 5–28.

Stalker, Peter. *The No-Nonsense Guide to International Migration.* Oxford: New Internationalist Publications, 2008.

Stratton, Jon. "'Welcome to Paradise': Asylum Seekers, Neoliberalism, Nostalgia and *Lucky Miles.*" *Continuum: Journal of Media & Cultural Studies* 23, no. 5 (2009): 629–45.

Suchsland, Rüdiger. "Interview mit Fatih Akin: 'Ich bin wirklich davon ausgegangen.'" *Artechock*, March 11, 2004, accessed March 12, 2012. http://www.artechock.de/film/text/interview/a/akin_2004.htm.

Suner, Asuman. "Dark Passion: Fatih Akin's *Head On.*" *Sight and Sound* 15, no. 3 (March 2005): 18–21.

Suner, Asuman. "Outside in: 'accented cinema' at large," Inter-Asia Cultural Studies 7, no. 3 (2006). Accessed 10 January, 2015. http://www.nbcfilm.com/uzak/press_screenasuman2.php.

Suvin, Darko. *Metamorphosis of Science Fiction: On the Poetics and History of a Literary Genre.* New Haven: Yale University Press, 1979.

Syrigou-Rigou, Eleni, ed. *Conversations with Lida: An Albanian Woman Migrant Speaks about Her Life.* Athens: Ekdoseis Anoihta Sinora, 2000.

Taneja, Prati, ed. "State of the World's Minorities and Indigenous Peoples: Events of 2009." *Minority Rights International Report.* July 1, 2010, accessed May 20, 2011. http://www.minorityrights.org/10068/state-of-the-worlds-minorities/state-of-the-worlds-minorities-and-indigenous-peoples-2010.html.

Tayeb, Fatima el-. *European Others: Queering Ethnicity in Postnational Europe.* Minneapolis: University of Minnesota Press, 2011.

Thompson, A. K. "Matter's Most Modern Configurations: Rivera, Picasso, and Benjamin's Dialectic." Scapegoat 2 (Winter 2011), 2–6. Accessed December 26, 2012. http://www.scapegoatjournal.org/docs/02/02_Thompson_MattersMostModern.pdf.

Ticktin, Miriam. "Where Ethics and Politics Meet: The Violence of Humanitarianism in France." *American Ethnologist* 31, no. 1 (2006): 33–49.

Todorova, Maria. *Imagining the Balkans.* New York: Oxford University Press, 1997.

Toubiana, Serge. "Interview with Michael Haneke." In *Caché.* DVD. Directed by Michael Haneke. Culver City: Sony Pictures Home Entertainment, 2006.

Tshimanga, Charles, Didier Gondola, and Peter J. Bloom. "Introduction: Examining Frenchness and the African Diaspora." In *Frenchness and the African Diaspora: Identity and Uprising in Contemporary France*, edited by Charles Tshimanga, Didier Gondola, and Peter J. Bloom, 3–19. Bloomington: Indiana University Press, 2009.

Tzanelli, Rodanthi. "'Not My Flag!' Citizenship and Nationhood in the Margins of Europe (Greece, October 2000/2003)." *Ethnic and Racial Studies* 29, no. 1 (2006): 27–49.

Udden, James. "Child of the Long Take: Alfonso Cuarón's Film Aesthetics in the Shadow of Globalization." *Style* 43, no. 1 (Spring 2009): 22–44.

Verstraete, Ginette. *Tracking Europe: Mobility, Diaspora, and the Politics of Location.* Durham: Duke University Press, 2010.

Vidali, Maria. "Living in a Policy Vacuum: The Plight of Albanian Immigrants in Greece." *Central Europe Review* 1, no. 21 (1999). http://www.ce-review.org/99/21/vidali21.html.

Vincendeau, Ginette. "*La Haine* and After: Arts, Politics, and the *Banlieue.*" *The Criterion Collection Film Essays.* May 8, 2012, accessed March 20, 2013. http://www.criterion.com/current/posts/642-la-haine-and-after-arts-politics-and-the-banlieue.

Volodina, Eleanora. "Interview with Fatih Akin." *Deutsche Welle Culture.* February 14, 2004, accessed May 11, 2012. http://www.dw.de/interview-with-fatih-akin/a-1114779.

von Busack, Richard. "Making the Future: Richard von Busack Talks to Alfonso Cuarón about Filming *Children of Men.*" *Metroactive,* October 1, 2007, accessed December 9, 2012. http://www.metroactive.com/metro/01.10.07/alfonso-cuaron-0702.html.

Voynar, Kim. "Interview: *Children of Men* Director Alfonso Cuarón." *Cinematical,* December 25, 2006, accessed December 29, 2012. http://blog.moviefone.com/2006/12/ 25/interview-children-ofmen-director-alfonso-cuaron/.

Ter Wal, Jessika. *Europe Day of Media Monitoring: Quantitative Analysis of Daily Press and TV Contents in the 15 EU Member States.* Utrecht: ERCOMER, University of Utrecht, 2004.

Warren, Kay. "Violence in Anthropology." In *International Encyclopedia of Social and Behavioral Sciences,* 16202–16206. London: Elsevier, 2002.

Weber, Beverly. "Freedom from Violence, Freedom to Make the World: Muslim Women's Memoirs, Gendered Violence, and Voices for Change in Germany." *Women in German Yearbook* 25 (2009): 199–222.

Weber, Beverly. "Headscarves and Mini-Skirts." PhD diss., University of Massachusetts, Amherst, 2006.

Weber, Beverly. *Violence and Gender in the "New" Europe: Islam in German Culture.* New York: Palgrave Macmillan, 2013.

Wheatley, Catherine. *Michael Haneke's Cinema: The Ethic of the Image.* New York: Berghahn Books, 2009.

Wihtol de Wenden, Catherine. "La crise de l'asile." *Hommes et migrations* 1238: 6–12.

Williams, Linda. "Film Bodies: Genre, Gender, and Excess." *Film Quarterly* 44, no. 4 (Summer 1991): 2–13.

Williams, Linda. *Playing the Race Card: Melodramas of Black and White from Uncle Tom to O.J. Simpson.* Princeton: Princeton University Press, 2002.

Williams, Raymond. *Modern Tragedy.* Stanford: Stanford University Press, 1966.

Wolmark, Jenny. "Staying with the Body: Narratives of Post-human in Contemporary Science Fiction." In *Edging into the Future: Science Fiction and Contemporary Cultural Transformation,* edited by Veronica Hollinger and Joan Gordon, 75–90. Philadelphia: University of Pennsylvania Press, 2002.

Zacharia, Katerina. "'Reel' Hellenisms: Perceptions of Greece in Greek Cinema." In *Hellenisms: Culture, Identity, and Ethnicity from Antiquity to Modernity*, edited by Katerina Zacharia, 321–54. Aldershot: Ashgate, 2008.

Zaimoğlu, Feridun. "Sex, Drogen und die Schocks der Moderne." In *Gegen die Wand: Das Buch zum Film*, 209–14. Cologne: Kiepenheuer Witsch, 2004.

Žižek, Slavoj. "DVD Bonus Features: *Children of Men* Comments by Slavoj Žižek." In *Children of Men*. DVD. Directed by Alfonso Cuarón. Universal City: Universal Pictures, 2007.

Žižek, Slavoj. "Multiculturalism, or, The Cultural Logic of Multinational Capitalism." *New Left Review* 225 (September–October 1997), 28–51.

Žižek, Slavoj. *Violence: Six Sideways Reflections*. New York: Picador, 2008.

Žižek, Slavoj. *Welcome to the Desert of the Real! Five Essays on September 11 and Related Dates*. London: Verso, 2002.

Index